Symbols

Paola Martani

Symbols

The Language of the Unconscious

Italian and Indian art sealed in Leonardo da Vinci.

Appendix by Professor **Chiara Rostagno**

Paola Martani

Harper Collins

First published in India in 2019 by
HarperCollins *Publishers*
A-75, Sector 57, Noida, Uttar Pradesh 201301, India
www.harpercollins.co.in

2 4 6 8 10 9 7 5 3 1

ISBN:978-93-5357-756-8

Typeset in 10/12 Baskerville
Design by Sayanti Bhattacharya

Printed and bound at
Nutech Print Services - India

When one directs one's gaze internally, a mandala will be found.

Paola Martani

// Acknowledgement

To my family: the invisible one that, from heaven, guides me and protects me. The earthly one that with love travels with me every day: Sema Anne, Irfan Baba and my lovely husband Umut Bilge. Thank you all.

Book Synopsis //

This book traces the historical development of Italian art and culture in the dramatically changing social and global environment that surrounded it. Starting from the Middle Ages and ending in the present era, the book focuses on the characteristics of different artistic schools and famous artists. It also makes insightful connections between the social climate and the artistic output of each era. This includes reference to the influence of various historical, psychological and philosophical movements. The analysis reveals how certain universal symbols exist in the human subconscious and how they are manifested.

The first part of the book consists of a concise exploration of the development of Italian art, including architecture, painting and sculpture, before the advent of photography. During this period it was the ultimate goal of the artist to faithfully represent reality. In the next part of the book, we see how, after photography made the ability of the artist to replicate reality redundant, artists found themselves free to move in new creative directions. Abstract and avant-garde art took off and artists also began to look at the inside of human beings rather than just the outside. This means that they searched for ways to represent the domain of the unconscious using symbols, formless shapes and innovated forms of colouring.

The book then considers the interconnectedness of art and psychoanalysis, drawing heavily on the insights and theories of Sigmund Freud and Carl Gustav Jung. There is a study of Freud's attempt to understand the personality of Leonardo da Vinci through his art and life history, and then this approach is compared to Jung's theories of universal symbols and archetypes.

The book concludes by presenting a detailed cross-cultural analysis of the mandala—a universal symbol that acts as a perfect example of how humans from all cultures and through time express subconscious archetypes in their creative outputs.

// Contents

Acknowledgement VI

Book Synopsis VII

Introduction 10

Part One

Art before Photography: The Art of Reality 15

Photography 23

Impressionism 30

Art after Photography: The Art of the Subconscious 33

Part Two

Art and Psychology in a Dialogue 43

Freud's Tryst with Art: Writings on the Art of Leonardo da Vinci as Insight into His Personality 48

Jung's Idea of Art: A Parallel with Indian Aesthetics 56

Symbols: The Language of the Unconscious 66

Contents //

Visual Excursus

Part One

Art before Photography 76

Photography 90

Impressionism 94

Art after Photography 96

Part Two

Leonardo's Art 103

Mandalas 110

Art, Traditional Mandalas and Drawings of Jung's Patients: A Comparison 114

About Jung's Patients 128

Appendix: Leonardo's Legacies—Chiara Rostagno 134

Bibliography 142

// Introduction

Every change, every detail in art is the representation of an idea. A thought takes shape, depending on the artist, in different forms. It could be in the form of literature, art, music, architecture or design. In addition, the historical period bears upon the particular thought—as if in a given place and moment, a common idea was circulating in the air. This idea can be traced through the different objects crafted by the persons present during that time. They create similar products with the same input, differing only in their use of different materials.

Let me evoke what Markandeya[1] said:
Lord of men, he who does not know properly the rules of chitra[2], cannot discern the characteristics of the image...without a knowledge of the dancing art, the rules of painting are very difficult to understand... the practice of dancing is very difficult to understand by one who is not acquainted with music...without singing music cannot be understood.[3]

There is an interdependence regarding the different experiences of the same phenomenon—an idea, a feeling—which comes to life based on the characteristics of different artists. Continuing the interpretation of Indian aesthetic philosophy, we see the figure of the artist—the Chitrakar. The human creative action is supposed to repeat the process of the creation of the universe in a sort of mimesis[4]—the artist is like a brahma, with the goal of creating a rival reflection of the universe through his artistic creation.[5] 'The image visualized by the artist is coming from a revelation of the truth of the universe.' A revelation of the truth of the universe takes shape not as a human invention, but as a visualization of what is supposed to be believed according to scriptures.

We introduce here a substitute of the universe, replacing the universe with the collective thought of the historical period in which we live and from which the genesis of the artist's beliefs take shape. We propose that there is a reflection of the society in the artistic creations. Starting from this conviction of interdependence between the arts and the society, we want to subsequently analyse the historical evolution of the transition from the nineteenth to the twentieth centuries, starting from a visual analysis of the art produced during this period, and reach an outcome of philosophical and psychological thought, like a circle, which closes and comes to its starting point. Following this circle leads us to an ancient art representative of the inner world and the beginning of time.

---

[1] (Sanskrit: मार्कण्डेय) an ancient rishi (sage), born in the clan of Bhrigu Rishi.
[2] Chitra is a picture or a painting.
[3] The *Vishnudharmottara* (Part III, Ch. 2, Verses 1–9).
[4] Mimesis (/maɪˈmiːsəs/; Ancient Greek: μίμησις (mīmēsis), from μιμεῖσθαι (mīmeisthai), 'to imitate', from μῖμος (mimos), 'imitator, actor' is a critical and philosophical term that carries a wide range of meanings, including imitation, representation, and mimicry.
[5] Prakriti creates, it is the 'creatrix'; means 'in the beginning', thus Prakriti literally means original and natural. It denotes the state of conditions at the beginning of creation, or the natural state of existence as it was at the beginning of creation. The opposite of Prakriti is Vikriti, meaning anything that has been modified, altered from its natural Prakritic state. Prakriti signifies the original and the eternal, while Vikriti represents its reflection or modification. Thus, only those that existed at the beginning of creation are natural or Prakritic. The rest are the modifications of whatever that existed naturally at that time. From this perspective, the natural world is not Prakriti but only a manifestation of it. The world emerges from Prakriti as a modification, transformation or projection.

At the start of the nineteenth century came the invention of photography. For centuries, the Western figurative arts had one goal—to represent the real and the concrete world. Now, a machine had been created, which was able to with a single click, capture a moment perfectly. The arts lost the purpose for which they were born. Photography easily surpassed the traditional art forms in accuracy and precision. People adopted this new technology quickly and artists were forced to find new ways to express and create.

In this scenario, artists soon realized that the camera was not able to represent the invisible world—the inner world and the movements of the soul and the spirit. At the same time, a variety of schools of art were flourishing. These included Dadaism, a deliberate movement to mock the art establishment, the later, Cubism, with its attempt to represent a three-dimensional world by disintegrating the figure into squares, which were then assembled together on a two-dimensional canvas. Later still came Surrealism, with the aim of externalizing the real functioning of thought—no longer bound by reason but free in its expression of the unconscious, and Futurism, with its unique ability to represent what could not be grasped in a photograph. Futurism represented the speed and succession of events, namely the flow of life, a confirmation of the philosophy of Goethe, for whom nature was a continuous passage from the formless to the form, an incessant metamorphosis. New forms of visual arts were seemingly born as compared with the previous Western forms of art, but can we really call them 'original' in real terms?

The Dhamma is not far, it's here with us. It has nothing to do with the angels of paradise or anything of that kind. It has to do with us, with what we are doing right now. See, sometimes there is happiness, sometimes there is suffering, sometimes pleasure, sometimes pain, sometimes love, sometimes hate . . . this is Dhamma. Do you understand? This is the Dhamma to know, you must investigate your experience.

—Ajahn Chah, Living Dhamma

After all, the Buddha himself did not invent the Dharma, but only rediscovered it—he rediscovered the natural order of things as they are, the way the world functions and he taught the knowledge or practices which allow us to live in this world in appropriate and harmonious ways. When we speak of the world or nature in Buddhism, we do not mean something 'out there', separate and independent of ourselves (that is, separate and independent of the subject that experiences it). We can wonder—after the invention of photography, were all the new artistic forms also 'rediscovered' in order to achieve a representation of the inner world?

To reaffirm the principle, we start with regard to the interdependence of the arts—not only must art reinvent itself quickly, but also recognize that time is beginning to flow much faster in every sphere. In the early 1900s, human reflection shifted its attention from the outside to the inside. The natural scenes described by Giacomo Leopardi[6], a refugee in his quiet country village, did not

[6] Giacomo Leopardi, 1798–1837 was a philosopher, poet, essayist and philologist.

seem to arouse interest any more; Giovanni Verga's verismo, in his frugal and beautiful Sicily, slowly gave way to something which could no longer be seen with the eyes. The representation of the external reality lost its primacy due to photography and also because of a speed of life too accelerated to allow time for one's thoughts to flow.

It was the beginning of the 20th century when artistic thought shifted its gaze from the external reality to the internal. This was also when Jung and Freud began to study the processes of the human psyche by linking them to the soul. It was also the time that had not yet fully experienced the 'fast century'. It was the end of a time in which life still moved slowly, giving time to the soul to develop its insights, complete its healing and walk its paths. The Great Wars had not yet created pain and disbelief in the minds of humans and the illusion of humankind's altruism remained intact, as Freud noted in his letters to Einstein. Indeed, at that time, this illusion may in fact have been the truth.

While psychology was beginning to illuminate the inner movements of human thought, the soul had to begin to adapt to an outside world which was moving more quickly and stridently. This adaptation was not easy, as Freud, in *Civilizations and Its Discontents*, does not forget to underline. And this was when this new speed had not even reached its midpoint, leave alone zenith. Today, we must cope with the pace and intensity of the present moment in which, in order to survive, people lose the time to listen, to feel or to even understand themselves.

We are in a century—unlike the 1900s—which is not only fast, but cruelly so. A century that looks with pity, and even contempt, at those few who still devote some time in the day to something which appears trifling—a few minutes of silence and peace in contemplation between the walls of a temple, in the pews of a church or in the halls of a mosque. This seems to be a period in history that teaches us to point fingers at those who have a voice which comes from within. It is customary to laugh at those who seek to understand the reasons for their emotions, and to mock and denigrate as primitive those who attempt to provide a medium to communicate with the invisible.

In a way, Freud did that in his non-spiritual analysis of the practices of totems and taboos. In his book *Totem and Taboo*, Freud compared the beliefs and practices of the 'savages' he studied with the way in which neurotics projected their mental constructions on the exterior world. Freud argued that the adherence of both neurotics and 'savage' people to ritual and a belief in the power of thought and ceremonial practices was a hangover from a primitive past. However, we can also argue that the people who populated the world with spirits to defeat death maybe did not have only an impulse to fight death, but in their slowness, had contact with that which we now no longer see.[7]

[7] The ideas of Jung were not the same as those of Freud. In his book *The Archetypes and the Collective Unconscious*, Jung writes that the primitive man does not care about the objective explanation of phenomena, but he feels the need, or rather, his unconscious psyche feels the irresistible urge, to trace every sensitive experience to a psychic happening—'To the primitive, it is not enough to see the sun rise and set—this external observation must contribute at the same time also a psychic event.'

This is what we propose to do in these pages, starting from the historical inflection that shows a change of course in the artistic journey, first through a visual analysis of the figurative arts, which are transformed from a snapshot of the real to an informal movement of colours in the inner world, then passing to the philosophical reaction that gives rise to the philosophy and psychology of the internal, which unfolds in two interpretations—one which is completely scientific and without faith and the other which links up with the past, the shamanic arts and the religions centred on humans and nature. At the same time, I wonder, how should we go about creating a link between the new surrealistic and the ancient primordial movements? How shall we prove that the new arts are simply the normal, forgotten and rediscovered expressions of the inner world?

In this historical period in which man needs his own space, in his attempt to assert himself, he shifts his gaze from the outside to the inside, reconnecting himself to steps he had forgotten and is now rediscovering. A connecting thread can be seen in the texts of Carl Jung, promoter of a psychology which sees the deep centre of the person in his potential unity in the archetype of the self and its symbols. This shows how the innovations that took place in the beginning of the last century in the artistic field are now just taking hold of the internal, producing what the shamanic art or the mandalas had already produced. In an attempt to show that the movements of the soul are symbolic, coloured, without clear and simple primordial forms, I remember what Antione de Saint-Exupery wrote: 'What is essential is invisible to the eye.'[8]

[8] Antione de Saint-Exupery, *The Little Prince*.

Part One

Art before Photography: The Art of Reality //

To imitate, with the highest possible fidelity, nature and human reality in its smallest details—the more successful the imitation will be, the better the work of art will be.
—Hippolyte Taine

A painting, a poem, a sculpture or any other work of art is always the outcome of an internal force, which dances between the notes of a historical epoch and the corresponding ideas conveyed by it. The work of art is not the product of an irrational creation, but is the product of its human and social environment. It conveys the idea and the mindset predominant in the historical period in which it is made. Depending on the circumstances, a work must be studied within its internal structure and in connection with the factors which have determined it—the social conditions and the spiritual climate. This allows us to grasp the significance of a given historical epoch. For many centuries, especially in the case of the figurative arts and architecture, the aim was perfection, understood as a faithful representation of reality, whether it was a face, a glimpse of nature or a landscape.

THE MIDDLE AGES

It will be useful to chart a visual course on a timeline which stretches from the 14th century (the end of the Middle Ages) to the late 19th century (before photography became widely spread). During this period, Italian art underwent many transformations, the most important of which are discussed here. We are faced with a transition in history which is emblematic of a transition from the Dark Ages to the Renaissance; it is a period in history in which different motivations behind all artistic production are evident.

Artistic representation at that time had been simplified because there was a certain reluctance for any kind of spatial expansion. The images were placed on a single plane,[9] were flattened out, and lacked three-dimensionality. In doing so, they were far from the reality which was perceived by the eye. In this period, art was identified in relation to a system of ethical–religious values. It was a time when God was the centre of attention and everything was foreign and different from the reality of man. After the 11th century, God was first celebrated through his creatures[10](and thus man, the main creature shaped in the image of God Himself, started to have importance again) and then, linking the human and the divine reality with the individuation of a feeling present in both humans and God, through love.[11] The gap between the two realities—that of God and that of man—began to reduce, giving space to art, which was rediscovering its dimensions. This is most evident in architecture, which had its thrust via two movements in art—the Romanesque and the Gothic.

The Romanesque movement was based on unity, in the sense that it presented a unitary vision of reality. It used symbolic forms and the language of symbols to represent God. The presence of sculptures became a necessary addition to architecture, serving both decorative and structural functions. Paintings and frescoes, inspired by

[9] In the early Middle Ages, a period ranging from AD 476 to AD 1000, the predominant artistic form was the sarcophagi, decorated with bas-reliefs.
[10] Let's remember Saint Francis of Assisi and The Canticle of the Sun (Praise of the Creatures).
[11] We remember all the poems of the movement 'Dolce Stil Novo' or the literature which developed in Sicily under the dominion of Frederick II of Swabia.

naturalism and a grandiose classical realism with a mystical imprint, tended towards a freer and more lively style during this period. They were characterized by sharp outlines and the use of strong colours. The figures had a plastic sense and were rendered in expressive, vivacious forms.

Gothic art[12] espoused an idea of the 'perfect' work—through his work the artist must succeed in creating beauty. It meant he must work for the divine moment of spiritual elevation and constantly search for perfection. Thus, Gothic art introduced a style that emerged in a more sophisticated manner from the Romanesque period—lines were lengthened and stylized, structures were lightened and forms became more ethereal, sweet and sinuous. In architecture, sacred constructions were required to surprise and astonish, pushing vertiginously towards the sublime, mirroring the human beings' attempt to touch the sky. Some of the formal elements that were used included piers, pinnacles, decorations and sculptures.

The highest expression of Gothic art was in the field of religious architecture. In clear contrast to the Romanesque style,[13] the Gothic style featured pointed arches, slender spires and stained-glass windows. Usually, the facade was topped by twin spires and had a large rose window[14] above the central door. Sculpture and painting were revived as an art form, thanks to the reforms carried out by Cimabue[15] and Pisano[16]. Sculpted figures were no longer confined to wall murals—they assumed greater dignity and a more defined volume as free-standing statues. Their fundamental characteristics were linearized form, sinuous features, expressive naturalism and a balanced composition of statues and reliefs.

The movement to understand art as a form of knowledge and as an experience of reality continued at increased speed. While Cimabue painted in a manner that was still medieval in style, Giotto's[17] figures were not stylized or elongated. They were precise and three-dimensional, with faces and gestures that were based on close observation. The figures were clothed not in swirling formalized drapery, but in garments that hung naturally and had form and weight. Giotto also took bold steps in foreshortening and had characters face inwards, with their backs towards the observer—creating a sense of space and depth. The figures occupied compressed settings with naturalistic elements. Forced perspective techniques were often used, so that the settings resembled stage sets. This similarity was increased by Giotto's careful arrangement of the figures in such a manner that the viewer appeared to have a particular place—and even an in-

[12] Originally the term 'Gothic' was used in the Italian Renaissance with negative connotations, indicating medieval art. Considered to be of little value, it was considered the work of barbarians.
[13] Characterized by the use of round arches, robust structures, and small windows.
[14] See the second last chapter on mandala, where this style of rose window is interpreted as a Christian form of the mandala.
[15] Cenni of Pippo, called Cimabue, was born in Florence around 1240 and died around 1302. He was responsible for the first structural reform of painting, similar to the reforms carried out in the domain of sculpture by Nicola Pisano. The reforms were based on the rediscovery of the classical Latin matrix and on the Byzantine iconographic tradition, and the result was expressed through the plasticity given to the chiaroscuro figures.
[16] Nicola Pisano (1210–80). His sculptures represent a synthesis of the different conceptions of Italian sculpture reworked in a plastic language—rich in human sensitivity and characterized by the presence of a formal compositional balance.
[17] Giotto di Bondone, born 1266-67/1276, at Vespignano, near Florence, Italy.

volvement in many of the scenes. Giotto's depiction of the human face and emotion sets his work apart from that of his contemporaries. The profound transformation carried out by Giotto concerned the figure of the artist, whose inventive capacity was enhanced. Art was no longer considered a technical or simply manual skill, as was the case in the past. Naturalism, with its depiction of reality, represented the possibility of interpreting nature, history and life. With Giotto, a new era was born.

HUMANISM

The end of the Middle Ages marked the revival of art, commerce and the study of ancient letters with a new, more critical perspective. In art, the Greco-Roman concept of balance and harmony prevailed (Classical Naturalism), but perspective was introduced in the realms of sculpture and architecture. The key idea was to bring man back to the centre of the universe. This was clearly anthropocentrism, i.e., man defined as the measure of all things. This occurred alongside the rediscovery of the studies of humanity and human values. Hence, this period is called 'Humanism'.[18]

A new language developed, based on experimentation and on the new conception of space. The basis of this new language was the perspectival view (the relationship to a particular point of view), the search for geometric rigour and the theory of proportions (the application of a systematic measurement of the relationship between the elements of a construction and the three different elements of the whole). Marcus Vitruvius Pollio, a theoretician of architecture in the 1st century BC, was used as a reference point for Renaissance architecture. A great innovator of the era was Filippo Brunelleschi[19] (Florence, 1377–1446), who was inspired by the models and the spirit of classical architecture and monuments. Brunelleschi is credited with the invention of perspective[20], understood as the application of mathematical principles and the visual perception to architecture.

Based on the reworking of the classicism of Nicola and Giovanni Pisano and of the naturalism of Giotto, Renaissance sculpture was founded on the basic tenets of Humanism. The main elements were naturalism—the careful characterization of the characters, depicted with psychological aspects; and classicism—an attempt not to imitate the models but to operate following the ancient aesthetic laws. In Brunelleschi's *Formella*, we see an artistic innovation. The

[18] 'Renaissance'—this word already suggests something which has to do with the recovery of the past.
In the Humanistic tradition of this vast period, the 'recovery of the ancient' meant a 'return to the classic forms'. Therefore, a careful study of ancient authors was carried out. The centre of this Renaissance was Florence, but it spread throughout Italy, although there was differentiation according to the different local cultural traditions. Even Rome experienced this great flowering when, to affirm the city's function as the capital of the Christian world and the seat of papal power, Nicholas V marked the 1450 jubilee by restoring the ancient monuments of the churches. This work of urban renewal was continued by Sisto Della Rovere, giving the city a monumental and classic style.

[19] In 1418, Brunelleschi won a competition for the construction of the dome of Santa Maria del Fiore, affirming the new position of the architect as a designer who was both personally responsible for his work and able to face formal technical problems from both theoretical and executive points of view. To solve the problems posed by the large diameter of the dome of Santa Maria del Fiore (about 45m), Brunelleschi invented a new technique, based on the Roman way of construction. He built the dome so that its structure was self-supporting, arranging the herringbone bricks so as to create a solid wall texture and adopted an ogival shape, emphasized from the outside by eight pointed ribs.

[20] The research of Renaissance artists on this powerful tool of drawing clarified the functioning of the ocular vision. This allowed them to translate what they saw with their eyes according to a logical system (which we call 'perspec-

figures in the foreground cross the borders of the frame projecting outwards, and the scene is fragmented into distinct episodes that find their dramatic centre in the gesture of the angel intervening to stop the hand of Abraham.

Humanist painting was characterized by the perspectival conception of space, the placement of figures in real space, the centrality of the human figure (represented realistically both in terms of the anatomical structure and the expressions of character) and the use of light (which highlighted the soft values of shapes, often interpreted purely volumetrically). The artist Masaccio (1401–1428) revolutionized painting by developing a sober and severe figurative language. He showed a preference for figurative psychological realism in the rendering of his characters. A precise perspectival framing characterized his work. Melodramatic episodes were given importance in the gestures and expressions of a few essential protagonists without giving too much importance to decorative digressions.

THE RENAISSANCE

Until the onset of the 15th century, the tendency of the figurative arts towards the representation of reality had been comprehensible through the observation of the works themselves. With Renaissance, we entered a period in which not only did the paintings show the purpose of art, but so did the theory behind the art. The reality that art was required to represent, was now expressed in the language of philosophy and literature. The chief characteristic of 15th-century art was the recovery of the concept of beauty and perfection. The artists recaptured the concept of beauty—understood it as the expression of perfection—by taking the classical models of ancient Greece as their base, enriching them with the ideas of Neoplatonism, and arriving at a reflection of beauty. This reflection was that all that was beautiful was good, just as what was good was also beautiful. Perfection and correspondence to the real became the basis for judging the creative capacity of the artist.

Through a revival of the ancient, glorious past of the Greco-Roman period, a model of beauty was defined. This was based on the preference for proper proportion and for representing forms as accurately as possible, as close to the real as possible. Finally, just like in Classical art, Renaissance artists sought a more perfect Naturalism. Thus, the search began for a perfect representation of the real world. One person who dedicated himself to the pursuit of a detailed study of the outside world's beauty in order to represent it better in art was Leon Battista Alberti.

Alberti (born in Genoa in 1404) fully embodied the ideal of a Renaissance man of culture and he was extremely versatile. He was one of the literati, a theoretician of art and an artist whose work was based on culture and theory. Alberti's goal was to make

tive'), enabling an exact configuration and representation of reality. The naturalistic quality of a work, in the pictorial field, can be understood as the most similar reproduction to that perceived by our optical-sensorial system. In fact, through our eyes, the visual rays sent to us from the outside world are collected. All of them converge in a single point inside the eye and are projected on an ideal plane. Put simply, with the use of perspective, three-dimensional reality is translated into two-dimensional representation. Therefore, the painter does nothing more than translate on a two-dimensional support the reality he perceives from the three-dimensional world which surrounds him. When the artistic reproduction of objects follows the same rules as our eyes, we obtain a naturalistic painting as the final result.

art noble, elevating it to the rank of liberal arts and transforming it to something above a simple craft. Alberti was more a theorist than a technician. His written works gave theoretical and scientific basis to artistic activity and promoted painting, sculpture and architecture to liberalis, that is, on the same level as the literature of philosophy.

Picturam expectamus eam quae maxime prominens et datis corporibus persimilis videatur.—*De pictura*[21] (We expect a painting which looks very much in relief and very similar to the data of the bodies.)[22]

Alberti tried to determine and classify the various constituent elements of the figurative form which must imitate and reproduce visible reality. He traced the rules that must be followed to create a painting which was a mirror of life.

With Alberti, the codes that an artist must follow to be considered an artist of value were written down. The rules that art must follow and the purpose to which it must aim were also laid out. The goal of the painter was to imitate real objects and to represent things as they were seen. Direct observation must be fixed and welded in a complete and clear form. The painter must paint, not on a white canvas, but as if the canvas was transparent like glass and the painter could see real bodies beyond the canvas and recreate them. In this manner, Alberti was searching for art intended to be a visual expression of living entities—objects that were present in time. Thus, the pictorial image was visible in its entirety in a single glance and the figurative image was nothing more than a mirroring of the observer's gaze.

What else can you call a painting but a similar embracing with art of what is presented on the surface of the water in the fountain?[23]

The painter composed artificial objects, but must create them in the likeness of the truth so that the painted images appeared true. Pictorial art was conceived as a mirror of reality, a route through which one could reach perfection and therefore, beauty. And that was the ideal which human life aspired to reach—perfect beauty. To achieve this goal, the rules were strict yet simple—pay attention to the sources of light, the way it falls and the reflections of colours. Through the techniques of chiaroscuro, the colours must be subordinated and unified in the light. Another rule was that the proportions and movements of the limbs of the figures must match those of the real bodies. Therefore, the subject of pictorial art was the real and its representation was curbed and attenuated by a time-consuming and rigorous work of artistic construction.

The artist elevated reality to a point where the rigid and violent contrasts disappeared. Visual representation and classical form merged into a perfection which reflected a superior unity of form. Beauty was obtained only when human reality and artifice came together harmoniously in unity.

[21] Composed by Leon Battista Alberti in vernacular Latin.
[22] Alberti, *De pictura*, p. 57.
[23] Alberti, *De pictura*, p. 47. [*Quid est enim aliud pingere quam arte superficiem illam fontis amplecti?*]

THE BAROQUE PERIOD (17TH CENTURY)

We begin our study of this ambiguous century by considering the Council of Trent[24], an event that gave life to a movement of extremely sophisticated artistic expression—the Baroque[25]. Aiming to affect the viewer emotionally and reinforce adherence to the Catholic faith, it was a spectacular, grandiose, but also ambiguous, art. While on one hand, the principles of Vitruvius were still extremely relevant, on the other, it was evident that Renaissance, Mannerism and Classicism were gradually declining. Their decline gave way to a new sensibility. This was a sensibility that emphasized tangible contact with reality, but also had a spectacularity which made it dynamic.

Based on the same principle that art was a mirror of reality, Baroque worked by recreating sacred images via an original form of artistic expression. The period also saw artists perfecting[26] Vitruvius's theory and displaying a profound realism. Realism was not the only expressive modality of the 17th century—an interest in multiple-genre painting developed. In addition to still-life, we see indoor scenes, objects, city views and moments from everyday life. Now, art began to celebrate not only the reality of nature but also the reality of human beings.

THE 18TH CENTURY

Even during the 18th century it is clear that the intent of art was to represent reality. In this century, sculpture generally traced the Baroque tradition of the previous century. The language of architecture was enriched—a prominent figure being Francesco Borromini[27] , who moved away from the ambiguity of Baroque style in order to restore clarity of intent to his buildings and to art in general.[28]

In the paintings of this period we see the passage from Baroque forms to Rococo style, the greatest accomplishment of which can be seen in Venetian painting, especially in the work of Antonio Canaletto.[29] The search for the perfect representation continued. We see many images of people immersed in nature (this portraiture and landscape artistry would become a profession in the next century, before the invention of photography)[30]. The genre, known as veduta[31],occupied a prominent place

[24] The Council of Trent was the 19th ecumenical council of the Catholic church, convened in reaction to the spread of the Protestant Reformation in Europe. The work carried out by the Church to put a stop to the spread of the doctrine of Martin Luther produced the Counter-Reformation. The Council of Trent lasted for eighteen years, from 1545 to 1563, under the papacy of three popes. It produced a series of statements supporting the Catholic doctrine that Luther challenged. With this council, the counter-reform of the Catholic Church and the reaction to the doctrines of Calvinism and Lutheranism were defined.

[25] The term derives from the Spanish or Portuguese definition of an irregularly shaped pearl. The adjective, meaning bizarre, was used to define a painting in which the rules of proportions were not respected and the composition was presented according to the caprice of the artist.

[26] The chiaroscuro contrasts enhanced by violent flashes of light, that accentuated the plastic sense of the bodies and underlined their dynamism. The colours were decisive and violent, standing out clearly on the dark tones of the backgrounds.

[27] Francesco Borromini, whose original name was Francesco Castelli, was an Italian architect born in today's Ticino. He was a leading figure in the emergence of Roman Baroque architecture. He died on 2 August 1667 in Rome but he influenced the art scene throughout the following century.

[28] His works are less decorative and more functional, with a language which anticipates the subsequent affirmation of the Neoclassical style.

[29] Canaletto, Venice, 1697–1768.

[30] Many painters produced mostly well-known aspects of the lagoon city to meet the needs of a rather varied clientele—from those who undertook the grand Italian tour to those who had never visited Venice, but who, sensitive to the charm of the city, wanted to decorate their residences with pictures of San Marco and the Grand Canal.

[31] The Vedutisimo developed particularly in Venice, following the great success of the series of etchings.

among 18th-century Italian artists. The forerunners of this style were the great decorators of the Papal palace in the previous centuries. These painters were in charge of representing and celebrating historical, political and religious events and setting them against the backdrop of the urban landscape of the city where the events had taken place.

THE 19TH CENTURY

The 1800s were a product of the perplexities and the dynamic forces that had pervaded the 1600s. It was the century in which historical change ultimately took place with full force. Characterized by resurgences, revolts and inventions, several diverse trends coexisted in the domain of art. The first of these, as if trying to give a sense of stability to a society undergoing mass change, was Neoclassicism—the attempt to reach a formal perfection through the inspiration of models from classical Greece. Realism and Naturalism were further developed. Realist art often featured subjects from the lower social classes and often faced a strong social criticism.

The push for a change, however, was too strong to be placated by an attempt to revive the values of the past or to be dominated by pictorial representation faithful to reality. The speed imposed by new mechanical inventions and technologies was too great, drawing attention to a world that was no longer bothered with the reality of the outside world but was giving strength to a new reality which had begun to make itself felt—sometimes even intangibly or invisibly—within the individual.

A movement was born in Germany at the end of the 18th century—Romanticism.[32] This spread in the subsequent decades throughout Europe until the first half of the 19th century, when it became a common reference for European culture—from novels to poetry, music, philosophy, painting and architecture. After the fall of the 'myth of the mind' at the end of the 18th century, Romanticism saw a rejection of the previous ideas and the search for an inner sanctity, which had been seemingly been lost. The Romantic person lived in the liminal space between the ideal and the real. As a consequence, his spirit was characterized by his pessimism and individualism, by his desire for freedom and affirmation of the individual with respect to the rules of society. Romantic culture enhanced the spontaneity of feelings, the free creativity of each person, while at the same time it was discovered that man had deep ties with the society in which he lived, and shared the feelings, culture and values of the society's tradition. The concept of a nation was born in this manner, a concept which becomes almost a religious value for the culture of the time.

It is not strange that a movement based on the inner force (or drive), which expressed the new mobility of man, developed in two opposite ways. The first of these was the search for a similar model as in the past, and the second was the desire to grow and discover a new model to properly articulate the movement's characteristics.

So we see a search into a previous period, one which abandoned the external reality in pursuit of an unseen, invisible force.

[32] This new culture spread, thanks to the Strum und Drang (impetus and assault)—a movement born in open polemic against the French Enlightenment. The term 'Romanticism' derived from the ancient French romaunt, meaning 'narration'. Narration indicates an adventurous and fantastic genre of literature which arouses particular emotions in the reader, although later, the word became synonymous with the sentimental.

However, even during that time, the artistic inspiration was coming from the outside, in the form of God. Romanticism also exalted religious values and, in particular, the widespread ones of Christianity. There was a re-evaluation of the cultures and values of the Middle Ages, a period in which the modern Christian civilization originated. There was also a re-evaluation of the nationalist artistic forms and the expression of feelings evident in Neoclassicism.

Painting was the most important innovative form of art during this period and it was based on great historical themes. The artist wanted to express feelings and emotions, hence his brush strokes were fluid and the play of light often dramatic. The painter David Friedrich (1774–1840) portrayed nature and nocturnal atmospheres that were corpuscular, melancholic and often in connection with the idea of death.

Painting is not really a language but instead a style. And this style begot a rather multifaceted movement, a new taste and a new manner of perception. The visual arts peaked at this stage of European cultural history, which was about to give way to the contemporary age. The concepts of man and nature, of soul and of religious sentiment, were all given full expression in an examination of the 'problematicness' and the depth of human nature.

Man did not yet have full awareness of the inner world as an autonomous dimension. Instead, this force was projected on the outside, into the relationship between man and nature. From the Romantic point of view, nature was the expression of God on earth, a form of greatness and power of which human beings were only a transitory manifestation. The sense of catastrophe that arose from the depths of the human soul created a feeling of agitation that could easily lead to horror, but sometimes, when man found a form of beauty in it, it led to the sublime.

The spirit used man to reach perfection, and man did this through art. Art now had a cognitive function—it was a privileged experience and a real organ of philosophy, capable of leading man to the Absolute. For this reason, the Romantic conception of art was based on overcoming the principle of imitation—art was not the imitation, but a creation, that is, a production of reality. It was incessant creativity, intuition and a knowledge of the infinite. It was the expression of the Absolute, of an independent power that led the genius to produce works with both consciously intended meanings and also meanings that were the effects of an unconscious production.

Sicily is the dot in 'i' of Italy. The rest of Italy seems to me only a stalk placed to support a similar flower.
—Friedrich Maximilian Hessemer, *Lettere dalla Sicilia*

Before examining how photography was born, how it has evolved and how its invention shaped the figurative arts and the millenarian intent of art itself, it is helpful to understand the background of the Italian artistic scene.

In the 1800s, the so-called Grand Tour[33] was in vogue—Italy was a destination where it was possible to have a real journey through history. The popularity of the tour allowed young and emerging Italian artists to earn from their passion. With their handheld casels, small canvases and watercolours, they sat outside the famous monuments, immortalizing them alongside majestic views of the Italian landscapes. They sold the paintings as souvenirs to tourists. There was also a tradition of commissioning a portrait from a well-known painter, often during a prolonged stop in Rome. The numerous painters, engravers and sculptors benefited economically from Italian tourism, both by selling their works and by offering their services as guides.

Photography was launched on 7 January 1839.[34] Daguerre's invention was greeted with great interest in Italy, where the press[35] acted as a sounding board. Demonstrations of the daguerreotype were held in Turin, Trieste, Milan, Rome, Naples and a number of other Italian cities.

There were immediate commercial prospects for this new technology. The travellers who wished to keep some souvenirs of the places they visited could buy a postcard—photographed by the camera and then painted by the artists, who, following the shadows, added the colours and reflections on the paper.[36] That stage was still a compromise—the machine was drawing the perfect border and the painter (colouring it only afterwards) was adding their skill and inspiration. Soon the camera, undergoing fast technological innovations, developed and became autonomous and started to entirely replace the work of the artist. The need to accurately and efficiently reproduce images of the many national monuments gave even more impetus to the development of the new techniques. In Milan, the photographer Alessandro Calluses began to take different shots of the city in 1839, but without doubt the first Italian to achieve the production of a series of views in a sys-

[33] The expression 'Grand Tour' seems to have made its first appearance in the guide *The Voyage of Italy* by Richard Lassels, published in 1670. It was a long voyage in continental Europe made by the rich, young European aristocracy from the 17th century. It could last from a few months to several years, and usually Italy was its destination.
[34] The date of the official presentation of the daguerreotype at Academy of Sciences in Paris.
[35] *Lucifer*, a Neapolitan newspaper, announced the invention on 6 February, while the *Piemontese Gazette* dedicated the entire issue of 6 March to the new technology.
[36] To understand the work carried out, we could look at the work of Silvia Camporesi (Forlì 1973), who, based on this technique, started to produce images—mostly self-portraits, but also interpretations of novels and mythological and religious texts—in which she exalted the landscape of Italy (the Italy that was disappearing—palaces, prisons, factories, and entire abandoned villages) using a technique that involved printing the camera images in black-and-white and then colouring them by hand in soft pastels which were easy to blend. As the artist herself stated regarding her work, 'This step, borrowed from the history of photography, has changed my relation with places—it is not a quick photographic reproduction any more, but an appropriation of ruins, obtained thanks to the time I dedicate working on each image' (M. Pedrini, 'La storia che non si smarrisce' in *Atlas Italiae*, pp. VI–XII).

tematic way was the publisher Ferdinando Artaria.[37] Between 1840 and 1844, he produced a series of 119 Vues d'italie d'après using the daguerreotype.

That century, thanks to the industrial and technological advances, moved quickly. If in the previous centuries there was time for a period of adaptation between one change and the next, now new developments came at a rapid pace. Technology improvements sped up the photograph development process and thus the portrait became a field of photography, a genre that acquired more and more popularity in Italy. The first portrait photographers were versatile and easily accessible to the customers. In addition to providing their equipments and travelling to the homes of the clients, they also ran stores selling machines and optical instruments of all kinds, with accessories and chemicals. Sometimes, they even gave lessons. New initiatives included the famous photographic walks—organized carriage expeditions during which group photographs were taken and then developed in the company's laboratories.[38]

In the beginning, the relationship between art and photography was a little controversial, as the overlap between the two fields created some conflict (which we will examine shortly). We can divide the dynamics between these two arts into two strands—one in which art sought to integrate photography as a support for improvement, and vice versa, in which photography sought the help of art to enrich itself; and the other in which the contrast resulted in a total separation.

Some artists[39] used retouching methods to enrich standard photographs with their own expressiveness and, at the same time, photographers collaborated with artists. In 1893, Vittorio, Leopoldo Alinari's son, published an article in the *Bulletin* against a new state regulation—the taxation of people who photographed paintings and objects in museums and state institutions. His photography shows were always popular, while the work he presented at international exhibitions received diplomas, medals and prizes. The beautiful pictures represented a new way of creating culture, which affected and stimulated art scholars. His photographs did not just portray paintings, sculptures and architecture, but also bound them to the interpreter. The photos were more readily available for the public to interpret than the traditional paintings of artists.

THE RELATIONSHIP BETWEEN ART AND PHOTOGRAPHY

The relationship between these visual arts was one of both love and hate. Initially, the new invention was received with scepticism. An entire category of painters who had made their living through portraits and the sale of their work to tourists on the Grand Tour lost their jobs, replaced by a machine which, with a single click, immortalized what they would spend hours painting.
The report from a commission to the French

[37] The work was a veritable catalogue of images of the most beautiful places of the country—Milan, Monza, Pavia and the lakes of Lombardy—followed by the most important tourist destinations—Venice, Florence, Rome and Naples.
[38] The Alinari brothers, Romualdo, Leopoldo and Giuseppe, were born in Florence. In 1852, Leopoldo opened a workshop in Via Cornus, where he started to produce portraits and, in 1854, founded the company Fratelli Alinari.
[39] Stefano Stampa, a painter and lover of photography, stepson of Alessandro Manzoni, created portraits of his loved ones. Antonio Sorgato used images of common people as models for his artistic activity; and the Alinari brothers (and Giancoma Brogi) started a trend of photographs of city scenes.

government on the invention of Daguerre began with a sentence spoken by the painter Paul Delaroche, 'From today the painting is dead.' But was painting truly dead, or was it now free to explore new territory, which, until then, had remained unexplored? Art certainly had now come to one of the critical moments of its evolution, but soon, in this time of fast adaptation, human creativity would show how a machine could not replace the human eye. But this took time, and thus art found itself faced with a dilemma. One, photography was perhaps the evolution of art itself, a new means of autonomous creative expression. Two, alternately, the advent of photography marked the start of the era of machines replacing the humans, just as the landscape and portrait painters of the 19th century had been replaced.

Heinrich Schwarz said, 'Photography is only the final product of a process that originated a long time before its invention; a phenomenon not circumscribed in the 19th and 20th centuries because the spirit of photography is much older than its history.'

As mentioned in the previous chapter, the intent of art for centuries had been the representation of the real. This can be traced back to the Greeks, for whom perfection was beauty, to the Renaissance era—a time when the principle was accepted that the work of art would be a direct and faithful representation of a real object. From this perspective, art and photography seem to be very closely related, as if photography was just a new step in the evolution of the perfection of art. Alberti, in *De pictura*, formulated the rules that an artist should follow to obtain a 'perfect' work. He expressed the theory of the visual pyramid and described some mechanical devices, such as the veil and the lattice, which would ensure that the visual scenes were mathematically correct.

In 1533, the concept of photography was concretely described by Giovambattista Della Porta in the book *Magiae Naturalis*. The light, he wrote, penetrated into the hole, produced an image on the opposite wall, clear but upside down. The picture became sharper when the simple hole was replaced by a lens. In the 16th and the 17th centuries, the room was reduced to a simple wooden box, 60 cm long, fitted in the front with a lens. The inside contained a mirror at 45°, and a second adjustable mirror constituted the bottom of the lid. The image was formed on a sheet of frosted glass. The image was then copied over on to a sheet of parchment paper, which served as a sketch for pictures that developed later.

Initially frowned upon by painters, who saw this invention as a possible competition, others used this technique as an aid to painting—as a support from which to produce their work. Examples are the famous views of Venice created by the painter Canaletto and those by the painters Ingres and Manet.[40] Many artists started to produce commissioned portraits, sending their clients to the famous photographer Nadar. Manet also used a photo for the portrait of Baudelaire and, Picasso himself used photography to study the values of surfaces. Picasso was also a photographer, using optical distortions of the wide-angle

[40] Among the most significant artists of Impressionist period, Édouard Manet (1832–1883) was influenced by the colours of Venetian art and Japanese prints.

lens to obtain particular visions of reality. Manet was undoubtedly a close observer of photography—in his famous painting *The Balcony*, he used the camera to paint people in the foreground and put those in the middle ground out of focus to accentuate the sense of depth. For the Dadaist photo-collages, images were taken mainly from current newspaper photographs and cut up unusually. The photo-collage was enriched by the use of pictorial techniques and the graphic union of the different images.

Now that realism was assured by the camera, painters could pursue their personal goals with new freedom.

However, some painters did not allow themselves to be involved in photographic reproductions. They took up the challenge and moved towards other paths, no longer focusing on the exterior and the reality, rather on the interior and the invisible reality. This allowed the possibility of the development of avant-garde movements such as Futurism, Expressionism, Cubism and Dadaism.

The goal was the highlighting of the phases of simultaneous movement, according to which a figure is not static, but multiplies, deforms and follows itself in the space through which it travels. In fact, if the photograph caught a moment that had passed and no longer existed, some painters wanted to represent (with reference to Goethe and his theory of metamorphic nature) the idea of the interconnection of moments, of a reality that is never identical to itself, in which there are no final forms, only continuous changes.

The advent of photography helped to free the painter of the need to imitate reality, thus offering the possibility of development towards a new dimension, which, in a society that was moving so fast, now needed care and attention. That was the dimension of the soul, which had no time to self-heal with the passage of time, but had to find a new path. This new art was interested in investigating what happened inside the emotions and inner mechanisms in order to overcome the emotions and inner mechanisms.

Art should not be created manually but must be found.
—Marcel Duchamp[41]

AN EXCURSUS ON ITALIAN PHOTOGRAPHY

Photography was fascinating to the Italian nobility. Prince Giulio Cesare Rospigliosi VI of Rome started collecting photographs, and others followed suit. Friends with most Italian and French aristocrats, Count Giuseppe Primoli assembled a considerable number of photographic pieces. He documented the sophisticated and elegant life of European nobility during the belle époque era. Travelling across Europe, the dynamic Count photographed Italian rulers during ceremonies and receptions. He even took photos of them on horseback and enjoying carriage rides. He was not an amateur—he had a refined taste and used modern photojournalistic techniques in his work. He was satisfied only when he portrayed his subject perfectly, using different angles to capture every reaction and uncover every detail. He was profoundly sensitive to the realities of

[41] I see this quotation as part of a step that brings together the Western conception of art with the Eastern idea that art is a discovery, not a new creation. The *Vedas* state that, 'The image visualized by the artist is coming from a revelation of truth of universe', i.e., shape is not a human invention, but a revelation and visualization.

life. He placed the curtain of his darkroom next to a group of American Indians and convinced them to be photographed. His lesser-known pictures of peasants, shepherds and shoemakers also showed the dire conditions endured by the poor people of Rome. His collection of cameras, darkroom equipment and glass sheets was carried by his servants and his brother Luigi, who accompanied him on his journeys. He produced more than 10,000 pictures. His most productive years were between 1888 and 1894.

In 1898, Italian photography leapt further forward when the 1st Italian Congress of Photography was held. The Turin Exhibition was held at the same time, and the National and International Exhibition was held in Florence in 1899 (where the 2nd Italian Congress of Photography was also held). Photographers, scientists and scholars gathered to discuss significant issues like the applications of picture-making. Anderson from Rome, and Philotheus—the inventor of the kinetograph (equipment responsible for film recovery, development and projection, patented in November 1895)—were among those in attendance. At the beginning of the 20th century, Realism was favoured in Italian photography and also in Italian literature. Giovanni Verga, a literary Realist, started taking photos in Sicily after learning the basics from Luigi Capuano. Despite the pictures being blurry and confused, they represented his aspirations to show people and their spirit. Verga's pictures reflect a strong connection with the French literary naturalism, which was greatly advocated by Emile Zola. Even Francesco Paola Michetti had a highly realistic style in his pictures of farmers. He used photography to create some of his greatest works and he was also influenced by the writing of Gabriele D'Annunzio.

THE FUTURIST PHOTODYNAMIC

The avant-garde style of experimental photography began in Italy before reaching the rest of Europe. Anton Giulio Bragalia, Arturo Bragalia and Carlo Ludovico Bragalia were responsible for its arrival. In 1911, the three brothers spoke of photodynamism as a concept for Futurist photography, influenced by Futurist cinema. Their creations were targeted at representing the deeper essence—the soul of matter. Physical movements were shown by controlling the exposure time and using experimental techniques in order to juxtapose multiple moments in one single photograph. The shift from one picture to another was shown in a series of images at regular intervals and by a sequence of superimposition of several figures. Anton Giulio Bragalia published his findings in 1913 in *Futuristic Photodynamism.* This new style also made a break from traditional academic photography. It suffered some roadblocks, however, as it received criticism from other Futurists. It did not truly begin to flourish until 11 April 1930, when Marinetti released the manifesto on Futurist photography in the journal *Futurism.*

PHOTOGRAPHY OF THE REGIME

Italy's Fascist Regime exploited photography in its own way. It used photography for propaganda, war and territorial expansion. The Regime relied heavily on pictures printed in newspapers and magazines and the Fascists were constantly checking for any problems with the material. This forced Italian photographers to self-censor their work in order to meet the demands of the newspapers who were commissioning them for photographs.

By using standardized techniques, the Regime's main focus was to photograph crowds and the political figures these crowds supposedly came to see and support. Depending on their purpose, the groups that came to hear speeches were photographed in two ways. First, to show vast crowds, they shot photographs from above, front and lateral locations, which helped to give a multiplication effect. The second technique was to shoot from the centre of the crowd, which made the photographer seem to be surrounded by a lot of people. The political figures were photographed using a lower angle, as if the politician was standing alone. The towering silhouette gave the impression of a heroic stature.

Photographs were of extreme importance. In 1942, the living conditions of the Italian people had degenerated. However, the Regime reduced the space allowed for pictures in newspapers, most probably to mask any visual symptoms of such degeneration. Additionally, laws were imposed to forbid the photographing of the areas that had been bombed by enemy planes.

THE PICTURE STORY

Many magazines started publishing picture stories. These were a set of images arranged in chronological sequence, along with captions in square boxes or clouds. Other than romantic-fiction and cartoons, these photo series were influenced by cinema and were quite ostentatious. These picture stories were initially called cineromanzo. These frames also provided a summary of films which were already playing in the cinemas. Predominantly, they provided for female audiences who wanted to re-live the movies in the absence of television. The last film in this series was *Last Tango in Paris* in 1974 by Bernardo Bertolucci. The first issue of *Grand Hotel* used illustrations by Walter Molino and screenplay by Julius Bertoletti, and was published on 29 June 1946. The name was the same as the Hollywood movie, and its story was from the novel *Souls Chained.* Luciano Pedrocci, who was a contributor to children's publications, replaced drawings with picture stories after seeing the success of the *Grand Hotel.*

These stories, with the help of Arnoldo Mondadori, led to the making of the 'Bolero film' (a format which the *Grand Hotel* also followed post-1950). This type of photo story captured the tribulations faced by a man and a woman who were in love but needed to cross obstacles in order to be together. It allowed even the barely educated to be close to literature. The photo stories were considerably successful and generated high revenues.

Many photo story actors became household names, such as Sofia Lazzaro (Sofia Loren) and Gina Loris (Gina Lollobrigida). Directors such as Federico Fellini were also given a platform. Television presenters such as Mike Bongiorno, Raffaella Carra and Pippo Baudo became famous. Singers such as Orietta Berti, Gianni Morandi, Albano and Romina Power also rose to fame. Classical stories from the Bible like Photographic Hagiographies of Saints and stories on the Christian Family were produced in 1959. *Launch* was a Roman publication which took hold of the market by telling stories about abortion and divorce. And even though fiction remained popular, the rise of television led to the downfall of the magazine photo-stories. Even then, the monthly sales for *Launch* publication were half a million in the 1990s, and in 2000 there was a free distribution of several pages of the story 'An Enemy to Win'. The former Miss Italy, Roberta Capua, and TV presenter Tiberius Timperi starred in it.

The minister of health also started a story about AIDS awareness, which was distributed on newsstands on 29 October 1999 and as a brochure in various clinics and hospitals. The photo story was (much later) launched on the internet.

// Impressionism

What we see in the movements of Impressionism and Post-Impressionism is perhaps the most visual example of the changing intentions of the world of art. We also see the human response inspired by the move away from Realism (which had been art's primary focus in the centuries earlier).

Impressionism was born from the rejection of both the contemporary pictorial traditions and the classic sentimental subject, which were both styles promoted by Academy of Fine Arts in Paris[42], technically meticulous and focused on the work of study. The Impressionist movement, although it still captured elements of concrete reality[43], grasped them in an innovative way[44], using undefined contours, blurred colours[45] and elements which were out of context or shocking to viewers.

The Impressionists rejected the traditional dictates, preferring to paint landscapes, street scenes and aspects of everyday life (instead of episodes related to classical history).

In art history, landscapes were not seen as being as important or as interesting as portraiture or religious themes. The artists, however, wanted to paint the outdoors in plein-air rather than in the studio, as they were interested in the effects of natural light rather than the exact design and description of the objects.

The Impressionists were the heirs of the experiences of great masters like Michelangelo, Tiziano and Caravaggio. They were inspired by the theories of Goethe[46], with his vision of a metamorphic nature and the existence of a unique and unreachable substance—and of Schopenhauer[47], who said that art is the intuition not of the object in its sensitive particularity, but of the idea in the object, and that art must look beyond the phenomenal world to contemplate the true essence of things.

The Impressionists were also extraordinary innovators, capable of using colour and light in revolutionary and powerful ways. The change in methodology gave rise to a

[42] The Academy imposed models to which all French artists would have to comply, and promoted the official exhibition of the Paris show (the route through which these models were made popular among the general public).

[43] Scenes from the bourgeois, carefree lifestyle, as well as from the realm of entertainment (such as cafés, dance halls and theatres), were among their favourite subjects. In their scenes of contemporary everyday life, these artists tried to capture a moment by pinpointing specific details such as light flickering on water, moving clouds or city lights falling on moving objects.

[44] By observing how the light reflects the colours, almost breaking them down, they put on the canvas short strokes of pure colour, juxtaposing the primitive primary colours so that they mingled in the visual perception only from a certain distance.

[45] The primary colours were placed in contrast to the complementary ones to enhance their intensity. In this way they obtained a higher brightness than what was usually produced by mixing the colours before applying them to the canvas.

[46] For Goethe, nature was a continuous passage from the formless to the form; it was amoral, it did not recognize anyone's rights, it overwhelmed everything and everyone, and did not distinguish between good and evil. Goethe's idea arose from the fact that he came from the century of English empiricism, during which thinkers such as Locke, Hume and Berkeley destroyed the concept of substance and the idea that there was something essentially stable. The new vision was a revival of the ancient Stoic and Epicurean conception and a denial of Platonism. The world was thought of as a continuous mixture from which all things were born and flow—everything was continually transformed into something else and there was no substantial thing.

[47] Art is a pure knowledge with which the genius looks beyond the phenomenal world (the world of appearances) to contemplate what is essential and permanent in reality- that is, the world of ideas. In music, in particular, art celebrates the essence of reality, that is, the incessant motion of the will. In fact, music is not a representation of ideas, but of will itself, and represents the supreme form of realization of the human spirit.

different style of painting. The new method involved applying paint in small touches of pure colour rather than in broader strokes. The rationale behind painting out of doors was to catch a particular fleeting impression of colour and light which would emphasize the artist's perception of the subject matter as much as the subject itself.

Since the beginning of time, styles and techniques of art have evolved. Each new departure has sprung from or been a reaction to the styles and techniques that came before it. Impressionist painters extracted pure or saturated colours from the palette. These have the maximum brilliance—they reflect exclusively the luminous radiations of their colour and totally absorb the others. Mixed colours, on the contrary, absorb the different light radiations of many different colours, resulting in the appearance of softer shades.

Manet has been often described as The Father of Modern Art and he displayed the subtle changes in the atmosphere of the period through his art. Manet, another great artist of the same movement, influenced the development of Impressionism by painting everyday objects. Pissaro and Sisley painted the French countryside and river scenes, whereas Degas painted scenes of ballet dancers and horse races. Morisot painted women doing everyday things and Renoir loved to show the effect of sunlight on flowers and figures.

Impressionist painters chose to represent reality and thus their paintings aimed to exalt the whole sensation of the fleeting moment. For Impressionists, reality was constantly changing in appearance. Objective Realism must therefore be replaced by the impression taken in a moment. The light changes every moment, things move in space—thus the vision of a moment is already different from the next moment. The fleeting moment of Impressionistic painting was totally different from the pregnant moment of Neoclassical and Romantic paintings—it captured perceptions and emotions, which gave their images a particular flavour of modernity. The movement, the energy in action, the vital intensity of things, could be reproduced through an immanent image of being, created and felt in the first person by the Futurist artist.

This movement began to show signs of the changing intention of art before photography really came into its own, but it still conformed to the idea of the representation of the real, depicting realistic images corresponding to those seen by the eye, even if enriched with odd details. For example, Manet distorted his scenes, abolishing the sense of volume, the light and dark and the perspective by using flat colours in strident combinations. However, women were still painted as women and the lines were well defined and corresponded to the previous model of representation of the real.

But after the invention and success of photography[48], this movement transformed into Post-Impressionism, a distinct movement that no longer focused on exterior appearances but on the interior world of the mind

[48] Impressionism rejected photography as an artistic expression, considering it an instrument intended to reproduce impartial and objective images from the world.

and the soul. The Post-Impressionists[49] did not reflect the texture of the objects of nature through colour and light effects, but instead, tried to embody a more subjective worldview. Vincent van Gogh (1853–1890) approached nature using vivid colours intended to produce very intense emotions. At first, he turned to social themes, as in his work *The Potato Eaters*, eventually moving to an introspective pictorial discourse in which both the brush strokes and the colours of the composition conveyed his inner moods. This can be seen in *Wheatfield with Crows* and *The Starry Night*, in which the art appears to be living in a whirling and dramatic movement.

Another painting technique that developed during the period of Impressionism was based on the combination of many tiny dots of colour, which, when viewed from a distance, created a sense of fusion, which produced a chiaroscuro effect—Pointilism[50]. The use of many small dots[51] of colour also gave the painting a greater sense of vibrancy. One of the leading exponents was Seurat (along with his student Paul Signac)[52], to whom the term was first applied with regard to his painting *A Sunday Afternoon on the Island of La Grande Jatte*[53].

In summary, it seems that as the emerging technology of photography surpassed the painter's ability to accurately reproduce a scene, art was freed to move in new directions. While early Impressionists experimented with light and colour, Post-Impressionist art moved beyond the confines of the concrete exterior world in order to explore, with a distinct abstract style, new dimensions and possibilities.

[49] This term is used to indicate the variety of painting styles which spread after Impressionism (particularly in France) between 1880 and 1905. The definition was coined by the critic Roger Fry in 1910, on the occasion of an exhibition held in London in which there were works by van Gogh.
[50] Paul Signac (1863–1935) was the head of this Neo-Impressionist movement.
[51] The equal-sized dots never quite merge in the viewer's perception, resulting in a shimmering effect like one experiences on a hot and sunny day.
[52] Georges Seurat (1859–1891) was a theorist and the promoter of the movement.
[53] In which the figures composed were from aggregate colour dots (reminiscent of a painting by Piero della Francesca).

Art after Photography: The Art of the Subconscious //

I believe in the future solution of those two apparently contradictory states, dreams and reality, in a sort of absolute reality, of surreality, if one can say so.
—Breton, *The Surrealist Manifesto*

Till this point in our study we have seen how the 20th century began with radical changes continuously in all fields of human life. The century was characterized by constant and rapid evolution, both because of scientific and technical developments as well as because of the rapid political and social changes. To handle these vast external changes, human beings were forced to take refuge in a slower dimension of nature—the inner dimension.

The changes affected the figurative language and the artistic experiences, which, with the advent of photography, had lost their purpose. Their new aim was to represent the invisible world—that sphere of psychic activity known as the unconscious.

All the materials for making art were in the conscious world and thus, art could not fully express the extent of the unconscious, which was both frustrating and endlessly liberating, depending on your point of view. However, the physical world and the subconscious one have a certain discourse and the subconscious is able to manifest itself in different ways, through some actions that each of us perform automatically without the filter of reason[54], such as the sudden emergence of memories or through repetitive habitual acts such as humming a haunting melody.

The profound transformations in art and culture during this era stem from the rediscovery of art's practical function, in which it must respond to precise requirements of rationality and usability, and at the same time allow the deep expression of the artist without any objective or rational logic. This thought underlay the Vanguard movement, begun by a group of intellectuals and artists who wanted to give their work an ideological motivation and send a message, often breaking with the past, of denunciation and renewal.

Here began a search on how the activity of a human being could become a part of a higher reality, to reconcile the two moments of existence—that of conscious (or wakefulness) reality and that of the unconscious (or dreams).

Among the major artistic movements of the first two decades of the century were Expressionism in Germany in 1920s, Cubism in France (1907), Futurism in Italy (1907), Abstractionism (1910), Dadaism in Zürich, Switzerland (1915), Italian Metaphysical painting (1917) and Surrealism in Belgium, France (1920). All these movements tended to break with the past by looking inside the human being instead of outside, each movement focusing on different internal motions.

[54] Without a doubt, the dream is the privileged manner through which the unconscious reveals itself in all its essence and meaning. In 1899 Freud published *The Interpretation of Dreams*, a revolutionary work in which the dream is seen as the tool for the reconstruction of unconscious psychic activity.

SYMBOLISM

Symbolism refers to the artistic movement which began in France in the late nineteeth century and interpreted the same attitudes of taste and sensitivity that characterized the symbolism of the literary field. In contrast to Impressionism and Naturalism, Symbolism conceived art not as a result of natural phenomena, but as a synthesis between sensory perceptions—a manifestation of the spirit. They shifted their interest from the object to the subject, from a passively perceived reality to a re-elaborated version of the artist's spirit. They used brilliant colours and strongly expressive lines to represent visions of remarkable emotions, sometimes tending to the macabre, inspired by literary subjects and religious mythology. The symbols used in their paintings were not mainstream iconography, but often personal, ambiguous and private.

It was Moreau's paintings, with their emotive, supernatural content, that excited most, the newly emerging Symbolism movement.

FAUVISM

This was a French artistic movement that developed between 1898 and 1908. The name 'Fauves' (French for the 'wild beasts') was used initially in a derogatory sense to indicate the use of colour by the painters when they exhibited their work in Paris for the first time in 1905. They abandoned the soft tones and hazy Impressionist style, preferring the bold and violent colours used by Dali and Post-Impressionists such as Van Gogh. The term 'Fauves' was never accepted by these artists, who felt that it did not reflect their lyrical and solar language. The strict contours and the simplified designs, matched with a dramatic and casual use of colours, exploited the expressive potential of the image rather than its resemblance to reality.

Fauvism can be classified as an extreme development of Van Gogh's style. Fauvism's central artistic concerns were the overall balance of the composition. The simplified forms and saturated colours drew attention to the inherent flatness of the canvas or paper. Within that pictorial space, each element played a specific role and the immediate impression of the work was of strength and unity. Furthermore, Fauvism valued individual expression. The artist's direct experience of his subjects, his emotional response to nature and his intuition were all more important than academic theory or elevated subject matter. All elements of painting were employed in the service of this goal. A representative of Fauvism was Henri Matisse[55].

EXPRESSIONISM

Expressionism[56] proposed a revolution in language. It found its first real historical example when, in Dresden in June 1905, some young architecture students formed a group called 'Die Brücke' (the bridge). A key element in their work was the emotional experiences of life. The goal was to create a portrait of reality according to the

[55] Henri Matisse (1869–1954)—his work represented the final break with the use of light and colour so that, for example, a woman's nose could be green if it contributed to the composition and expression of a painting. He said, 'I do not paint women; I paint pictures.' He saw colour as a personal expressive element—subjective and totally independent.

[56] Expressionism was a cultural current that arose in Germany at the beginning of the 20th century as a reaction to Impressionism and Naturalism. It originally established itself in the field of fine arts, then spread to literature, music and films.

emotions that it aroused in us. There was an aversion to the Realist focus on objects and an abolition of three-dimensionality. The philosophy of the group was based on the spontaneity and the immediacy of the expressive form, in opposition to the bourgeois conventionalism. The formal features of the artistic production included deformed and exasperated expressive images, irony and caricatures of reality, the use of marked contours, broken lines, inspiration from primitive art, graphic works based on the contrast of wide black and white tonal masses, and strident colour contrasts. However, in Berlin, in 1913, on the eve of the outbreak of the First World War, the group disbanded due to artistic differences.

While the artists focused on emotive and interpretive art, Expressionism was not restricted to the domain of painting. It played a large role in cinema, theatre, literature and dance. All production was characterized by an exaggeration of form, which added to the emotional effect.

CUBISM

Cubism[57] refers to a 20th-century painting movement started by Pablo Picasso[58] and Georges Braque[59] which revolutionized the way subjects were represented in paintings. Instead of faithfully describing the world around them, the Cubist painters used basic geometric shapes to synthesize a single composition from different points of view, which in reality could not be adopted simultaneously.

We can distinguish two phases of Cubism. The first is Analytical Cubism (1909-1910), characterized by accentuated fragmentation of plans and geometric shapes which are almost dissolved, and the use of dull colours and monochromatic compositions. The second is Synthetic Cubism, developed from 1912, which implements a partial recovery of the colour and shape, which is now completely released from the traditional conception of space.

The basic principles of Cubist painting are the negation of perspective vision, the realistic definition of volumes, the breakdown of volumes in faceted planes, the possibility of multiple views, decomposition of figures into their constituent elements and an interplay between bodies, objects and the surrounding space. The artists abandoned perspective, which had been used to depict space since the Renaissance, and also turned away from the realistic modelling of

[57] This term was used for the first time by the critic Louis Vauxcelles, who, on reviewing some works of Braque in 1908, commented that were formed from cubes.

[58] Spanish artist Pablo Picasso (1881–1973) moved to Paris in 1904 and on entering the environment of the poets and intellectuals, soon became a promoter of radical change in artistic conceptions. In 1907, along with Braque, he outlined the principles of Cubism. In 1914 he moved to the South of France and, after a trip to Italy, began a Classicist recovery of figurative language. After the war, he devoted himself intensively to graphics and ceramics, yet also to politics through participation in the Conference for Peace, for which he produced the drawings of his famous *Dove of Peace*.
His so-called Blue Period lasted from 1900 to 1904, during which he produced different Post-Impressionist works in sombre tones. The Rose Period, marked by the use of oranges and pinks, lasted from 1904 to 1906. In *Les Demoiselles d'Avignon* (1907), Picasso addressed the problems of volume, making this the work with which he equated the birth of Cubism.
His paintings featuring broken, free images were a radical leap from the sculptural tradition of modelling (carving or moulding) to a new technique of assemblage.

[59] Georges Braque (1882–1963), greatly influenced by Cezanne, became the founder of Cubism. Typical of his productions were still-lifes featuring musical instruments, created in relation to the guidelines of Analytical and Synthetic Cubism.

figures.
Cubists explored open forms—piercing figures and objects by letting the space flow through them, blending background into foreground and showing objects from various angles. Some historians have argued that these innovations represented a response to the changing experience of space, movement and time in the modern world.

Cubism paved the way for non-representational art by putting new emphasis on the unity between a depicted scene and the surface of the canvas. These experiments were taken up by the likes of Piet Mondrian, who continued to explore their use of the grid, abstract systems of sign, and shallow space.

FUTURISM[60]

The Futurists proclaimed a break with the past and an adherence, through expressive anti-traditionalist forms, to the dynamism of modern life. They held a positive attitude towards new technological achievements. The first Futurist manifesto appeared for the first time in *Gazzetta dell'Emilia* on 5th February 1909. It was one of the first important Modern art movements centred on Italy. It advocated the destruction of syntax, which was to be replaced by the use of free speech in poetry and prose. In February of 1910, the '*Manifesto of the Futurist Painters*' was published, which was followed by the '*The Futurist Painting: Technical Manifesto*'[61] and the '*Architectural Manifesto*' in 1914. In subsequent years, further manifestos were released, one for each of the individual art forms. The Futurists gave geometric shape and colour to that which was invisible and not measurable physically—the forces, movement, speed, sound, noise, light and smell.

Umberto Boccioni[62] was one of the signatories of the *Manifesto of Futurist Painters.* He strongly affirmed the need to destroy the worship of the ancient past of Academic Formalism, and believed in the need to exalt every form of originality, however daring or violent. *Elasticity*, his painting depicts the pure energy of a horse, fully expresses the artist's reflection on the theme of movement and the environment.

Futurist ideology influenced all types of art. It began in literature but spread to every medium, including painting, sculpture, industrial design, architecture, cinema and music. Futurism emphasized the dynamism, speed, energy and power of the machine, and the vitality, change and restlessness of modern life. The Futurists were fascinated by new visual technology, in particular chrono-photography, a predecessor of animation and cinema, which allowed the movement of an object to be shown across a sequence of frames. This technology was an important influence on their approach to showing movement in painting, encouraging an abstract art with rhythmic, pulsating qualities.

[60] Futurism was an artistic cultural movement founded by Filippo Tommaso Marinetti in 1909. Those who took part included musicians, writers, photographers, sculptors and designers.
[61] We remember Giacomo Balla (1871–1958), whose artwork marks the transition to Futurism. His focus on dynamic movement is evidenced in *Young Girl Running on a Balcony* (1912).
[62] Born in Calabria (1882–1916).

ABSTRACTION

Abstract art[63] deliberately abandoned the representation of the reality of objects, instead pursuing the expression of visions of structure and form via free and fantastic creations of decorative and symbolic value. The creation of the abstract image, which had already begun with Impressionism and Cubism (which promoted a four-dimensional geometric representation of the world), was finally brought to completion. Great exponents of the style were the Swiss artist Paul Klee[64], Kandinsky and the Russian Vaslij, who, in 1912, declared the absolute independence of artistic creation from the world of objects. The works of Piet Mondrian[65] also have to be remembered in this context.

Abstractionism has been the phenomenon that has influenced the development of art in the 20th century the most, both as an artistic form accomplished in the two directions (the representation of pure emotion and of geometric conceptualization) and as an influence exercised on the representation of reality. By 'Abstractionism' I mean an artistic form which completely severed the link with the imitation of reality, instead proposing the overcoming of the traditional figurative canons through the direct representation of states of mind and intellectual concepts, using colour and shape in complete autonomy from reality. In this sense, Abstractionism is a child of the same circumstances which led Contemporary art to revolutionize the traditional aesthetic canons. Stylization and the dissolution of form are taken to extreme consequences in Abstract art, until the definite escape from the constraints of figurativity is reached. The lack of 'real' references generates an interpretative ambiguity. Consequently, there is a confusion between the purely decorative aspect and the deeper meaning of the work of art, which tends to lose its transcendence in order to be inserted neatly into the everyday.

Abstraction has, since the earliest times, always been present in art. It is born from the human peculiarity of being an interpreter of the world, seeking to synthesize it in signs, concepts and symbols. Art itself is an abstraction, as is writing and language. Apart from this, the artistic forms, once they have reached a degree of imitation that cannot be overcome technically, tend to pass through stylization and deformation. The most obvious example is represented by the evolution of the representations of the Mother Goddess from the Palaeolithic era onwards. Abstract, geometric or fantastic motifs have always been used in architectural and ceramic decoration. In Arab art, abstraction is ever dominant. Modern art is crossed by a constant tension towards abstraction; Mannerism was the first manifestation of this tension. Faced with the formal perfection of the Renaissance mas-

[63] Abstract art was born in Monaco in 1910.

[64] Paul Klee's works are preserved in the Civic Gallery of Modern Art and Contemporary Art in Turin, at the Museo del Novecento in Milan and at the International Gallery of Modern Art in Venice.

[65] Piet Mondrian (1872–1944), a Dutch painter and theorist, approached Cubism by creating a series of paintings on the theme of the tree. His work was based on the simplification and decomposition of the organic form. His Abstractionism became increasingly stringent in his later works, which were centred on the progressive subdivision of the plane in space and entrusted solely to lines and colours. The works *Composition*, and *Composition with Black, Red, Gray, Yellow and Blue* are preserved in the National Gallery of Modern and Contemporary Art in Rome.

ters, the Mannerists turned to a stylization of forms aimed at fusion; colour claimed its autonomy from adherence to reality, exerting constant pressure on form. The art that followed, while remaining linked to the imitation of nature and the aesthetics of beauty, has continued this progress.

Abstractionism, as an artistic phenomenon of the 20th century, represents the definitive surpassing of Classical figurativity and is built on the relationship with the observation of truth, through the creation of a new dimension in which there is no continuity between order and chaos.

DADAISM

The aim of Dadaism[66] was to demystify all the values created by culture using actions inspired by the ideas of primitivism, that is, rational creative spontaneity. The name 'Dadaism' came from Tristan Tzara (who coined the word), and has no meaning. The philosophy of the movement was to refuse all rationality and rational motivation, and instead identify the madness and the show in the artistic act. The paintings, sculptures, collages (the French term for a technique based on the re-composition of fragments of different materials on canvas using glue) and the photographic processes of Dadaism highlight the great importance attached to language as a source of creativity.

Dada artists are known for their use of ready-made objects, everyday objects which could be bought and presented as art with little manipulation by the artist. The use of the ready-made raised questions about artistic creativity, the very definition of art and art's purpose in society. Dadaist artworks present intriguing overlaps and paradoxes in that they seek to demystify art in the populist sense, but nevertheless remain cryptic enough to allow the viewer to interpret the work in a variety of ways. Some Dadaists portrayed people and scenes representationally in order to analyse form and movement. The key to understanding Dadaist work lies in reconciling the seemingly silly, slapdash styles with the profound anti-bourgeois message. Tzara especially fought the assumption that Dada was a statement, yet Tzara and his fellow artists became increasingly agitated by politics and sought to incite a similar fury in Dada audiences.

METAPHYSICAL PAINTING

Metaphysical painting refers to an artistic trend of the 20th century in Italy, which emerged in 1910 as a result of the production of paintings by Giorgio de Chirico.[67] This trend leveraged the effect of surprise through the use of unreal and fantastic images. The setting was highly important—a razor-sharp scene without anything deformed and unrecognizable, with cool colours and highly contrasting light and shade.

[66] This was a literary and artistic movement that was born simultaneously in Switzerland and America around the year 1916.

[67] Giorgio de Chirico (1888–1978) was the creator of compositions in the Classical style set in large, deserted, twilight scenes, made even more disturbing by the insertion of external elements such as puppets and dummies. In the National Modern and Contemporary Art Gallery in Rome you can admire *Hector and Andromache* (1917) and *The Disquieting Muses* (1925), and in the Museo del Novecento in Milan, you can admire the beautiful portrait of *The Prodigal Son* (1922).
The Red Tower and *Piazza d'Italia* are the among the first of de Chirico's paintings—striking because of their simplicity. Many of his paintings show architectural scenes—buildings with porches, streets lonely and deserted. But his

The setting announced solitary presences—squares, towers, statues, buildings, still lifes and small figures of men who appeared to be under a spell. Metaphysics was never a movement, but a pictorial intellectual experience.

SURREALISM

Surrealism established itself in Paris as a cultural and artistic movement in the 19th century, although the first 'Surrealist Manifesto' was not written until 1922 (by the poet André Breton (1896–1966). The term 'Surrealism' was coined by Apollinaire and taken up by Breton. It meant a dream dimension beyond the real. Inspired by the principles of metaphysical painting, but mostly by the theories of Freudian psychoanalysis, the Surrealists affirmed the need to express, even in a waking state, the unconscious forces of humans. In the field of visual arts, the primary artists were: the Italian painter Paolo Uccello and the British artist and poet William Blake. In the mid-1920s, many painters began to adhere to Surrealism, including Salvador Dali, who approached the movement in 1930 but was accused of pursuing private business interests. Paul Klee and Pablo Picasso both showed strong adherence to Surrealist principles. Two authentic Surrealist masterpieces are *The Birth of Liquid Desires* by Salvador Dali and *The Empire of Light* by René Magritte.

Surrealism is a pure psychic automatism—the actual functioning of thought—which we propose to express verbally, in writing or in any other way. Surrealist thought operates in the absence of any control exercised by reason and outside of any aesthetic or moral preoccupation. Surrealism is that part of us which becomes alive when we dream—which emerges and expresses itself even while we are awake. Thought, devoid of inhibitions of an aesthetic moral character, is free to wander. Once that superior reality—surreality—is achieved, waking and dreaming are reconciled and interpenetrate in a harmonious and profound manner.

Max Ernest, quoting Ducasse (1846–1870), known under the pseudonym of Compte de Lautréamont, describes the process of creating Surrealist art as, 'As beautiful as the casual meeting of a sewing machine and an umbrella on an operating table.' The beauty comes from the mating of apparently irreconcilable realities on a plane that is apparently not convenient. The Surrealist beauty comes from finding together two existing real objects that have nothing in common and are in a place equally alien to both. The unexpected vision surprises for its absurdity and because it completely

visions of reality are different from the reality that the observer understands. In the paintings the light is the actual colour of objects, the sky features unnatural colours, the shadows that contrast with the bright areas are excessively long. The perspective is almost always deliberately deformed, thus the space has an unusual appearance. His scenes are dominated by the absence of life, containing the absolute silence. The atmosphere of these paintings is similar to that of a dream or a vision. *In Italian Square* we see two tiny human figures in the background and a train with a steam engine passing by. At the centre, on a low pedestal, sits a statue—a statue in a square is a great thing, says De Chirico, because it represents the human form and yet is still marble and permanent.
The Red Tower was the first painting sold by De Chirico. In this painting, behind a wall on the right, you see an equestrian statue that is similar to those often found in Italian markets, especially in Turin. We can say that representations of De Chirico exceed reality in the sense that they go beyond it. The spaces and objects that come from our experience are shown to us with new aspects, which surprise us and confuse the things we know and enhance them with mysteries and secrets.

contradicts our certainties. The ways and techniques devised by Surrealist painters to achieve an automatic painting independent of the processes of rational control were numerous. Rubbing, grating, etching and collage—the image that derives from the methods is always free from the will and can be used across objects and forms—the rationality of the forms becomes surreal by their co-association.

Surrealist emphasis on the mysterious, the marvellous, the mythological and the irrational was an effort to make art ambiguous and strange. Fundamentally, Surrealism gave artists permission to express their most basic drives like hunger, sexuality, anger, fear, dread, ecstasy and so on. Inspiration was taken from Sigmund Freud's work on dreams.

TRENDS IN CONTEMPORARY ART

'Informal' art, defined as Abstract Impressionism, is placed alongside Expressionism, Dadaism and Surrealism in claiming that art is only the creative act which enhances the inherent expressive possibilities of the materials used. Moreover, by refusing the rational composition of images and considering artistic expression to be a result of chance and unconscious spontaneity, the artist must create art with a continuous attitude of experimentation. Examples can be found in the work of Piero Dorazio and in Arnaldo's installations *Freccia di Luce* (The Spear of Light) in the city of Terni, *Colonna del Viaggiatore* (The Traveller Column) at Spoleto and *La Palla di Pomodoro* (The Golden Sphere) by the seaside in Pesaro.

NEO-CONCRETE ART

This term refers to a form of non-figurative art which aimed at turning abstract ideas into 'concrete' realities. The ideas were first theorized in 1930 by Van Doesburg, who aimed at integrating architecture, sculpture and painting using mainly geometric composition.

Imitation, or realistic representation, has been one of the goals of figurative art since the earliest times—the ancients called it mimesis. During some periods, artists have striven to create the effect of an illusion, with images that seem to extend the real, 3D space of the viewer. At other times they have striven for Realism—an impression of social reality. In the 20th century, the opposite of Abstraction is best thought of, in the broadest sense, as 'Figuration', though some Abstract Expressionists considered any residual presence of the figure, such as is seen in Miró or early Rothko, no matter how abstracted, to constitute Figuration [68].

Art, a term which comes from Latin roots, means a skill or a technique. 'Art' is a study of the technique itself. The graphic, pictorial, print-, sculpture- and image-based forms of art are all essentially a means of communication, involving listening with the eyes. The observer, thanks to shapes, colours and movements, as well as associations, dissociations and strong provocations, is involved in the author's visions, emotions and feelings.

Although photography the often blamed for the disappearance of figures in modern painting, the real reason has more to do with the experimental, self-expressive and avant-garde urges of artists. The Impres-

[68] A key example is *Christina's World* (1948) by Andrew Wyeth.

sionists were the first to allow the figure to fade in importance upon the emergence of a new stress on the surface. It is perhaps significant that the term 'Impressionism' was first applied to these artists as a form of criticism, because their paintings only left an impression of the actual forms being depicted. Although the figure did not have the dominant presence in 20th-century art that it did in previous times, the art of this period was better able to represent the human beings not only in their physical aspect but in 360 degrees—as beings whose reality was not limited by the physicality of the body but was unlimited, infinite and rich as only the inner universe can be.

Expressionists put human figure at the centre of the style devoted to celebrate human yearnings and anxieties, while the other avant-garde artists created an art which was for humans—making their everyday objects look strange and, at the same time, revealing the unconscious in order to enable an exploration of their intimate interiority.

Having traced the development of art from the Middle Ages to the 20th century, in the following part of this book, the complex interrelationship between the interior and the unconscious, and its expression in art is explored in greater depth.

Part Two

Art and Psychology in a Dialogue //

Art is the manifestation of human imagination and creative skills in a tangible form; it is a vessel for beauty and emotional expressions. Prior to the 17th century, art was seldom differentiated from crafts or the sciences, and it was certainly not considered suitable only for individuals with particular skills or mastery. However, this changed when 'fine arts' began to be distinguished from acquired skills such as the decorative or applied arts. Today, visual expression can take the form of painting, sculpture or architecture (among others), and in a much broader sense, the fields of musical theatre, cinema, dance, literature and poetry can also be considered art forms.

Psychology, on the other hand, is the scientific study of the human mind and its functioning. It seeks to understand the mechanisms behind our behaviours. Psychologists have paid considerable attention to the phenomenon of the conscious and the unconscious mind, as well as how our experiences interplay with our thoughts and emotions.

The psychology of art is an attempt to unite these two domains through a study of how we perceive and understand art. Its aim of art psychology is to trace the mental processes of artists as they create their work. Although Aristotle was one of the first great thinkers to consider the relationship between art and psychology, it was Sigmund Freud who first applied the principles of psychology to the world of art, the artist and the audience. He defined artistic activities as powerful instruments for the psychoanalytic analysis of personality and attempted to provide explanations to great works of art through an examination of the life of their creators. He even dedicated himself to studying the life of Leonardo da Vinci to understand the motivations behind his most famous works.

Freud firmly believed that life was all about subduing one's wants and desires, and that this subjugation found a channel of expression in artistic imagination. Thus, an artist was essentially an individual who acknowledged his desires via imaginative-artistic expression. He wrote, 'Art is an intermediate realm between reality, which refuses to countenance wishes, and the world of fantasy, which realizes them.'[69] The energetic person 'is one who succeeds by his efforts in turning his wishful phantasies into reality', whereas the artist 'can transform his phantasies into artistic creations instead of into symptoms...the doom of neurosis.'[70]

By this, Freud meant that the artist diverts himself from reality because he cannot bear to renounce the desires that society frowns upon. Instead, he lets his desires be realized in fantasy, then translates his fantasies back into reality via artistic media. The products are accepted by people as precious representations of reality. Thus, in a certain way, the artist becomes the hero, the king, the creator, the beloved—that he craves to become. This is a summary of the Freudian hypothesis of sublimation—essentially a claim that a search for compensation and fulfilment is responsible for the great human endeavours in the arts, political world and sciences. The process of creation results in satisfaction and allows the channelling of

[69] Eric Samajda, *Freud and Culture*, 2015.
[70] Sigmund Freud, *Five Lectures on Psycho-Analysis*, 1995, p. 81

underlying grief and disappointment. Freud believed that this process could be identified and examined by means of psychoanalysis.

In general, the artist is considered a kind of a performer—one who creates a piece with a certain frame of mind, bringing to life a part of his lived reality. Art is provocative and it is understood differently by each person based on their specific context. This raises questions on the authority of the artist as a genuine entertainer, because the source of the enchantment varies depending upon the audience. The same art piece is bound to create different reactions in different people. Freud attributed the cause of the differing reactions to the same art piece to the unconscious.

A young archaeologist, Norbert Hanold, discovered a bas-relief in a museum of Rome; he was so attracted to it that he was very pleased to be able to obtain a perfect plaster cast to hang in his studio in a German university town, so that he could study it thoroughly. The image reproduces a young girl, who, in the act of walking, lifts her garment up a little, so as to leave her feet uncovered in her sandals. One foot rests completely on the ground, the other behind is raised and touches the ground only with the tips of the toes, while the sole and the heel rise almost perpendicularly...Dr Hanold, professor of archaeology, had not found in the bas-relief anything remarkable for his science...the fact is that he had been attracted to something...He finds there something 'modern', as if the artist had in the street portrayed the 'live' image. He attributes to the girl depicted in the act of walking a name—Gradiva, the advancing one.[71]

The enthusiasm for the image of the young lady in the picture had no relevance to his scientific study, yet it aroused the youthful classicist such a great deal that he felt it demanded further investigation.

But what was the cause of such an arousal? According to Freud, 'It is very understandable that, in the unconscious of Hanold, the girl's manner of walking sparked an identification with a playmate of his youth.'[72] The image triggered in Hanold a sense of the 'return of the removed', that is, a resurgence of a forgotten childhood memory. This is alluded to in the name that Hanold himself attributed to the girl, 'the advancing one'.[73]

This example reveals how, through images, an individual can unintentionally experience what he/she has been subconsciously searching for 'against every expectation and every intention'.[74]

How one interprets art depends upon where one has come from and where one plans to go. The image is given a meaning from the historical context of the 'self' of the spectator. And, likewise, the image can acquire as many meanings as the number of spectators it has. Besides, there may be images that are meticulously created but which have no lasting impact on the viewer (and vice-versa). An image can also help people derive meaning from a memory they may otherwise be unable to express.

[71] Sigmund Freud, *Delusion and Dream in Jensen's Gradiva*, 1907.
[72] Ibid.
[73] Ibid.
[74] Ibid.

In opposition to the Freudian perspective, Carl Gustav Jung believed that it was problematic to trace art back to the psyche of its creator. Jung reconnected to Indian aesthetics, considering the artist's product as a contemplation and rediscovery of universal truths.

He argued that, in prehistoric times, the artistic impulse in the mind of the humans existed undifferentiated from other cultural sensibilities; art in itself had no particular meaning—it existed like nature. The creative process, on the other hand, was something different. It arose out of the same psychological conditions as a neurosis. The content of this creative impulse originated from the unconscious; therefore it extended beyond the individual.

Jung suggested that one's personal experiences did not have much to do with the creation of art, thus hinting that art was supra-personal—something that rose above the individual concerns of the creator.

Jung's association with art was essentially ambivalent. From one perspective, he gave enormous significance to art and to the artist, but at the same time he described art as an autonomous process, demonstrating little consideration for the individuality of the creator.

Jung's words hint at a kind of jealousy with regard to artistic creation. Both he and Freud shared a particular dislike of contemporary art, which they considered unattractive and devoid of any emotional stimulation. They believed that art was best viewed from the sidelines and that the goal of art was not only to mirror reality but also to steer the conscience. In their opinion, contemporary artists were marching towards the oblivious without being mindful of their actions. On account of a lack of genuine conviction in the objectivity of the psyche, these artists were creating images that depended on the persona of the artists for their interpretation rather than on the psyche of the individual viewer.

For Jung, 'the oblivious' (Freud's 'unconscious') was an example of an ancient, shared creative energy. He linked it to allegories of the spirit, the female, ill-will and the male part of the female. Rather than referring to the individual oblivious, Jung spoke of an aggregate oblivious.

The procedure of individuation happened through the creation of images which, in contrast to Freud's conclusion, were not signs alluding to known things, but rather alluding, in a general, obscure way, to that for which there was no other satisfactory articulation. The disparate ideas contained within each work of art allowed for the clarification and examination of one's mental procedures—this was the 'psychology of art'.

PSYCHOLOGY OF GESTALT

The Gestalt school of psychology emerged in the early 20th century in Germany, moving later to the United States. In opposition to Structuralism, the key principle of Gestalt psychology was that the mind could form a perception (of a scene, image, artwork, etc.) that was different from the aggregate of the individual parts. Connections were made between conscious experience and cerebral activity. Proponents of this school explained that the viewer of an artwork, while mentally generating this 'whole' image, subconsciously picked up cues that established a connection between the mental state of the viewer and that of the artist. Gestalt psychology depended upon taking the physical reality of the phenomena as the initial starting point for analysis, and then exploring how it was positioned in contrast to the phenomenal reality (what is seen).

German perceptual psychologist Rudolf Arnheim believed that art was a means of expression and a medium through which one could perceive the meaning of life using colours, patterns and shapes. He defined vision and perception as processes of creative and active understanding. He said that we organize perceptions into structures and forms with which to understand them. He also indicated that artists could utilize structure and shading to incorporate signals into their work.

Perpetual shape is the outcome of an interplay between the physical object, the medium of light as the transmitter of information, and the conditions prevailing in the nervous system of the viewer...The shape of an object we see does not, however, depend only on its retinal projection at a given moment. Strictly speaking, the image is determined by the totality of visual experiences we had with that object, or with that kind of object, during our lifetime.[75]

POST-FREUDIAN PSYCHOLOGY

Freudian psychoanalytic hypothesis had a significant impact on the work and lives of avant-garde artists, despite the fact that Freud, owing to his Classicist orientation, had a low opinion of Contemporary art, including Surrealism and Expressionism. He maintained that in order to discuss art, one needed to maintain an exact harmony between oblivious elaboration and cognisant (pre)elaboration (i.e., between oblivious substance and artistic structure).

There were a number of different post-Freudian advancements regarding the place of psychoanalytic research in art. For example, Ernst Kris proposed the hypothesis that art enables its maker to give structure to the driving forces and profound clashes inherent in their life. Following the idiosyncrasies of a particular style would enable a 'controlled regression at the service of the ego'. A similar process would be generated in the viewer's psyche, which would result in a kind of re-creation of the work through the distinguishing proof procedures effectively recognized by Freud. Art was thus understood as a product of an ancient mental architecture, existing to give structure to the shapeless through an artistic language that enabled us to address and expose what we were unable to internally characterize.

Marion Milner, another post-Freudian commentator, proposed that images were the only means by which a child could express internal psychic processes.[76] He posited that art was a means through which one could connect with one's unconscious.
We have seen in this chapter that the psychology of art is a rich and multifaceted theoretical field. Uniting the practitioners is the desire to forge links between the inner

[75] 'The Intelligence of Vision: An interview with Rudolf Arnheim'.
[76] Borla, *Madness removed by healthy people*.

world of the artist or spectator and the outer visual-physical world of concrete objects and observable phenomena. The common theme running through all of the previous discussions and perspectives is that one cannot understand a piece of art simply by trying to describe and explain the physical piece itself. Depending upon the school of thought employed, the artwork could be understood as a product of the childhood experiences and the supressed emotions of the creator, or it could also be argued that the artwork had no fixed meaning because the perception of it is entirely subjective—a product of the emotional and perceptual systems of the audience. If we are to adhere to the school of Gestalt psychology, we must acknowledge that a piece of art is something entirely set apart from the individual components of which it is comprised, perhaps, as Jung argues, a product of a universal ancient creative energy that runs through every being.

Every input to the human sensory system, including the visual, is experienced as an interpretation of the constant flux of the phenomenal world. The most important message to take from this overview of the relationship between art and psychology is that no one person can ever hope to define the ultimate meaning of an artwork.

// Freud's Tryst with Art: Writings on the Art of Leonardo da Vinci as Insight into His Personality

With regard to these artists, I am one of those philistines and lumaconi (snail) that you (Oscar Pfister, author of the booklet on the psychological and biological bases of expressionist painting), *put to the pillory in its introduction.*
—Sigmund Freud

As can be gathered from this quotation from Freud—who is known as the father of psychoanalysis—he did not look favourably upon Impressionist and Surrealist art. Paradoxically, many cite him as the founder and connoisseur, despite the fact that at a personal level he had a considerable impatience with Contemporary art, and on the theoretical level he believed that to be able to talk about art, you had to maintain a precise balance between unconscious processing and processing of the preconscious. That meant that you needed a balance between unconscious content and artistic form. Freud stated adamantly that the Surrealists had failed to give the preconscious image a structure which derived from the unconscious. The same form of sculpture[77], which developed at the transition between the nineteeth and the twentieth centuries, and which preferred to leave a little margin for the imagination of the viewer by remaining unfinished, was put to the pillory by Freud.

Art constitutes an intermediate realm between reality that frustrates the desires and even the fantasy world that satisfies them—a domain in which the aspirations to the omnipotence of primitive humanity have remained so to speak... The artist is originally a man who diverts himself from reality because he cannot adapt to the renunciation of the fulfilment of the impulses that reality initially demands, and lets his desires of love and glory be realized in the life of fantasy. However, he finds the way back from the world of fantasy into reality because, thanks to particular attitudes, he translates his fantasies into a new kind of real thing, which is accepted by men as a precious representation of reality. Thus, in a certain way, he truly becomes the hero, the king, the creator, the beloved, what he craved to become and this without going through the laborious and tortuous path of the effective transformation of the external world.[78]

Freud investigated the reasons and processes involved in artistic expression, with particular reference to the artist's personality. He considered art to be a fulfilment of desire in the face of a reality, which was too frustrating and unsatisfactory, and in this respect he considered it to be a game for children or a fantasy for adults. Such fulfilment involved both the production process and artistic fruition. He believed that art was also homologous to the dream. He was convinced that the artists had discovered the unconscious before science. Freud proposed to read the work of art (like the dream) as a bipartite text, distinguishing between manifest content (the text or the form of the work) and latent content (its unconscious meaning). In the second half of the 1920s, Freud's attitude towards reality assumed the character of a sort of disillusioned humanism. His aesthetic theory inclined towards a conception of art understood, above all, as defence and consolation in the face of an existence filled with frustration and trauma.

[77] For example, Auguste Rodin (1840–1917) left partially intact the pieces of stone from which he carved, to give the impression, as Michelangelo did, that the figure slowly grew from the stone.
[78] S. Freud, *Essays on Art, Literature and Language*, Turin, 1991.

BRIEF OVERVIEW OF FREUDIAN THEORY

A fundamental concept in Freudian theory is that of sublimation, understood as the ability to satisfy a desire (especially sexual) through a shift of its goal—finding satisfaction not in its natural field but in sectors that do not encounter moral or social censorship and that are valued socially, like art or science.

Originally, sexual drive is not for reproductive purposes but for pleasure. This manifests itself in the infancy of humans, when the child reaches pleasure through genitals and stimulation of other erogenous zones of the body, and are assigned to the task of limiting it. As the passion evolves, it passes from object-specific love and the autonomy of the erogenous zones to the primacy of the genitals in the service of reproduction. In the course of this evolution, a part of the excitement is initiated by sublimation.
In relation to this evolution, there are three degrees of civilization:
1st: The liberated drive to operate regardless of the goals of reproduction.
2nd: The repressed drive of all which is not needed for reproduction.
3rd: Only reproduction is admitted as a sexual goal—it corresponds to civil morality.

According to Freud, a number of individuals do not satisfy society's demands. For these people, the development of the drive from auto-eroticism to object-love has occurred differently. From these disturbances originate deviations from the sexuality typical of a civilization. For example:

• Perverts: Infantile fixation to a temporary sexual goal has prevented the primacy of reproduction.
• Homosexuals: The sexual goal has been diverted from the opposite sex.

If the harmful effects of the deviation are minor, this must be attributed to the complexity of the drive, which means that even when some parts of the drive are excluded from evolution, they are still structured in a usable form. Their affinity to sublimation for the purposes of civilization is so strong that it leads to inversion. In the effort to regain control of their impulses, these individuals consume all the energy they would otherwise use in civilization—they are inhibited on the inside and paralysed on the outside. This can have two outcomes:

• The victims remain afflicted and so they must suffer the consequences of their deviation.
• After attempted but unsuccessful repression, the uninhibited drives are manifested in other, harmful ways.

Such individuals are likely to suffer from nervous psycho-neurosis. Freud defines neurosis as the negative of perversion, because neurosis is the formation of behavioural or psychosomatic symptoms as a result of repression. For the neurotic individual, there is a limit beyond which their constitution cannot adapt to the demands of civilization. Individuals who try to overcome their constitution simply succumb to neurosis.

Neurosis can also be the result of traumatic past experience, according to Freud. Traumas are experiences on one's own body or sensory impressions. In the first five years of a child's life, certain traumas may be experienced. In the subsequent five years, the child goes through a period of latency, during which these experiences are suppressed. Then during puberty, alongside the sexual development of the child, these experiences are likely to resurface, often resulting in neurosis.

The common characteristics of neurotic phenomena can be understood as follows:

1. The effects of the plot are of two types: positive—attempts to remember the plot (fixation to repeat)—and negative—they pursue the opposite purpose; nothing is remembered, a defensive reaction.

2. Their expressions are the illusions that can become inhibitions and phobias.

These contribute to the determination of character. All these phenomena are compulsions, independent of the other psychological processes. They are not influenced by external reality. When the internal reality prevails over that external, we have a state of psychosis.

For example, a little boy who shares the bedroom with his parents as a child must consequently hear and observe their sexual encounters. At first, neurosis erupts after the first spontaneous nocturnal pullulation, with insomnia as a first symptom. This single symptom is a compromise, an attempt to defend against those perceptions, an attempt to establish curiosity. The child begins to excite his penis with his hands and to undertake sexual assault on the mother, identifying with the father. This goes on until his mother forbids him to continue and her threats to him that his father would be emasculated leads to trauma.

He ceases his sexual activity. He does not identify with his father but fears him instead, identifying himself with his mother and clinging to her as a shield against his father. He becomes a model boy at school, so far showing latency. But the arrival of puberty coincides with the re-emergence of the neurosis. He has lost the sensitivity of his penis, he does not try to touch it, he does not approach a woman. He only has sadomasochistic fantasies. He hates the father who has brought him failure in life. He does not want to succeed in the profession that he had been pushed into by his father and only after his father's death does he find a wife. A totally selfish character emerges, a copy of the image he has from his father—the return of the removed.

FREUD'S APPLICATION OF HIS THEORY TO ART

In 1906, Freud wrote *Delusion and Dream in Jensen's Gradiva*, in which he tried to arrive at an understanding of the work (the novel *Gradiva* by Wilhelm Jensen) in the light of the life of the author, especially with regard to his childhood psychological activity. The book is an example of medical criticism and an excellent example of psychoanalysis. It could be seen as a kind of psychological novel, where the jurisdiction of psychoanalysis is extended to artistic phenomena. Then, in 1910, Freud wrote about a childhood memory of Leonardo da Vinci, another instance of his psycho-biological method applied to art. Freud seems to be more concerned about the psychological, existential and artistic difficulties that could be seen in Leonardo's complete works. Also, he undertook reflection on the destinies of his partial drives.[79] Freud proposed that an imperfect sublimation[80] of these desires was the reason behind Leonardo's turn to studies of a scientific nature.

In my first memory of my childhood, it seemed to me that, being a cradle, that a kite (eagle) came to me and opened my mouth with its tail, and many times struck me with its tail in my mouth.[81]

Freud dedicated himself to studying Leonardo from 1909 to 1910.[82] In his writings he tried to delineate the figure of the painter, starting from a dream[83], which Leonardo mentions in his manuscripts (see above). Freud worked towards a biographical reconstruction:

His illegitimate birth subtracted him until about five years from the influence of his father and left him at the mercy of holding the seduction of the mother of which he was the only comfort. If we start from his kisses to an early sexuality, we can think that he entered a phase of infantile sexual activity... The overwhelming of an energetic removal puts an end to this childish exuberance...Leonardo can live in abstinence giving the impression of being asexual. Then, when the waves of puberty's excitement will overwhelm him, they will not lead him to disease...Most of the needs of the sexual drive can sublimate...in the thirst for universal knowledge... The removal of love for the mother will cause this part to be pushed towards a homosexual approach and manifests itself as an ideal love for children. In the unconscious continues the fixation of the mother...But for the moment it remains in a state of inactivity...From an obscure childhood Leonardo emerges before us as an artist, a sculptor painter, thanks to a specific talent presumably reinforced by the early awakening of the drive to look into the early years of his childhood...In the flourishing of youth, Leonardo seems to work at first without any inhibition. A period of virile creative force and artistic productivity in Milan, where the benevolence of destiny found him in Duke Ludovico il Moro, a paternal substitute. But soon...the inevitability of sexual life is being imposed, the activity and the capacity for rapid decisions begin to fade, the tendency to ponder and linger appears already as a disturbing element in the 'cenacle'...Leonardo becomes a researcher; at first still in the service of his art, and later autonomous and far from it. With the game of the father's substitute protector, this regressive substitution gains further ground. After he became impatient with the brush... The childhood past had taken his hand. But the research effort seems to bear within itself the traits that characterize the activity of unconscious impulses. That is insatiability, inflexible rigour, the lack of adaptability to real circumstances. At the height of his

[79] According to Freud, the sexual drive (or 'drives'—the drive is in fact formed of a number of parts) is more developed in humans than in other animals. It has had enormous influence on the operation of all civilizations.
[80] The faculty of sublimation is the exchanging of the original sexual goal/drive with another which is no longer sexual.
[81] Leonardo da Vinci, *Atlantic Codex C-61*.
[82] S. Freud, *'Essays on Art, Literature and Language'*.
[83] Freud recalls that childhood memories are actually fantasies born later. Thus, it is important to understand the cyclical development of the subject.

life there was a new transformation. Deeper layers of his psyche became active again for the benefit of his art. He met the woman who awakened in him the memory of happiness, the sensual ecstasy enclosed in his mother's smile, and under the influence of this evocation he rediscovered the love that supported him at the beginning of his artistic attempts, when he created smiling women with his brush. He painted Mona Lisa, Madonna and Child *and the series of mysterious figures distinguished by an enigmatic smile. With the help of his oldest erotic impulses, he celebrated the triumph of overcoming the inhibitions that weighed on his art.*[84]

To verify his hypothesis on the instinctual development of Leonardo, Freud was forced to go back to the artist's childhood and examine his family situation. He came across the famous memory (see above), which he used in the title to his essay, 'Leonardo da Vinci and a Memory of His Childhood'.

Freud's essay made use of an extensive bibliography[85] but it still contained an error—the term used by Leonardo was 'nibbio', but it was translated in the text used by Freud as 'vulture'. Freud gives two explanations—reducing it to a passive oral sexual act reminiscent of the memory of breastfeeding, or as the image of the Egyptian goddess Mut, who was depicted with an image of the vulture. The vulture in ancient times was considered to be an entirely female species fertilized by the power of the wind, and thus was a symbol for the birth of Christ, whose mother was a virgin impregnated by the Holy Spirit. And since Leonardo—an illegitimate son—was the son of only his mother, he was thus also the son of a vulture. The vulture is the mother, while the tail is the penis, which the child has thought of as a sexual attribute of the mother. The discovery that the mother was deprived of it brings disappointment. On 17 June 1910, Jung first saw the vulture silhouette in the drapery of the Madonna in a painting in the Louvre.

Eric Neumann commented in 1959:
Against the background of archetypal relationships, the bird with the infantile fantasy of Leonardo, considered in his creative unity of mother-breast and father-foul, is symbolically a vulture, even if Leonardo called him a kite. . . . For this reason we are perfectly right if we keep the term vulture, which Freud chose by mistake, because it was precisely for this gaffe that his acute intuition penetrates to the core of the question.[86]

Freud divided the psychological personality of Leonardo into two types—a placid, indulgent, benevolent side, full of passion for everything that interested him, and an ambivalent side, which condemned war and bloodshed, called the humans 'the first animal amongst animals', and yet designed weapons and drew images of death by hanging (for example, the drawing of Bernardo Bandini hanged). Freud then confronted Leonardo's sexuality but proposed that what appears to be a rejection of sexuality in his works is not entirely so. In fact, in the work *Angelo Incarnato* (The Angel Incarnate)[87], we clearly find an erotic background and

[84] S. Freud, *Leonardo da Vinci and a Memory of His Childhood,* 1910.
[85] The texts mainly used by Freud are Fumagalli, Marinoni, Richter and Smiraglia Scognamiglio.
[86] Erich Neumann, *Art and the Creative Unconscious.*
[87] It should be noted that the design of the penis of the angel has a different colour than that of the figure; it could therefore have been a joke played by one of his students.

St. John the Baptist[88] also has a sexual background. Moreover, Leonardo had presented sexual organs several times[89]—it defines the scientific side of Leonardo's sexuality. The artist converted his sexual drives into a thirst for knowledge.

Freud himself recognized the limits of his sexual drive theory. Similar existential situations can have different (and even opposite) results—sublimation, artistic expression versus repression, neuroticism, but excluding a priori any reference to the life and the psychology of an author or an artist is equivalent not only to reducing art to its history or to its language, but to erasing any trace of individuality. Psychoanalysis is not a tool with which we can solve the problems of art in a definitive way, but it can add elements of understanding rather than factors of certainties. Whatever the case may be, Leonardo would never have failed to be what he was—his genius remains undisputed.

Whether he was sexually inactive or a homosexual, in Leonardo's later life, perhaps as a consequence of exclusive maternal tenderness received in infancy, his love for 'mother' is replaced by love for 'son' and thus the 'son' becomes the object of his gestures of love. In fact, Leonardo surrounded himself with beautiful children. His assistants were known for their physical appearance rather than for their artistic skill. He often used his assistants as models and he looked after them carefully. He loved youngsters in a manner that his mother loved him. This form of narcissism, as Vasari says, is also found in his attitude towards his works of art, which he often neglected as his father had neglected him in the beginning years of his life. On the analysis of sources, Leonardo could be defined as a 'sensually non-active homosexual'. However, at twenty-four, Leonardo was indicted and prosecuted for sodomy following an anonymous complaint on the basis of the testimonies of contemporaries.

When Freud analysed Leonardo's later life, he again returned to an exploration of the relationship between the artist and his mother. Freud believed that the famous smile which can be seen on the faces of so many women in Leonardo's paintings was the smile of his mother. Leonardo rediscovered this smile when he was fifty years old and met Lisa Gherardini (who was the model for his famous *Mona Lisa*). Freud argued that the *Mona Lisa* was a representation of none other than his mother Caterina, from whom he was taken away when he was five years old.[90] One thing that Freud still did not know (it was reported years later) was that the landscape behind the *Mona Lisa* is similar to a tributary of the Arno which comes from the mountains of Vinci—maybe the artist wanted to reconnect with his mother in the place of his happy childhood. Regardless, the smile certainly fascinated Leonardo so much that he reproduced it in other works, such as *St John the Baptist* and *The Virgin and Child*.

Freud's work on Leonardo is one of the most enlightened examples of the use of psycho-

[88] Created 1508–1513, now in the Louvre.
[89] Let us remember the serious errors of anatomy in Leonardo's female figures.
[90] According to Freud's reconstruction, Leonardo would have spent the first years of his childhood exclusively with his mother, before going to live with his father and his father's young wife at the age of five.

analytic science for biographical research. Indeed, Freud wrote to Jung in 1909, *'I've had an idea since I came back. The mystery of Leonardo's character has suddenly become transparent to me.'* [91]

Despite this, it must be remembered that because of the lack of information about the private life and the infancy of the great Renaissance genius, the uncertainty and fragmentary nature of the material available, the length of time that separates Freud's attempt to illustrate the personality of Leonardo from the era in which he lived and worked, Freud does not aim to provide definitive explanations. At the end of the essay, Freud reiterates the general limits that psychoanalysis can reach in the field of biography:

Let us understand the inevitability of the person in question having had a certain reaction and not another. . . . We must admit here a certain degree of freedom which cannot be solved further with psychoanalytic means. [92]

In his psychoanalysis of artists, Freud highlighted, above all, the role of the unconscious mind, at times risking privileging the psychopathological traits of the creator over their artistic talents. For Freud, Leonardo remained an undisputed genius.
His tribute to this great artist was a duty and not just a trivial matter. In his essay on Leonardo, the artist's childhood and its relation to his body of work, he never disregarded the genius of the Renaissance master. With a firm grounding of an appreciation of Leonardo's work, Freud then went on to unravel and reveal, layer by layer, a methodological approach to studying the art of da Vinci. He revealed how childhood experience and its psychosexual nature can be seen, not as defining factors of art, but as subtle inspirations. In this manner, Freud demonstrated his intellectual method and also paid homage to da Vinci in the best way that he knew.

[91] Freud in a letter to Jung, 17 October 1909.
[92] Freud, *Un ricordo d'infanzia di Leonardo da Vinci.*

// Jung's Idea of Art: A Parallel with Indian Aesthetics

The exclusive orientation towards personal factors, which is required by the search for personal causality, is not admissible for a work of art, because here it is not a human being but the creative process that goes beyond the individual.

It is a thing with no personality and for which, that which is personal cannot be a criterion of judgement. The true work of art derives its particular meaning from the fact that it has succeeded in freeing itself from the narrowness and obstacles of what is personal, leaving far from itself every caducous and contingent element of pure personality.
—C.G. Jung, *Psicologia analitica e arte poetica*

This quotation reminds us of Indian aesthetic beliefs. The philosophical debates outlined in this chapter have little of the Occidental thought and negligible agreement with the interpretation of art which we have seen so far. The ideas explored in this chapter have a more Oriental bearing and are attempted to be modelled on the ancient thoughts of India. We will articulate the Jungian creed through parallel concepts—first those presented by the psychoanalysts, and then those of their Indian counterparts, creating a mirror which will allow the reader to draw the similitude and dissimilitude.

We will now immerse ourselves in this line of thought, starting from the birth of this conviction in Jung's life.

It all began after Jung's theoretical divorce from Sigmund Freud. Jung felt that the Freudian methodology (which traces everything back to psychological antecedents) risked moving away insensibly from the subject and making each artist a clinical case and every work of art a disease. This led Jung into a period which he called 'inner uncertainty'. During this period, Jung experienced a profound loss, which he considered equivalent to the loss of the soul.[93]

I could finally immerse myself in the world of mystery—which included the trees, a body of water, the swamp, stones and animals, the library of my father. But I was isolating myself more and more from the world, with a slight feeling of bad conscience.[94]

Characterized by a strong introversion, to recover the lost piece of his soul Jung had to descend into his own unconscious,[95] which induced him to sever relations with the academic world and all the stability which he had held onto until that moment. Searching into the details of his existence, Jung founded a form of research that he later called 'active imagination'.[96] To give expression to this inner narrative, Jung used collage[97] and,

[93] C.G. Jung and Aniela Jaffe, *Memories, Dreams, Reflections*, pp. 212–213. This phrase refers to the shamanic practices by which the shaman is called by the spirits, generally during a psychological collapse. Through this he learns what his faults are, how to self-heal them, and gains the wisdom to see into other souls (remember that one of the tasks of the shamans, according to tradition, is to treat patients by recovering lost pieces of souls).
[94] Ibid., p. 58.
[95] The profound disorientation led him to a voluntary descent into the 'kingdom of mothers', that is, to that dangerous confrontation with the unconscious.
[96] Analytical psychology has a method called 'active imagination' which consists of giving tangible form to the images of the unconscious and expanding them to consciousness. It consists of focusing attention on emotions, and more generally, on the unconscious phantoms (so-called monsters) brought to consciousness, and on letting them develop freely, without the consciousness influencing them, but interacting with them, giving life to spontaneous images. In other cultures, shamanic ones for example, it is the practice of being able to walk in the three invisible realms (infe-

inspired by childhood memories, he built a miniature village from stones as a part of an almost ritual experience. The game was a sort of rite d'entrée, which allowed him to make contact with an 'incessant flow of fantasies' coming from the 'underground'.[98]

Learning to activate his 'active imagination', he began to visualize a descent into another world. The contents of some dreams and visions were really disturbing (rivers of blood, floods, storms, glaciations) and apparently subjective. In fact, in the autumn of 1913, Jung had a series of prophetic visions of the imminent war:

I realized that a terrible catastrophe was approaching: I saw the violent yellowish waves, the fluctuating rubble of civilization works, the countless dead, and finally the sea turned to blood. . . . An internal voice told me, 'Look carefully, it's all true, it will be so.' [99]

Jung's fantasies in those times were populated by biblical figures such as Salome and Elia, which the scholar later recognized as personifications of some archetypes. Subsequently, another image emerged from his unconscious, developing naturally from Elijah and manifesting itself in a dream. This was Philemon, who teaches Jung the 'reality of the soul', becoming his inner guru, his 'psychagogue'. These apparitions are well known to the shamans, who call these ancient entities guides, or animals of power. Often these entities change shape when the shaman is ready for a more complete revelation. Jung's dreams and visions ceased in the summer of 1914 during the First World War. In search of the meaning of those images, he considered the idea of the whole experience as having something to do with art. It is interesting to note that the seductive hypothesis had been suggested by an internal female voice.[100]

I gave her the name of Philemon. Philemon was a pagan, but wrapped in an Egyptian-Hellenistic atmosphere, with a gnostic colouring. Her image appeared to me for the first time in the following dream: There was a blue sky, but it looked like the sea, not covered by clouds, but by clods of brown earth. It seemed that the clods were moving away from each other and were letting the blue water of the sea be seen. This water was, however, the blue sky. Suddenly, from the right, a winged being hovered in the air. He was an old man with taurine horns. He carried a set of four keys, holding one as if he were about to open a lock. He was winged, and his wings were those of a kingfisher, with their characteristic colours. Failing to understand this dream image, I painted it to better see it. In the days when I was busy painting I found a dead kingfisher in my garden near the lake shore! I was

rior, characterized by animals of power; superior, where the guiding spirits reside in human form; and the concrete world with its energetic facet). In the Indian and Buddhist tradition, it is the process of rediscovering the universe through the rediscovery of oneself.

[97] Invited to give his opinion about contemporary art, Jung did not hesitate to call it 'black magic'. He was referring to the breaking of the rules of art by avant-garde artists, but despite this he used a technique used by such artists (collage) to express his inner movements.

[98] 'Then I abandoned myself. Suddenly it was as if the ground was sinking, in the true sense of the word, under my feet, and I fell into a dark depth,' C.G. Jung, *Ricordi*, p. 221. Here he recalls the description of the classic shamanic journey, a descent into the subterranean world.

[99] C.G. Jung, *Ricordi, sogni, riflessioni*.

[100] A voice which he had initially recognized as his patient and subsequently as his soul; a typical and archetypal part of a human's unconscious.

stunned, as only rarely do we see such birds around Zurich. He had recently died, at least two or three days, and he had no signs of injury. Philemon and the other images of my imagination gave me the decisive conviction that there are things in the psyche that are not produced by the ego, but are produced by themselves, and have a life of their own.

The results of Jung's confrontation with the unconscious found their first realization in a collection of six small volumes bound in black leather, *The Black Books*. The contents were later transcribed into a large volume in folio, bound in red leather and called *The Red Book.*[101] The 'Records' inform us that *The Red Book* was accompanied by a series of paintings, circular in form or 'mandalas'[102], which had been created since 1916.

The debate between art and science had profoundly marked Jung's life and his relationship with the supernatural dimension, since he, during his journey into his mind, felt the need 'to obey a higher will'.

Philemon and the other figures of my imagination gave me the decisive conviction that there are things in the psyche that are not produced by the self but are produced by themselves and have their own life.[103]

Just like a guru, Philemon became an aspect of his higher self.[104]

In 1916, Jung entered into dialogues with the dead as a response to a spiritual invasion felt at his house in Küsnacht:
The whole house was inhabited by a crowd of people, as if it were crammed with spirits. They crowded right under the door, and there was a feeling of not being able to breathe properly. I was naturally tormented by the question—'For God's sake, what is it?' Then they shouted in chorus, 'Let's go back to Jerusalem, where we did not find what we were looking for.'

These words correspond to the first few lines of *Septem Sermones ad Mortuos.*[105] The crowd of spirits felt by Jung disappeared when he decided to write the sermons.

Then it began to flow uninterruptedly from me, and in just three evenings I had already written everything. As soon as I had taken the pen, all that crowd of spirits had vanished.[106]

According to Jung, his soul had withdrawn into the unconscious, which corresponds to the mythical land of the dead, the land of

[101] In *The Red Book*, Jung attempted an artistic elaboration of his fantasies in a highly sought-after language and style using the Gothic script (following the example of the medieval manuscripts).
[102] By mandala I mean a circular image that can be drawn or painted, but also modelled or even danced (think about the dances of native Americans and of dervishes). Often this form contains a quaternity and appears, as Jung discovered following his personal and clinical experience, in states of disorientation or psychic dissociation. The Navaho sand ritual paintings can be considered, like the Tibetan configurations, real mandalas. It seems that both respond to clear needs of the 'curative' type, aimed at finding a spiritual balance (even if their beauty and harmony unequivocally bring them closer to art). At the time of personal confrontation with the unconscious, Jung used these circular forms in his paintings instinctively, without caring about their meaning. Only a few years later, at Chateau d'Oex, where he drew drawings on his album daily, did he begin to conceive the mandala as a 'cryptogram of the self', a sort of mirror of the global personality, which is harmonious only when everything is going well.
[103] Jung, *The Red Book*, p. 225.
[104] In the shamanic tradition they are called guiding spirits.
[105] Jung wrote this over only three evenings.
[106] Ibid., pp. 234–235

the ancestors. Since then, it became increasingly clear that the dead beings represented the ancestral traces of the unconscious, 'the voices of the Inexplicable, of the Irresolute, of the Increment'.[107]

Jung drew a circle in his notebook every morning, a mandala, and used this to identify his current psychic situation.[108] He began to understand that artistic representations, in this case mandalas, were a mirror of the totality of the psyche.

Through Jung's writings, his mandalas and his fantasies, he came to the conclusion that his invisible inner voices, while representing the crowning of his experience in the abyss, concerned all of humanity. Most of the subsequent Jungian scientific production[109] was a continuous amplification of the imaginary productions which emerged in that period, a theoretical translation of his upsetting personal story.

This is why we are paying attention here to the imagery. This imagery is at the root of the exploration of the collective unconscious and it is also the basis of interest in art and creativity. Jung fits significantly into the debate on the relationship between psychology and art, creating a combination of the archetypal aspect with the cultural and personal aspects of artistic production.

For Jung, the work of art is a production process that goes beyond the individual, because its meaning cannot be found in the human condition which produced it. Starting from this concept, I would like to trace its similarities with Indian aesthetics.

Jung says that it is imperative that the work of art be given its due. It is necessary that analytical psychology exclude any prejudice of a clinical nature. The work of art is not a disease and therefore requires a completely different perspective than that of a doctor.[110] The meaning and character of the work of art, in all its forms, are within it and not in the human conditions that came before it. We could say that the work of art uses humans and their personal dispositions simply as a nutritious medium, using their energies as it pleases and modelling itself according to what it wants to become.[111]

Similarly in India, the image visualized by the artist comes from a revelation of the truth about the universe. Shape is not a human invention, but a revelation and visualization.

This ontology mirrors the analytical psychology consideration of the creative impulse as an autonomous complex that has a psychic life independent of consciousness. The origins of the creative work are not to be found only in the personal unconscious of the author—because in this case it would be symptomatic art and not symbolic (think of the artist's neurosis)—but must be sought in that sphere of unconscious mythology whose primordial images are generated by those properties common to the collective

[107] Jung, *The Red Book*, p. 236.
[108] Through these drawings he could observe his psychic transformations day after day.
[109] His science was the only means to extricate himself from that chaos. Otherwise his fantasies would have led him to assume an attitude of mere contemplation, away from the moral obligation to bring them back to reality.
[110] The risk of Freudian hermeneutics is represented by the psycho-biological temptation—the reduction of the work to the life of its author.
[111] C.G. Jung, 'On the relation of Analytical Psychology to Poetry'.

unconscious of humanity.

In this regard, Jung specifies that:
There are no innate representations, but innate possibilities of representations that place defined limits on the most audacious fantasy, there are categories of the activity of the imagination, in some way a-priori ideas of which existence is not demonstrable without experience.[112]

These images appear only in the formed subject as the regulating principles of its formation, which means that we cannot reconstruct the primitive model of the primordial image except by means of conclusions drawn from the finished work. The primordial or archetypal image is a figure, demon, man or process, which is repeated throughout history whenever the creative fantasy is exercised freely.

Similarly, according to ancient Indian sensibilities, only art which conforms to the rules given in the canon (*sadhana*[113]) is really beautiful, what does not obey is not beautiful.

It is at its outset, a mythological figure. Examining it from within, we note that it is in a certain way, the result of innumerable experiences typical of all past generations. The psychic residues of countless events of the same type could be seen. It represents an average of millions of individual experiences and gives an image of psychic life, subdivided and projected into multiple forms of the mythological pandemonium.[114]

When the creative fantasy is exercised freely, then these primordial images, in which the very voice of humanity resounds, are unleashed. The artist who employs them is elevating the precarious to the eternal, as if he were speaking with a thousand voices.

The artist can only express what is in him, what he is. It makes no difference whether or not the same thing has been expressed a thousand times before. There can be no property in ideas. The individual does not make them, but finds them.[115]

This vision of things might seem problematic when compared with the Western idea of art, for where is the place of originality?

The concept of art for art's sake is completely external to Indian thought. The artist's goal is not to express himself, nor is it to create beauty—the beauty is the topic and the topic is the beauty. Nothing is independent. The originality is not a problem—the artist must have incorporated all the rules, all the formulas and have understood them in order to be able to use them while adding his own spirit and also something new. This is the non-duality of copying and creativity in new hands. The freedom of the artist is not limited by the prescription of the tradition, and his creativity is developed freely within the rules themselves.
The art of the *raga*[116] (Indian classical music) is very useful in understanding this con-

[112] C.G. Jung, *Analytical Psychology and Poetic Art*, 1922
[113] Sadhana can also refer to a discipline undertaken in pursuit of a goal, or to instructions to carry out a certain practice.
[114] C.G. Jung, *Analytical Psychology and Poetic Art*, 1922
[115] Ananda K. Coomaraswamy, *'Understanding the Indian Art'*, *Introduction to Indian Art*, 8, p. 80.

cept. The musician chooses only three or four notes out of an available seven to use during his performance.

For the first part, called *alap*[117], he will have the complete freedom of improvisation. In the second section, called *jhor*[118], the music will start to play, and in some cases the voice of the singer will also follow (the musician must improvise according to the rhythm of the music and the voice). In the third section, called *jhalla*[119], the climax of the piece, there is a display of virtuoso (musicians who excel in musical techniques or execution) using advanced playing techniques, and in the fourth and final section, or *gat*[120], the fixed composition is introduced, and with it takes place a dialogue between the instrumentalist and the drummer, as well as improvised flourishes on the prepared melodic line.

The artist will be in a condition of freedom during the improvisation of the piece, without forgetting the rules and techniques of the raga. He will follow the structure but explore it at the same time. The ideas of originality, individuality, self-expression and freedom are fallacious—the freedom is to conform to the ideal form.

INDIAN ART AND JUNG'S ARCHETYPE

Every relationship with the archetype, lived or expressed, is moving in the sense that it acts by releasing in us a voice that, mediated by the artist, works on the education of the spirit.

The artist tends not to heal his wounds through a progressive adaptation with the collective, but, keeping them open, he uses his suffering as a means to bring about the healing force of creativity from the depths of his psyche.

The correlation between psychic suffering and art (concluded from my experience of analysing artists) is not a part of a causal approach, which considers the work of art as a product of the disease, but is a discovery that comes from within a perspective which views every event and every psychic phenomenon as part of a project whose meaning must be discovered.

For the artist, the act of creation is an attempt to discover and affirm his identity. It heals the splits and wounds, is a way of relating to his unconscious and is a potential present in every human being, a fact that all Jungians essentially agree on.

The concept of the artist as an individual has been thought in two very different ways: In the modern view, the artist is a special or even abnormal kind of man, endowed with

[116] Each Indian musical composition is based on a raga (or raag)—the execution is extemporized on the seven allowed notes (sa, re, ga, ma, pa, dha, ni).
[117] The *alap* is the opening section of the raga performance. It takes the form of melodic improvisation, unmetred with a slow tempo.
[118] *Jhor* is the second section of a raga. Here the tempo has increased to steady or medium pace, there is a regular pulse, an introduction of a metre and the music becomes more elaborate.
[119] *Jhalla* is the third section of a raga. The tempo increases to a fast and lively pace, the beat is now exciting with complex rhythms. This is the highest point in the piece.
[120] *Gat* or *bhajan* is the last section of a raga. The tempo is moderate-fast, the tabla-drums are introduced, and the rhythm cycle and fixed composition are introduced.

a peculiar emotional sensibility that enables him to see what we call beauty.[121]

So we convince ourselves that the artist is almost a prophet, that art is something too beautiful for this world, and that 'the artist is an individual, expressing himself, and so it has become necessary to have books written about every artist individually.'[122] We separate the artist from the manual worker and are not used to conciliating the production of the art with the products of manual work. One has a level close to perfection, and the other is something too brutal to be even compared to art.

However, these distinctions do not apply in India.

That kind of idealism that glorifies the artist who pursues a personal ideal of beauty and strives to express himself, and suffers or perishes for lack of patronage, would appear to Indian thought far more ridiculous or pitiable than heroic.[123]

The names and peculiarities of individual artists, even if we could recover them, would not enlighten us—nothing depends upon the genius or requires the knowledge of the individual psychology for its interpretation. To understand it all, we must understand experiences common to all men of the time and place in which a given work was produced.[124]

In the psyche, which is a place of creative capacity and activity, creativity is connected with both its constructive and destructive aspects. When the individual acts to generate something, he animates the realm of the imagination—that intermediate zone between the individual and the external world, that reflective moment in which events are transformed into images.

The creative imagination is therefore considered a fundamental psychic component that depends upon taking care of the soul and its images, a care that characterizes the approach of the archetypal school of art. The profound relationship between creativity and individuation, the vision of the work as a place where the artist takes care of his psychic wounds and works on his own transformation, can not only be seen through a mixed approach to art, which begins from different theoretical perspectives, but in many cases can also be cultured within one—an initiatory model that traces the dynamics of death and rebirth in the artistic product to the centre of initiation rituals.

This model makes visible the creative function of the psyche (particularly active in the artist), whilst also suggesting that the relationship between art and psychotherapy deserves some serious consideration.

Jung was among the first, if not the first, to introduce artistic activities into psychotherapy, in particular drawing and painting. We see evidence of this in his self-analysis, such as the draft of *The Red Book*—the contents of his dreams and fantasies beautifully crafted with drawings and poetic texts, de-

[121] Ananda K. Coomaraswamy, '*Understanding the Indian Art*', *Introduction to Indian Art*, 8, p. 78.
[122] Ibid.
[123] Ananda K. Coomaraswamy, '*Introduction*', *Introduction to Indian Art*.
[124] Ibid.

veloped with the technique of active imagination.

When we consider Jung's appraisal of the artistic domain, connected or not with the vicissitudes of self-analysis, we must also remember the design of the mandalas, the drafting of the *Septem Sermones ad Mortuos* and the building activities with the stones, all of which Jung considered to be material rich with symbolic value.

Once the image is fixed, the problem of its elaboration begins for the analyst. This elaboration proceeds along two directions—the principle of understanding, which aims to immediately extract the sense from the image, and the principle of representation, which invites us to enrich it and develop its shape.

All of these practices, which I have been doing for some time now in my analytic work with some of my patients, are useful and sometimes necessary exercises of amplification of the image, because they focus it better, they specify the traits and the implications, allowing it to carry out the therapeutic role that is contained in its image quality, and that, in synthesis, is that of translating into a perceptible form pulsing, affections and emotions.[125]

However, the danger presented by this Jungian approach is the tendency to consider the work, especially the form of visionary creation mentioned by Jung, as a terrain in which the action of the different archetypes must be traced. Splitting personal, archetypal and cultural elements and favouring only one of these factors does not allow for a full understanding of the artistic product.

Stopping at the examination of the creative process, Jung comes to establish a polarity that he designates as a contrast between symbolic and non-symbolic. He says that in the face of creative intention, which arises and develops as an autonomous force in the artist, one can react in two ways, either by trying to identify oneself with it and shaping it as much as possible according to one's own intention (which will result in more complete forms and aesthetically satisfactory results), or by welcoming the substantial extraneousness of the work as a process that cannot be completely guided or assimilated.

This same principle is expressed through the identification of the artist with his product—the necessity for the artist to identify with his creation is emphasized throughout the sadhana canon.

The rites that the artist must follow in order to create art, are central to the sadhana. To be able to identify completely with the concept that he wants to express, the artist must purify himself through spiritual exercises and work alone. Only through meditation and concentration will the artist be able to visualize the art piece. He will have to realize this by turning himself into a form of clairvoyant. This visualization can occur during sleep, or even during the day, using a yantra or a mantra.[126]

There are three ways to go about this visualization: 1) Attentive observation of the

[125] C.G. Jung, *L'uomo e i suoi simboli.*

[126] To enter the trance state, shamans often use percussion; Jung calls this process 'active imagination'. In any case, in all these means, concentration and constancy are used to enter the subterranean world.

rules 2) Concentration and meditation, and 3) Awareness.

Markandeya replied Prakrti and Vikrti (come into existence) through the (variation in) form of the Supreme Soul. The form of Him (which is) scarcely to be perceived is called Prakrti. The whole universe should be known as the Vikrti of Him, when endowed with form. Worship and meditation (of the Supreme Being) are possible (only when He is) endowed with form. The best position of the (Supreme) Soul (however) is to be imagined without form. To see the worlds (He) possesses eyes closed in meditation. This concession being made, life in its entirety becomes fit for artistic representation, and the realm of imagination is as close within the reach of the artists, as nature that surrounds him, for tradition guides him in the one case and observation checks and inspires him in the other. [127]

In *Sukranitisara*[128] the importance of the contemplative act is underlined in the statements 'When the visualization is done the artist can start to work'[129] and 'When the sample has been formulated, he can realize on the wall what has been visualized.'[130]

The third step, the awareness, is the result of the first two steps (the visualization and the work). The awareness (or understanding) comes from the replacement of the duality of the subject (creator of the knowledge) and object (knowledge) with a non-duality in which subject and object are one.

None of the products of art can be attributed to a specific being—behind an artisan there is the knowledge of an entire population. Everything will become clear if it is kept in mind that the form is not a human invention, but, as said earlier, a revelation and a visualization. Art is based on social dynamics, not on private choice. It is not the expression of some particular personality or of some individual idiosyncrasy; it is the human being, as the external and universal self, who is expressed. It is this supra-individual level from which the artist derives his vitality. What he produces is not the result of his observation of humans and things in the world but what he sees in his mind as the archetypes, iconographic images and portraiture of standardized types of human beings. As Ruskin clarified, the 'virtue of originality is not newness . . . it is only genuineness'.[131]

In the Indian tradition, the practice of art is acquired from previous generations. When the only point that matters is the topic, originality is not a virtue, just as copying is not a crime. 'Originality and novelty are never intentional. Changes in form, distinguishing the art of one age from that of another, reflect the necessities of current theology.'[132] Artistic tradition is a living entity, not restricted to a specific sector but applied across different domains of life. Similarly, 'there are no distinctions of fine and applied or decorative art and no insurmountable barrier dividing the art of the

[127] The *Vishnudharmottara* Part III, Ch. 40, Verses 1–19.
[128] One of the classic canonical scriptures
[129] *Sukranitisara* VII, 74, p. 116.
[130] Ibid., 3, p. 158.
[131] V. Raghavan, *The Aesthetics of Ananda Coomaraswamy*.
[132] Ananda K. Coomaraswamy, *'Introduction'*, *Introduction to Indian Art*.

folk from the canonical arts'.[133] The artist is not a special kind of person, but every person is necessarily a special kind of artist.

In India, art is understood as being mixed with everyday life in a completely different manner than it is understood to be in the Western world. Coomaraswamy describes this mindset by saying, 'Art was an integral quality inhering in all activities,[134] entertained by all in their daily environment, and produced by all in proportion to the vitality of their activities.'

This can be understood if we move our axis from the love we have for art for art's own sake to the love we have for life in general, until we reach the point of seeing all everyday products as beautiful. This beauty can be found in their utility and the fact of their being a product of many lives which, one after the other, seeks to improve the quality of their existence. 'A race producing great art, however, does so, not by its love of art, but by its love of life.'[135] Anything well made can be beautiful, just as anything which responds to a human need and which can be used daily can be considered a work of art.

[133] Ananda K. Coomaraswamy, *'Introduction', Introduction to Indian Art.*
[134] Ibid.
[135] Ibid.

Where does the representation of the un-representable come from? Where does the visual image come from when it has to represent the universe, or the unconscious, or things that do not pertain to the phenomenal world and are visible only to the eyes of the psyche, of the soul?

I start from the Indian concept of aesthetic philosophy, as discussed in the previous chapter. According to that, there is no subject-object distinction between the artist and the art he produces. He does not discover something new but merely uncovers an already existing truth. We can expand this idea by adding that as the artist always keeps the goal of his work in mind, the viewer cannot touch the beauty of the product without an ideal emphatic vantage point. He cannot reach the stage of acceptance (sādharana) of the passions, which make the subject come alive without integrating in his imagination its meaning (atha-bhāvana). The idea is that the artist is a man who is being seen in the world, who is making miniature universes that are representations of the entire cosmos.

The artwork guides the viewer to achieve such a realization. The vision of beauty is a pure act of contemplation and a conscious identification with the mind's interior. Beauty is based on canonical tradition. What the rules of the canon dictate is not the final image of the product, but what process has to be followed. It is not the external shape—subjective and impermanent—but the inner form—permanent and communitarian, even universal. The artist is not obligated to express only himself. His goal does not have an aesthetic direction, but it is informed by aesthetic and philosophical knowledge. He must express certain truths, the origin of which is the universe. Thus beauty is not independent from the subject, beauty is the subject as the subject is beauty.

As we can clearly see, the distance between the visible and the invisible (adjectives that are typically used to distinguish between the human or earthly dimension and the spiritual or heavenly dimension) merge into one in this philosophy. This concept is based on the idea that the human being contains the universe within himself. In this direction, after having dealt with Jung's beliefs about art, it is necessary to address the language of the unconscious. Interestingly, numerous cultures, whether they are near or distant at the spatial and temporal level, seem to have the same form of expression—symbols and mandalas—that act as continuous references to one's inner life.

THE MANDALA

Mandala is a word that derives from the Sanskrit language, meaning a magic circle, a circumference and the centre. Typical mandala images consist of circular figures, inside which there are other geometric shapes such as squares and triangles. There is significant diversity of images, but all follow a precise geometric ratio.

Mandala-style images are typical of Hinduism and Buddhism, and represent the universe and its origins. They are thought to be useful for meditation, personal development and the growth of one's spirituality. They can be made with fabrics, colours, powders and sand, and can be used as a plan when building temples. The Mandala has always been used to induce meditation and to consecrate places or moments in the life of a person.

The mandala has always been present in the history of all cultures.[136] It is present in nature,[137] in architectural constructions, in rituals and in religions. Ancient populations used the circle as a protective element, an enclosure to defend a person or to strengthen his spirit, and the first drawings that children of every culture begin to make are shaped like circular spirals. Across most of the civilizations in our history, we invariably see symbols expressed through circular drawings.

In some churches, mandalas are imprinted on the floor mazes[138], which represent the link between the Mandala and the inner journey that each of us can follow to achieve spiritual betterment. In Christian culture,[139] mandalas are present in the church in the form of roses and rosettes. They are most often present in Gothic cathedrals, which represent the aspiration to totality and to inner order. The rosettes spread and collect the light in such a way that, at times, entering a cathedral, one has the impression of having entered a large Mandala. With them, while contemplating them, we get in touch with our inner selves.

The best-known Mandalas are of Tibetan origin,[140] and these have assumed a deeply spiritual connotation. The Buddhist Mandala is a dynamic concept, in which places, figures and objects are represented in an analytical and detailed manner. According to Buddhists, the Mandala represents an imaginary temple that embodies the birth of the cosmos, its contemplation and the interiorization of the image. The disciple can reach a mental state in which they are free from the bonds of materialism and free to direct their own actions.

The mandala is widespread in most religions and has the important task of bringing man back to the Divine Creator. Greeks, Egyptians and the Navajo built Mandalas in an attempt to represent the illusion of earthly life with all its ephemeral and transitory components and for the purpose of describing the magical symbolism of the universe and its construction within the eternal circle of existence. The equivalent of the mandala in India is the yantra. These are more schematic, use geometric figures and Sanskrit letters and contain no representations of places or people. The body can participate in the realization of a yantra using yoga postures that promote meditation.

In modern times, the greatest scholar of the Mandalas was Carl Gustav Jung,[141] and even today he remains the main point of academic reference in this regard. Jung was,

[136] Ancient graffiti with circular patterns has been found in Africa, Europe and North America.
[137] In fruit, in stones, in flowers, in trees, in the sky, etc.
[138] For example, the labyrinth of the Cathedral of Chartres (built around AD 1200) was traversed on foot, or even by crawling, in order to obtain indulgences. It symbolically represented the journey to the holy city of Jerusalem.
[139] Examples of mandalas can also be found in Christianity in the early Middle Ages—they generally feature Christ at the centre and the four Evangelists (or their symbols) at the four cardinal points.
[140] There are many kinds of Tibetan mandalas, each of which has a specific function to help the disciple learn the Buddha's teachings. Each mandala has its own rituals, prayers and mantras. The work of building the mandala ends with a ceremony that sees the destruction of the mandala—meant to remember the transience of life and its rebirth. The sands and coloured earth that are used to make the mandala are distributed to those present at the ceremony, so that they may enjoy the benefits of the mandala themselves.
[141] In 1938 in Darjeeling, Carl Jung had the opportunity to discuss the mandala with a lamaic Rimpoche named Lingdam Gomchen at the monastery of Bhutia Busty. Gomchem explained the Mandala to Jung as a dmigpa, a mental image that could be built up only by the imagination of a fully instructed lama. He also said that no Mandala was

in fact, the first from the West to study the mandalas and recommend them to his patients. He spontaneously came across the therapeutic potential of the mandala during a phase of profound journey of self-analysis.

I began to understand the Mandala drawings. . . . There, every morning I sketched in a notebook a small circular pattern, a mandala, which seemed to correspond to my intimate condition of that period. With the help of these drawings I could observe my psychic transformations from day to day. . . . When I began to draw the mandalas, however, I saw that everything, all the roads I had followed, all the steps taken, always brought back to a single point, that is, in the middle. It became increasingly clear to me that the mandala is the centre.[142]

The central point of the mandala image can be taken to represent the unconscious of man; it is the centrifugal force that pushes it to experimentation in the external world and the centripetal force that brings it back for introspection in the internal world. It is a matter of ritual, a reiterative process, requiring meditation to realign one's inner mandala.

Jung noticed that, when he asked his patients to draw mandalas, the images changed along with the change of psychological state that the person was experiencing. He also noticed that, despite the different cultures and personalities of the patients, particular forms were common in their images, in particular the circle and the central point. He considered these symbols as archetypal figures of the collective unconscious, which he differentiated from the individual unconscious. The individual unconscious belongs to each individual and is formed by the personal experiences of each person. Within this is the collective unconscious, formed of that which has not been personally acquired and experienced. To the collective unconscious belongs inherited common primordial images, which contain within themselves the symbolism of the birth of man and the world. These primordial images can re-emerge through the emotions of an individual.

For Jung, these radial or spherical images are none other than the exteriorization of the collective unconscious. According to Jung, it is not religion that invents the sacred, but it is the sacred that is projected in the mind of man so that he can make it the instrument with which to build religion. Every human faith is, by definition, contingently bound to the subjective beliefs of the individual. But every faith is promoted by something extra-human, something present in the very essence of man. The metaphorical symbols of any faith seem to reflect the truly fundamental structures of the human mind and these symbols remain largely unaffected by cultural contexts. Often, the basic structures

like any other—they were all different. He told Jung that the mandalas found in monasteries and temples were of no particular significance as they were simply external representations.
Jung has returned several times to the mandalas in his writings, such as in *Psychology and Alchemy* (1944), *The Philosopher Tree* (1945/54), *Mandala Symbolism* (1950), *What Are the Mandalas* (1955), and *Mysterium coniunctionis* (1955–56). These texts investigate another universe, one made of images, in which mandalas play an introspective, reflective and coordinating role, leading to the process of individuation, then of separation, then of union, then again individuation, in a dialectically swirling process which never ends and through which man can search for his own self.

[142]Jung, *Erinnerungen*, p. 199.

are of a graphic rather than a verbal nature; in this situation, symmetry in representation plays a fundamental role.

We must see the mandala from a Jungian perspective and realize how they can prove to be epiphanically useful both for understanding the hidden part of our self and for solving the inner complexes that we cannot see because of our psychological blindness. The paradigm of the journey that contemporary man is destined to follow expands to embrace the cosmos. It embraces the archetypal universality that marked us in primordial times and which we carry within us like a genetic code. Mandalas, therefore, take on an impersonal meaning, deriving directly from their archetypal co-location in the collective unconscious, where the universal psychic nature generates a Mandala that is coherent with its condition, integrally connected with the subject through emotions—on the surface and beneath it.

Things that have such distant roots in the history of humanity, like the mandala, naturally touch the deeper layers of the unconscious, a place where conscious language turns out to be impotent. One cannot acquire these unconscious strata by education—it is innate. It can also be seen as a universal library of human knowledge, the transcendental wisdom that guides mankind. Such knowledge can re-emerge[143] from the obscure depth of oblivion to express the greatest presentiment of consciousness and the supreme intuition of the spirit, and thus it is possible to merge the oneness of the consciousness of the present with the most remote past of life.[144]

The mandala, as a structure rooted in the unconscious, represents the movement between the inside and the outside—forces which lead to the exploration of the external world and to our interiority. The centre of the Mandala, from which everything begins, is like the centre of one's soul, where one can regain energy and harmony.

To design a mandala means to create a mirror of our inner world at that particular moment of our life. The use of selected geometric shapes,[145] colours,[146] numbers,[147]

[143] Jung stated that the religious life must be linked with the experience of the archetype of the collective unconscious. Thus, God himself is experienced like an archetype on the psychic level.

[144] Jung, *Kommentar*, p. 36.

[145] The circle represents the beginning and end of all things, the square represents stability and solidity, and the triangle represents a union of the body, mind and spirit. The union of two equilateral triangles represents the seal of Solomon with the four elements—earth, air, water and fire. The cross is an ancient symbol expressing a connection between the spiritual and the material world and the union of the opposites. The star represents the divine—a symbol of personal identity. The flower is the symbol of the recovery of inner growth. The sun is the symbol of energy and life force. The tree symbol represents the force of life, with its roots indicating home and the people we are emotionally attached to.

[146] Red is the colour of fire, representing life and warmth. Using red symbolizes passion, action and strong emotions. It can also mean anger, hate, ire. Blue is the colour of the sea and the sky, and thus expresses calm, serenity and harmony. Green is the colour of nature, and reminds us of nature's cyclical rebirth. It is a relaxing colour that leads to reflection and gives a sense of security. Yellow is the colour of the sun and light. It expresses joy, life and relationships with others. Orange is born of the union of red with yellow. It is the colour of the rising sun. It represents joy, willpower and suggests the resolution to problems. White contains all the colours, so it is a symbol of perfection. Using this colour evokes simplicity, purity, innocence and links to sacredness and transcendence. Black is the absence of colour. It is the colour of darkness, evil and mystery. It is a symbol of sadness and death. It also represents aggressiveness and pessimism. Pink is born of the mixture of red and white. It represents delicacy and it is a colour associated with femininity, tenderness, fragility and vulnerability.

[147] 'One' symbolizes the individual as a unit. It can be a sign of egocentrism. 'Two' represents the dualism between body and spirit. It expresses alternation and conflict. It can mean a desire for comparison with important people.

everything belongs to a personal choice which evokes our inner reality. Even the mode of colouring can indicate something about us. For example, one who starts colouring from the centre and moves outwards will be a person who is sure of himself and his centre. In contrast, one who starts colouring a Mandala from the outside and moves inward may be insecure, with little confidence in themselves and in the world.[148]

The Mandalas are representative of both the whole of humanity and of the individual—they are the golden flower[149] from which the collective unconscious is able to germinate in the personal unconscious. In its graphical reproduction, the mandala manifests a quadrature pattern. The quadrature of the circle is an archetype symbol that represents the decomposition of the initial chaotic unit into the four elements and the subsequent reassembly into a higher unit. Quaternity is the pattern for all the images of God, because if the definitive and decisive idea of completeness is the circle, then its ordinary division is into quarters. An archetype is an innate tendency that transforms the individual consciousness. It is a trait defined more through a drive than through inherited content and images. It is a matrix that influences human behaviour as well as ideas. It also has a bearing on ethical, moral, religious and cultural levels. Thus, archetypes are inborn tendencies that shape the human behaviour, and although Jung stressed the necessity of free personal creation of the mandala, he explained that these archetypal patterns would always reemerge, reflecting the patterns of the universe unfolding in absolute consciousness.

Individuation, for Jung, meant realization of the self. It is the process through which one becomes oneself—a self that is indivisible and unique. It is an expression of uniqueness and self-sufficiency at a microcosmic level. Jung discovered this process during his confrontations with the unconscious and especially when he was painting his first Mandalas.

Jung wrote about these initial moments in his autobiography:

My Mandalas[150] *were cryptograms concerning the state of the self, which were pre-*

'Three' is considered the perfect number. It represents the relationship between body, mind and spirit. 'Four' represents the pursuit of balance and harmony, and the contrast between the divine and the material world. 'Five' expresses the desire for psychophysical balance. It recalls the meaning of the five-pointed star—the man who expands to occupy his space and his reality. 'Six' is a number with a strong female symbolism. It is, therefore, the number of creativity and balance. 'Seven' represents the closure of a cycle and the search for a new equilibrium. It indicates a transformation and inner activity. 'Eight' can signify organization and a balanced, harmonious personality. 'Nine' indicates the need for synthesis and harmony between the physical body, the mind and the spirit. It represents the mystery of human existence. 'Ten' is the number of our fingers, of the Ten Commandments, the number that recalls perfection, realism and morality.

[148] The use of the Mandala can help us achieve spiritual and inner growth, or to find a balance in a particular moment or period of our life. The Mandala, beyond all the archetypal, religious and sacred symbolism, is an image of ourselves—the realization and contemplation of which can increase our degree of consciousness and awareness.

[149] '*Il segreto del fiore d'oro*' is the text that, in the rediscovery of the meaning of alchemy and of all the related processes of the collective unconscious, began the psychological confrontation with the East.
The golden flower is a Mandalic symbol which Jung had already observed in the work of his patients; he describes it as a flowered Mandala drawn from above, that is, like a regular geometric ornament. It appears as a flower that grows from a luminescent coloured plant—a solar wheel based on the number four.

[150] Jung designed his first Mandala in 1916, when he was aged forty-one, using the simplest form—a circle with a centre. Every day he created another and studied its symmetry, which he considered a revealing sign of his own psychic equilibrium. When prey to strong and disturbing emotions, the circle was altered; when the creator was in harmony with himself, the circle was balanced.

sented to me anew each day. In them I saw the self, that is, my whole being. . . . The self, I thought, was like the monad which I am, and which is my world. The Mandala represents this monad, and corresponds to the microcosmic nature of the psyche.

The question arose repeatedly—what is this process leading to? Where is its goal? From my own experience, I knew by now that I could not presume to choose a goal which would seem trustworthy to me. It had been proved to me that I had to abandon the idea of the superordinate position of the ego. After all, I had been brought up short when I had attempted to maintain it. . . . I was being compelled to go through this process of the unconscious.

I had to let myself be carried along by the current, without a notion of where it would lead me. When I began drawing the mandalas, however, I saw that everything, all the paths I had been following, all the steps I had taken, were leading back to a single point, a mid-point. It became increasingly plain to me that the Mandala is the centre. It is the exponent of all paths. It is the path to the centre, to individuation. During those years, between 1918 and 1920, I began to understand that the goal of psychic development is the self. There is no linear evolution; there is only a circumambulation of the self.[151]

Of course, this idea was not unique to Jung. In *Psychology and Alchemy*, Jung writes about how psychotherapeutic work can be interrupted when the symbol is recollected. In some cases, the process extends beyond the realm of psychotherapy. It seems that psyche tends towards a target beyond the conscious interest of the ego. That target is in some dimension what the ego does not know about. It is the realization of the self, or uniqueness, as previously mentioned. This led Jung to look for specific elements of the individuation process in other case studies—patients or close relatives. The book *Psychology and Alchemy* illustrates, with the help of dream interpretation, this very centring process which leads to the self (in the case of a patient who has no prior initiation).

The years when I followed the internal images were the most important era of my life, in which everything was decided. It all started then, and the later details are just additions and clarifications. All my back activity consisted in elaborating what in those years had sprung from the unconscious and had first overwhelmed me. It was the raw material for the work of a lifetime.[152]

In an attempt to understand Jung's dramatic journey 'to the other pole of the world', we have seen what mandalas are, from a Jungian perspective and how they can prove to be epiphanically useful for understanding the hidden part of ourselves. Jung's journey became a paradigm of the journey which contemporary humans are destined to undertake—one which expands to embrace the cosmos, a universal symbolism that is also registered in us as part of our own DNA. Consequently, mandalas take on an impersonal meaning, deriving directly from their archetypal co-location in the collective unconscious, where the impersonal psychic

[151] Carl Jung, *Memories, Dreams, Reflections*, p. 196.
[152] Ibid.

nature acts as an intelligible and universal connector for every individual who, with autonomy and dynamism, generates a mandala consistent with his own condition, connected integrally through his emotions.

Similar to the visionary art of William Blake, the symbols, colours, numbers and geometric forms of the Mandala work together to produce a representation, not of a visible reality but of inner movements. The images create a chain which is not limited to the individual but which unites all human beings throughout time and space. The language spoken by our interior, by our soul, by our unconscious, is thus—a language of symbols.

I paint to evoke a changing language of symbols, a language with which to remark upon the qualities of our mysterious capacities which direct us toward ultimate reality. An artist is a prophet and seer, not a painter, or craftsman, or design maker, or reporter or entertainer . . . the artist has the superiorly searching perception with which that world outside of man's contamination can be penetrated and the truth drawn out from it. —Morris Graves [153].

[153] Morris Graves: *Selected letters*, University of Washington Press; First Edition (January 30, 2013).

visual excursus

Part One

// Architecture

// Medieval Period [i]

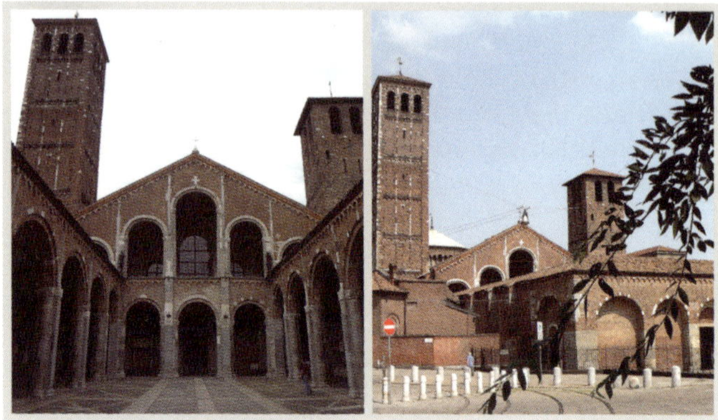

The Basilica of Sant'Ambrogio [ii]

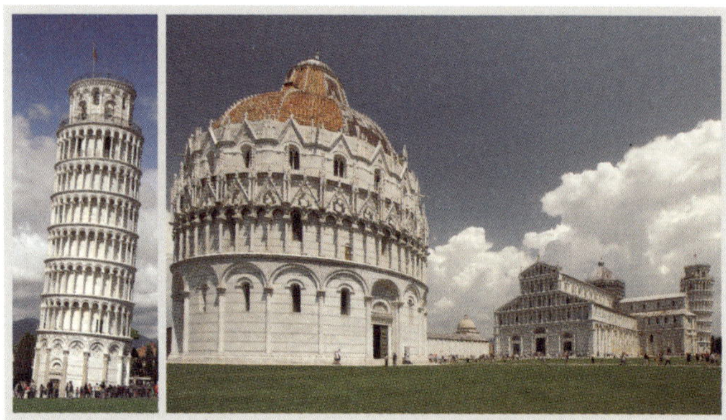

The Tower of Pisa and the Bell Tower of the Cathedral of Pisa [iii]

[i] The architecture of this period included the Romanesque French, and Gothic styles. The constructions had a predominantly religious purpose—churches, cathedrals and monasteries, for example.
[ii] ***Basilica di Sant'Ambrogio*** - One of the oldest churches in Milan, it was built by St Ambrose in 379–386, in an area where numerous martyrs of the Roman persecutions had been buried. The initial name of the church was Basilica Martyrum. Considered a prototype of Romanesque architecture, this basilica is built in brick on the earlier Paleo-Christian basilica. Preceded by a deep quadriportico, it has a gabled facade and a plan with three naves. The central nave is covered by vast cross vaults. In front of the presbytery, covered by a barrel vault, there is an octagonal dome.
[iii] ***The Tower of Pisa and the Bell Tower of the Cathedral of Pisa*** - The architects involved in these constructions included Bonanno Pisano (who started the work), Giovanni di Simone (who continued the project) and Tommaso Pisano. The tower began to bow during construction due to the subsidence of the land it was built on. However, thanks to recent engineering works, the leaning has been partially reversed and the tower is not in danger of falling. The Romanesque style characterizes the four monuments of the Pisan square—the tower, the cathedral, the Camposanto and the baptistery. Here Galileo performed his first experiments related to his theory of gravity.

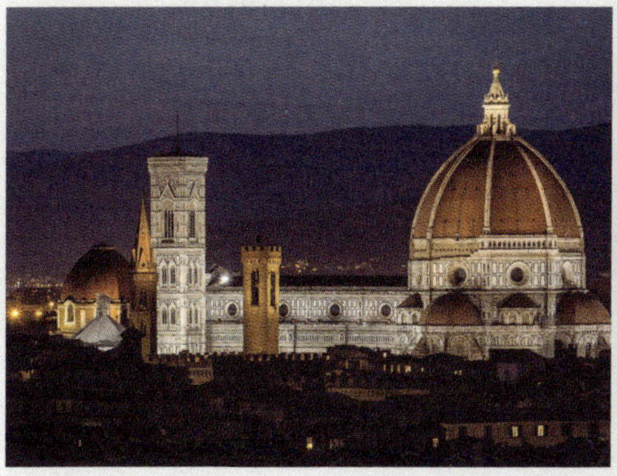
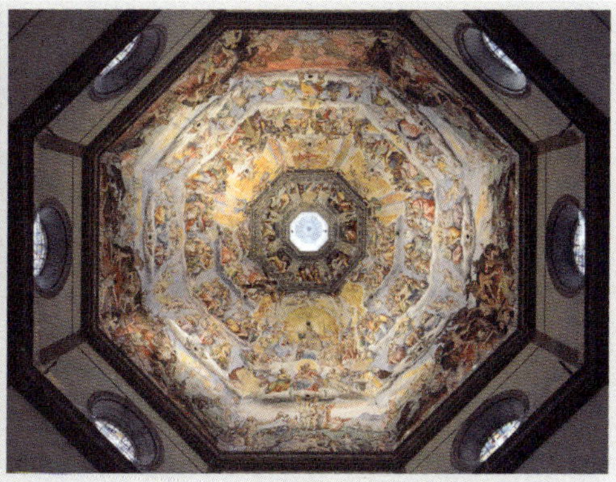

Santa Maria del Fiore [iv]

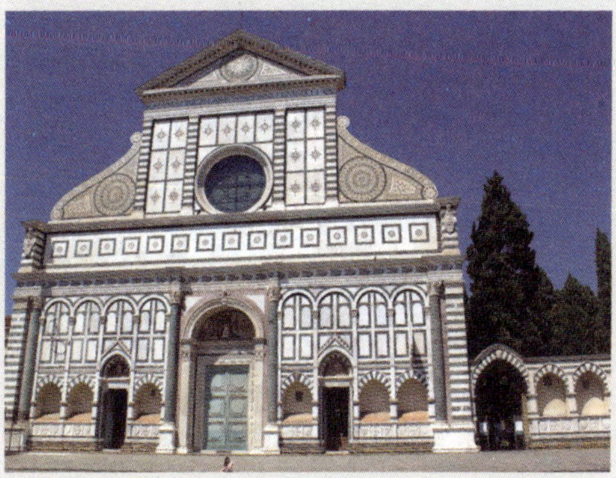

Santa Maria Novella [v]

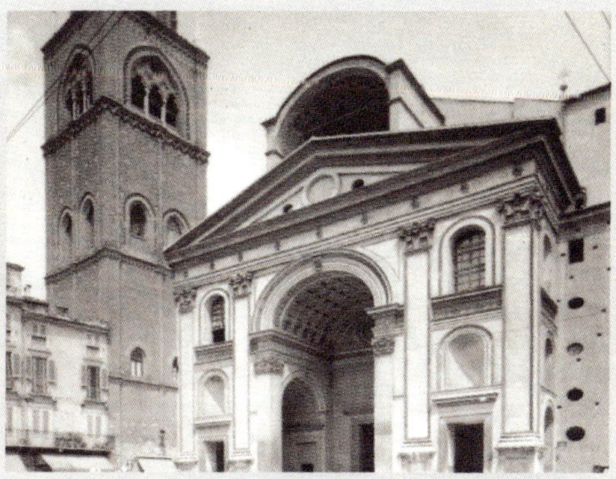

Basilica of Sant'Andrea [vi]

[iv] ***Santa Maria del Fiore*** - The construction of Santa Maria del Fiore was begun in 1296 and was structurally completed by 1436. It was built in the Gothic style, to a design of Arnolfo di Cambio, with the dome designed by Filippo Brunelleschi. Brunelleschi designed the dome to be self-supporting, and affirmed the new position of the architect as a designer responsible in person for his work, able to face formal technical problems under both theoretical and executive points of view. He is credited with the invention of perspective, understood as the application of mathematical principles and visual perception to architecture.
[v] ***Santa Maria Novella*** - The facade of the Santa Maria Novella (in Florence) was designed in 1450 by Leon Battista Alberti. The motif featured geometric coloured marble according to the classical laws of harmony and modular relationships based on the square. In 1470 Alberti added a triangular pediment between the two large scrolls of the facade.
[vi] ***Basilica of Sant'Andrea*** - This is a Mantuan minor basilica. Its construction began in 1472 according to the designs of Leon Battista Alberti.

// Renaissance [vii]

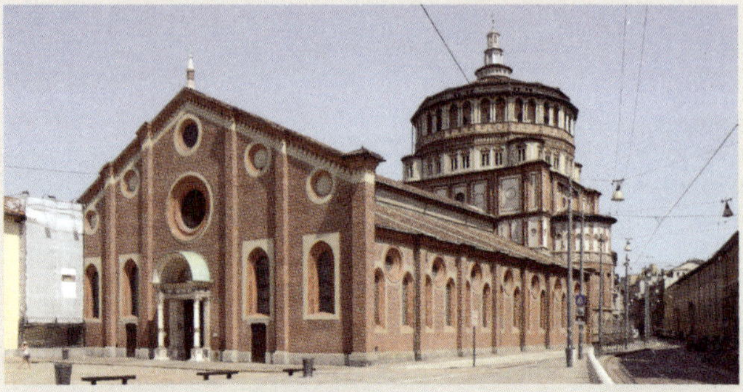

Santa Maria delle grazie [viii]

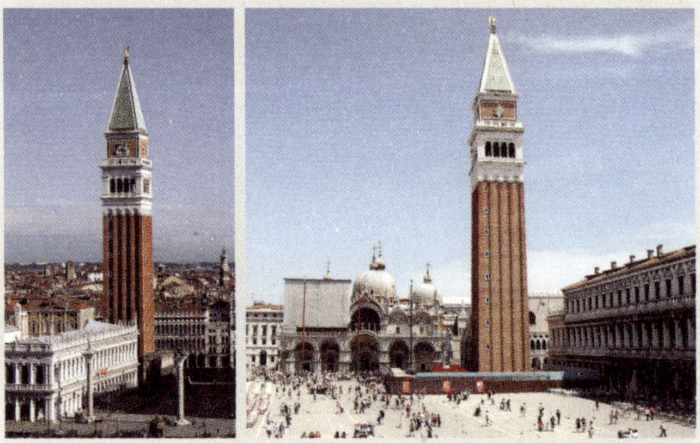

Campanile di San Marco [ix]

[vii] ***The Renaissance period*** saw a deliberate resurrection of Greek and Roman architectural traditions. Two major exponents included Donato Bramante and Sansovino. Donato Bramante (b. 1444) was an architect working in Lombardy and Rome. Bramante was a great innovator in the Classical sense, synthesizing the laws of configuration (founded on the relationship between the historical situation in the use of Classical orders and their combinations) within structures carefully calibrated from the point of view of spatial relationships. Sansovino (1486–1570) was a Florentine architect and sculptor who acquired a taste for the Classical style of Bramante and Raphael in Rome. He adapted it to the particular conditions of the urban character of Venice. He should be considered the main figure in architecture in Venice in the 1500s. Out of his work, of particular interest is the loggia of the Venetian bell tower.

[viii] ***Santa Maria delle grazie*** (Holy Mary of Grace) - Built between 1492 to 1497, this church and Dominican convent in Milan, northern Italy, is included in the UNESCO World Heritage sites' list. Bramante worked on the crossing and the dome as well the transept apses and the coir with apse.

[ix] ***Campanile di San Marco*** (Canpanièl de San Marco or St Mark's Campanile) - This is the bell tower of St Mark's Basilica in Venice, Italy, located in the Piazza San Marco. It was built by Sansovino and completed in 1549. It is one of the most recognizable symbols of the city.

// 1600s [x]

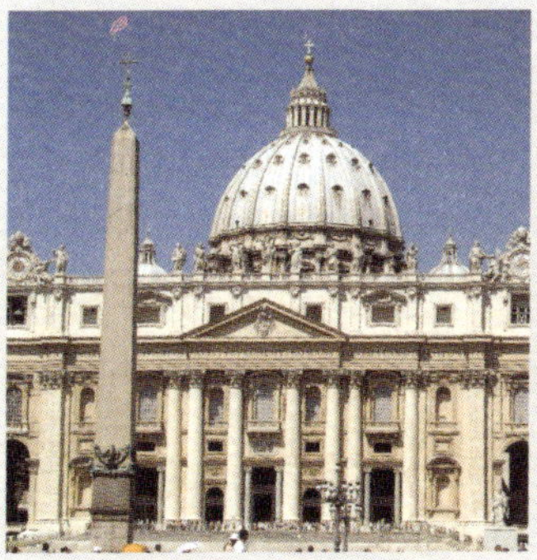

Papal Basilica of St Peter [xi]

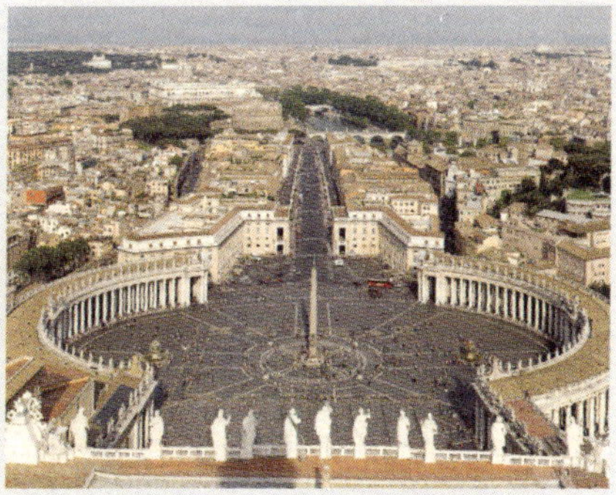

Square in front of St Peter's Basilica [xii]

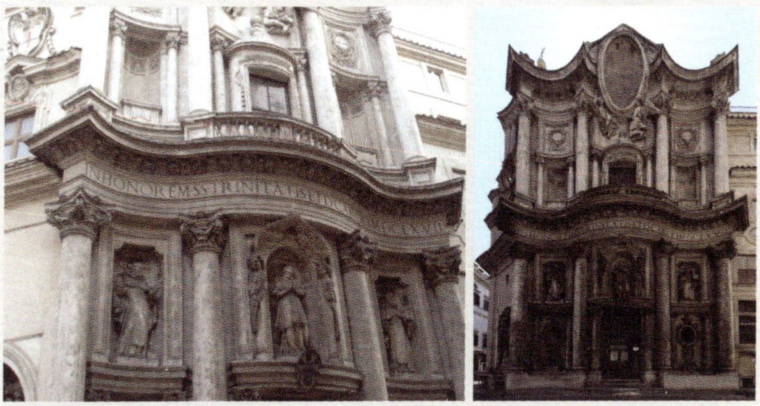

San Carlo alle Quattro Fontane [xiii]

[x] Two architects famous during the **1600s** were Lorenzo Bernini and Francesco Borromini. Bernini (1598–1680) was an architect, sculptor and set designer who, without denying the classic balance of the Renaissance tradition, modified its forms with Baroque sensibility and an original scenic and spectacular taste. His life was devoted to different popes, especially Pope Urban VIIIth Borromini (1599–1667), unlike Bernini, always remained outside of the courtly world. He dedicated himself exclusively to architecture, a domain in which, through his religious fervour, he was able to combine an extraordinary technical expertise with a profound cultural education. In his work, the space is dynamically designed and low-quality materials are used, such as brick masonry, white plaster and stucco decorations, rather than marble and precious materials.

[xi] ***Papal Basilica of St Peter*** - Located in the Vatican, St Peter's Basilica is an Italian Renaissance church in Vatican City. It was designed principally by Carlo Maderno (1607–1612), who was a master of the Baroque style. His taste can be defined as preparatory, a connecting element between the Renaissance architecture and the successive innovations in architectural language.

[xii] ***Square in front of St Peter's Basilica*** - Pope Alexander VII charged Bernini to design this. In 1657, Bernini designed the oval square delimited by an architraves portico. It featured a series of 284 columns, crowned by 140 statues of saints. The portico was inserted on two wings which connected it to the facade. With this colonnade it appears that the Church of Rome welcomes and embraces all the faithful, creating an architecture which connects the basilica to the city.

[xiii] ***San Carlo alle Quattro Fontane*** (Saint Charles at the Four Fountains) - Also called San Carlino, this is a Roman Catholic church in Rome, Italy. The church was designed by the architect Francesco Borromini in 1638.

// 1700s [xiv]

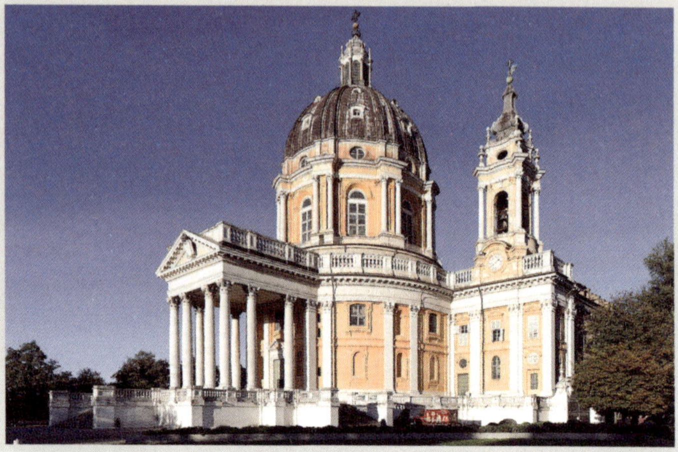

Basilica of San Superga [xv]

// Neoclassical Architecture [xvi]

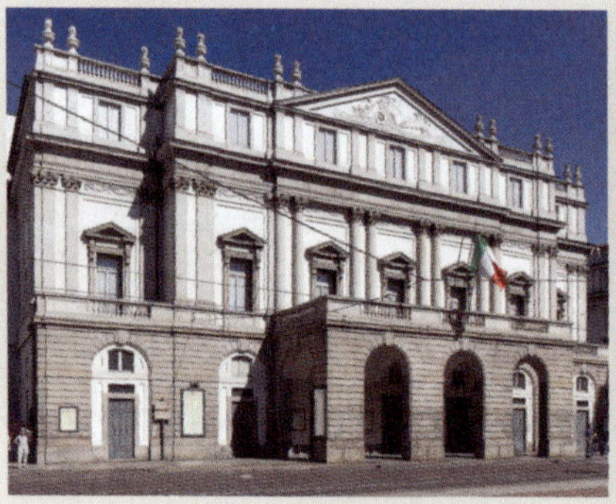

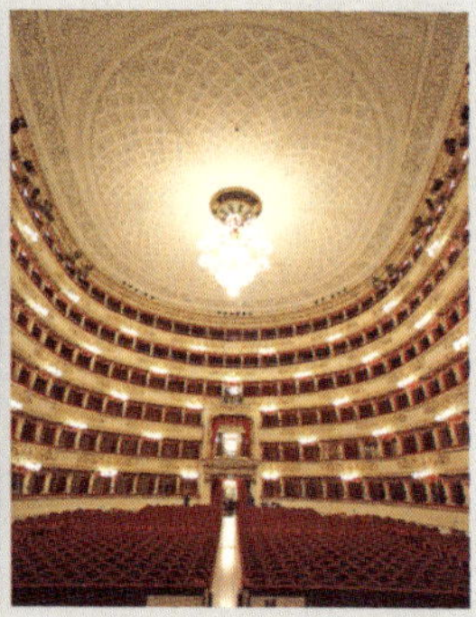

La Scala [xvii]

[xiv] Towards the middle of the century a different orientation of architecture can be observed: less decorative, more functional, with a language that anticipates the subsequent affirmation of the Neoclassical era.
[xv] ***Basilica of San Superga*** - This was built between 1717 and 1730 for Victor Amadeus II of Savoy. It was designed by Filippo Juvarra and located at the top of the hill of Superga, overlooking the city where Prince Eugene of Savoy had defeated the French. It was funded by Duke Vittorio Amedeo Secondo di Savoia after the siege and the battle of Turin in 1706, and is dedicated to the Madonna Delle Grazie.
[xvi] **Neoclassical architecture** was the product of the 18th- and 19th-century revival of the Classical principles of design. Much of the work was inspired by Andrea Palladio. Giovanni Antontio Medrano and Alessandro Pompei were among the early pioneers of this style in Italy.
[xvii] ***La Scala*** - Giuseppe Piermarini worked in Milan, renovating and constructing the Teatro alla Scala. Funding for the construction of the theatre came from a group of Milanese families who continued to support Piermarini. He began in 1776. A fire destroyed the previous theatre, The Teatro Regio Ducale, after a carnival gala. The site chosen was that of the church of Santa Maria alla Scala, which was demolished to make way for the theatre. The theatre was used not only as a place of entertainment but also for the public life of the owners, who used it to host their guests, to enjoy their meals and gambling. It was inaugurated in 1778.

// Sculpture

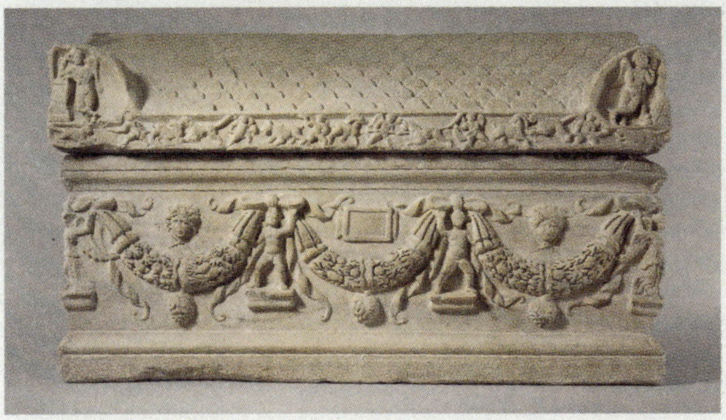

Sarcophagi [xix]

// Medieval Period [xviii]

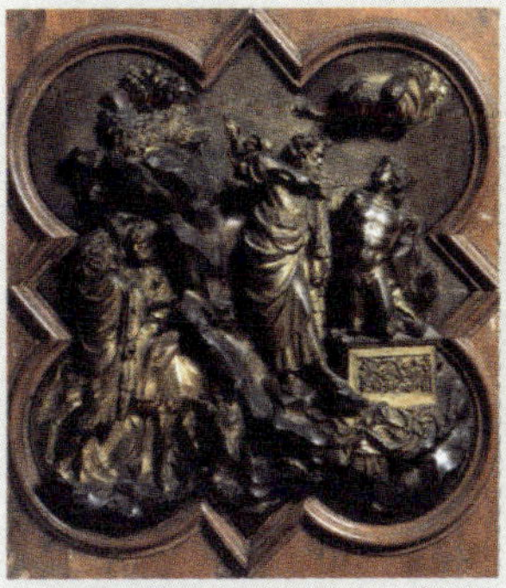

Sacrifice of Isaac [xx]

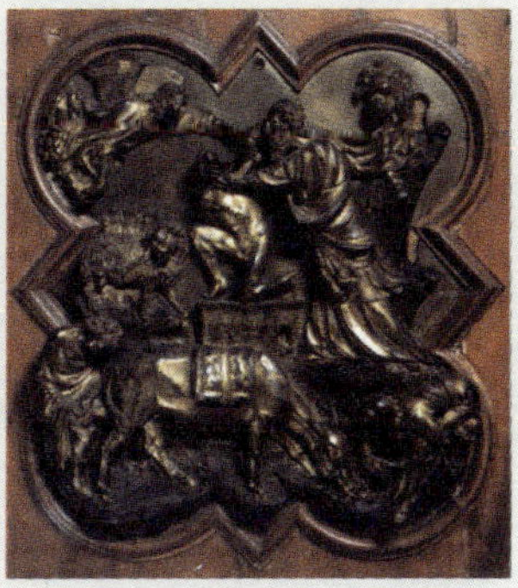

Sacrifice of Isaac [xxi]

// Humanism

[xviii] During this period. statues became less popular as sculptural forms, whereas reliefs, carvings and carved panels became more dominant.

[xix] ***Sarcophagi*** (tombs) - These were made in Ravenna in the 15th century. In the domain of sculpture, figures were represented mostly frontally, in static poses, with little sense of perspective, and as rough bodies with fixed features. There was no psychological characterization—the features appear all the same, as ecstatic stereotypes. The only sense of perspective was in the context of the social standing of the characters—the most powerful characters were represented as the biggest; the least powerful as the smallest.

[xx] ***Sacrifice of Isaac*** - This is a bronze tile made in 1401 for a competition to design the door of the Baptistery in Florence, by Lorenzo Ghibertini. The scene takes place within a unitary space which gently slopes towards the bottom of the tile itself. The figures appear almost in pose and the reference to the ancient style is expressed in the elegant nude figure of Isaac.

[xxi] ***Sacrifice of Isaac*** - In this sculpture, also called 'Formelle', by Brunelleschi (1401), we see an innovative character. The figures in the foreground cross the borders of the frame—projecting outwards—and the scene is fragmented into distinct episodes, which find their dramatic centre in the gesture of the angel intervening to stop the hand of Abraham.

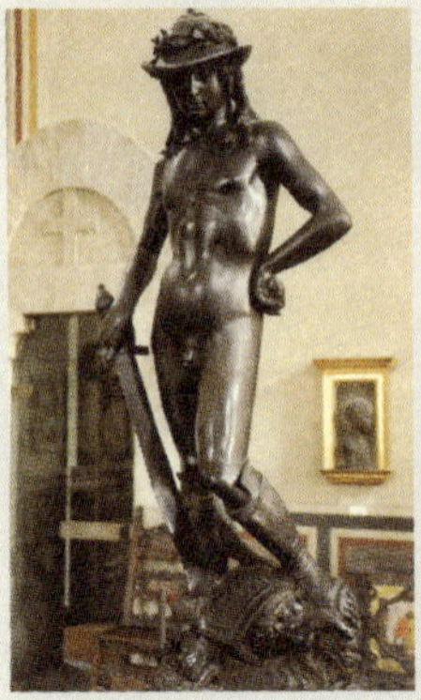

David - Donatello [xxii]

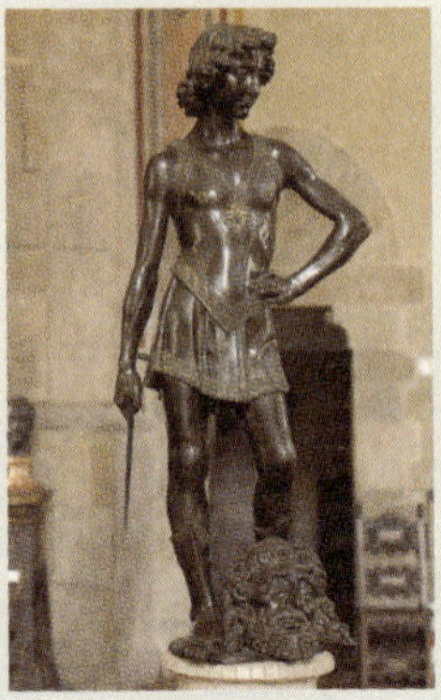

David - Verrocchio [xxiii]

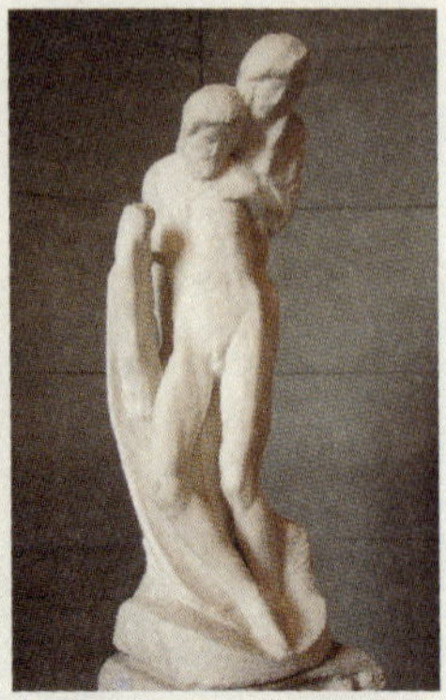

Rondanini Pieta [xxiv]

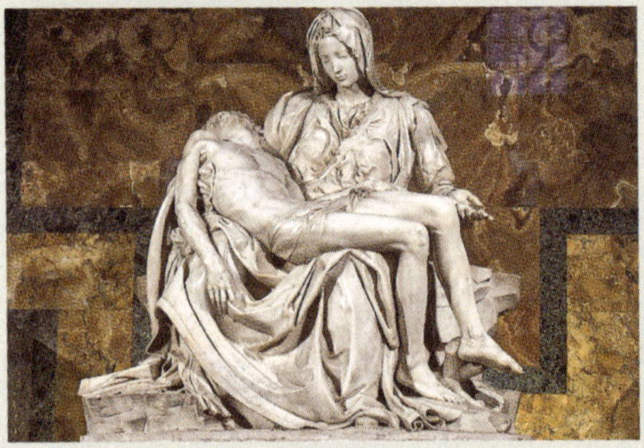

Pieta of St. Peter [xxv]

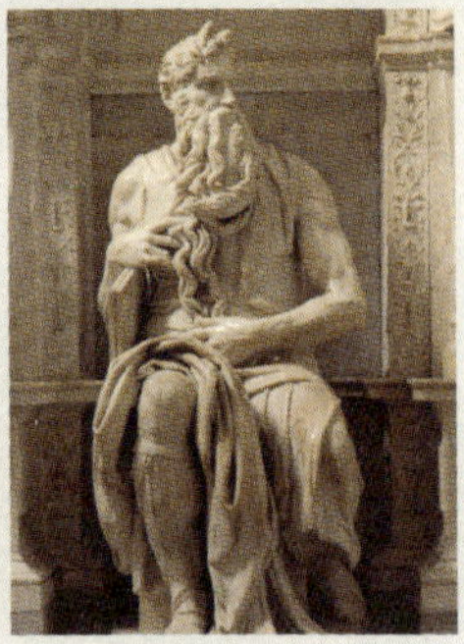

Moses [xxvi]

[xxii] ***David*** - Donatello - This is the title of two statues of the biblical hero David by the Italian early Renaissance sculptor Donatello. They consist of an early work in marble of a clothed figure (1408–1409), and a far more famous nude bronze figure dating from the 1440s or later (pictured here). Both are now in the Museo Nazionale del Bargello in Florence. Although inspired in a striking manner by Classical models, Donatello conferred the freedom of divine inspiration upon his work. He was original in the irregular centring of his compositions, in his continuous modulation of light and shadow, and in the deeply thoughtful attitude of his work.
[xxiii] ***David*** - Verocchio - Andrea del Verrocchio's bronze statue of David was most likely made between 1473 and 1475. It was commissioned by the Medici family. It is sometimes claimed that Verrocchio modelled the statue after a handsome pupil in his workshop, the young Leonardo da Vinci. Verrocchio's sculptural work shows a pictorial tendency which accentuates the chiaroscuro aspects and the soft play of the light of the surfaces. His bronze David contrasts with Donatello's thoughtful statue. His version shows the bold image of a young man with a slightly unstable pose.
[xxiv] ***Rondanini Pieta*** - The 'unfinished' dramatic masterpiece (1564), reflects the spiritual tension that animated the last years of Michelangelo's life—the dilution of his heroic vision of man and the awareness of the presence of cosmic pain. The sculpture is of the Virgin Mary mourning over the emaciated dead body of Christ.
[xxv] ***Pieta of St Peter*** - This composition by Michelangelo (1497–1499) is in pyramidal form on a block of Carrara marble. It shows the Virgin depicted as a young woman supporting the dead Christ on her lap. One of the details that is most surprising in this sculpture is the extremely youthful aspect that the artist has given to Mary's face. It is likely that, according to the intentions of the sculptor, the Madonna represents the whole of humanity.
[xxvi] **Moses** - This work of Michelangelo (1506) represents the biblical character at the moment when, having come down from Mount Sinai with the tablets of the law, he sees the Jews worshipping a golden calf. In the Bible, Moses is said to have been struck by a fit of rage, but the Moses carved by Michelangelo is portrayed in an attitude of self-control, of solemn calm. The tension of the muscles and the veins, the position of the body and the furious gaze makes it one of the most admired sculptural masterpieces of all time.

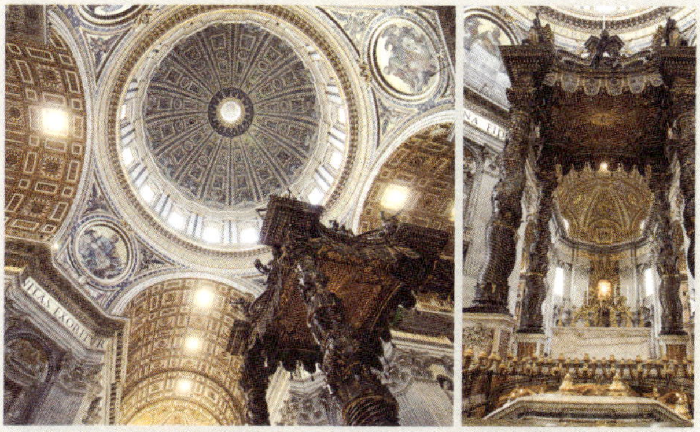

St. Peter's Baldachin [xxviii]

// 1600s [xxvii]

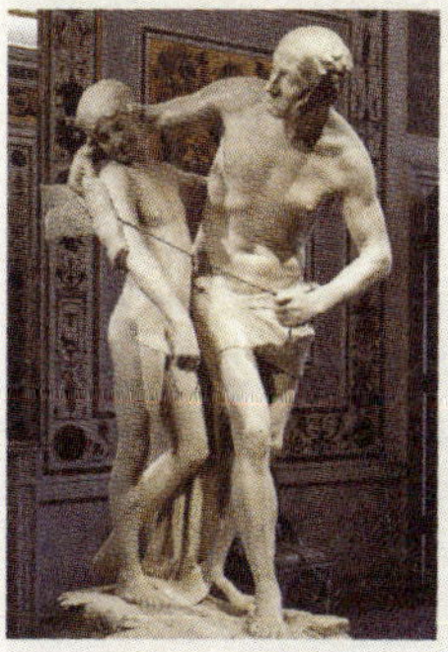

Daedalus and Icarus [xxx]

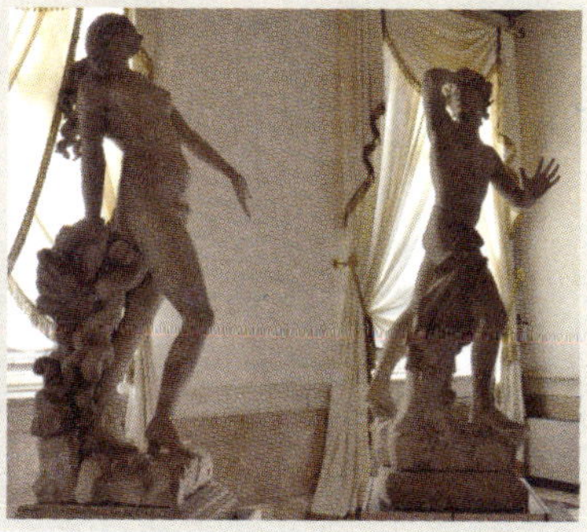

Orpheus and Eurydice [xxxi]

// 1800s [xxix]

[xxvii]The Baroque architectural style is characterized by the magnificence and richness of the materials used—marble gold stucco.

[xxviii] ***St Peter's Baldachin*** - This is a large Baroque sculpted bronze canopy over the high altar of St Peter's Basilica in the Vatican City. The baldachin is at the centre of the crossing and directly under the dome of the basilica. Designed by the Italian artist Gian Lorenzo Bernini, it was intended to mark the place of Saint Peter's tomb. Commissioned by Pope Urban VIII, the work began in 1623 and ended in 1634.

[xxix] Neoclassicism was a current which developed between 1750 and 1830, and was based on the theories of Winckelmann, a German architect and author of *The Ancient History of Art*. He considered the history of art to be the result of certain political, social and intellectual forces placed at the base of creative activity, and thus the result of succession evolutions. A significant boost to this current came from the archaeological excavations carried out in Pompeii and Herculaneum. The principles of Neoclassical art were the balance and stability of the forms—this equilibrium model defined Greek-Roman art. The Neoclassical cultural centres in Italy were in Rome and artists included Antonio Canova in Milan, Jacques Louis David in France and Francisco Goya in Spain.

[xxx] ***Daedalus and Icarus*** - Another of Canova's famous works (1779), it is based on the story of a maze which Daedalus, a skilled artisan in Athens, had built for the King of Crete—a building from which it was impossible to escape, that is, the labyrinth. This complex imprisoned the Minotaur, a monster who was half-man and half-bull, the son of Queen Pasiphae. The Athenian hero Theseus entered the labyrinth and killed the monster, but in revenge, the king locked Daedalus in the maze, along with his son Icarus. To escape from there and from the island of Crete, Daedalus created a pair of wings with wax and bird feathers for himself and Icarus. Father and son managed to fly away from the island, but although his father advised him to fly low, Icarus ventured higher and higher until the heat of the Sun melted the wax of his wings and Icarus fell into the waves. That sea still bears his name—the Icarian Sea near the island of Samos in Greece.

[xxxi] ***Orpheus and Eurydice*** - Antonio Canova produced his first commissioned work—a pair of statues showing Orpheus and Eurydice (1775–1776) at the age of just sixteen or seventeen, for his patron, Senator Falier. The subject came from the antique legend of Eurydice, wife of the singer Orpheus, who died from a snake bite. Orpheus was so downcast that he resolved to bring her back from the underworld and set off to Hades to charm the gods with his music. He was successful and was permitted to take Eurydice back with him to Earth on the one condition that he not look at her on the way. But Orpheus could not resist looking back to see if she was following him and thus lost her for ever.

// Painting

// Middle Ages [xxxii]

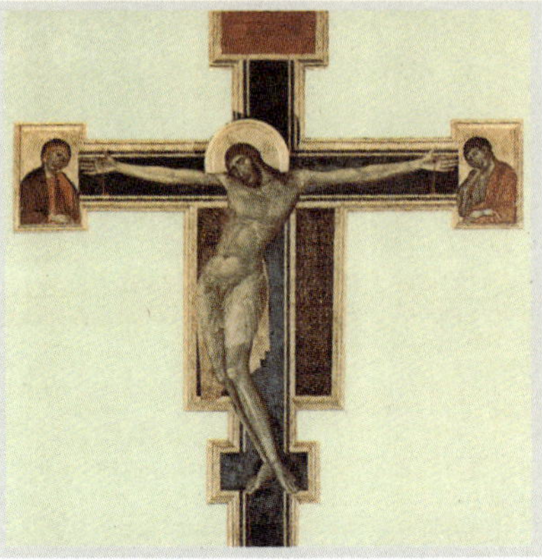

Crucifix of Santa Croce [xxxiii]

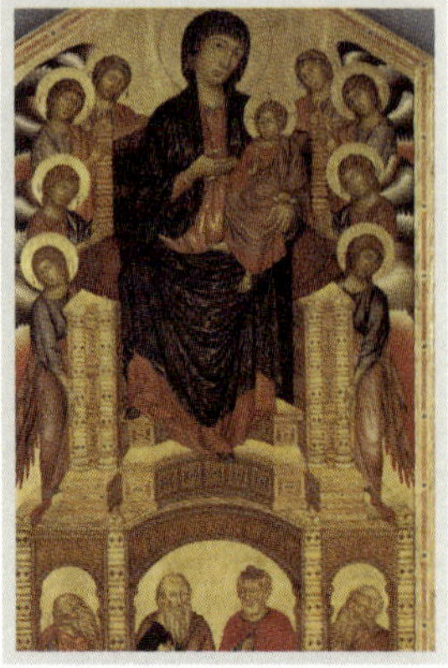

Madonna [xxxiv]

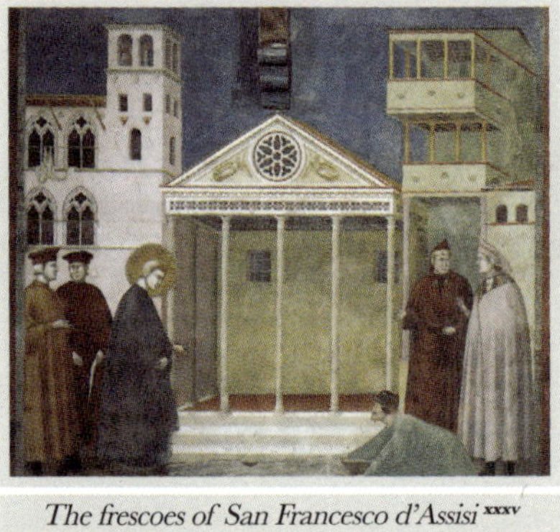

The frescoes of San Francesco d'Assisi [xxxv]

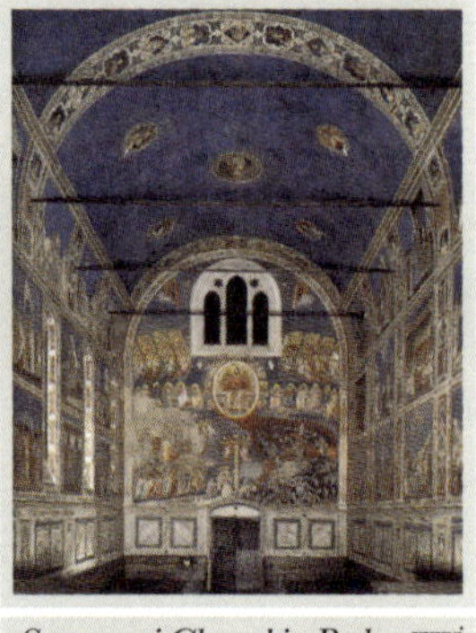

Scrovegni Chapel in Padua [xxxvi]

[xxxii] Painting and fresco, inspired by Naturalism and grandiose Classical Realism with a mystical imprint, tended towards a freer and more lively style during this period. The stylistic features of Romanesque painting were as varied as ever, with Byzantine and Ottonian influences. Typical characteristics of Romanesque aesthetics included sharp outlines, use of strong colours, a plastic sense of the figures and expressive, vivacious forms.

[xxxiii] ***Crucifix of Santa Croce*** - From the church of Santa Croce in Florence, this was made by Cimabue in 1288. It is characterized by the use of chiaroscuro and a dramatic representation of the position of the body of Christ. It demonstrates the beginning of an artistic evolution which went beyond Byzantine style.

[xxxiv] ***Madonna*** - Cimabue created this for the church of The Holy Trinità of Florence in 1284. It shows Madonna portrayed in the foreground, surrounded by angels and prophets. She is depicted with more human features than was typical of the Byzantine style.

[xxxv] The frescoes of ***San Francesco d'Assisi*** - Giotto di Bondone's work represents a synthesis of the different artistic visions of his time, from the Byzantine Romantic tradition to the taste of Gothic and the recovery of early Christian classical art. The profound transformation carried out by Giotto concerned the figure of the artist, whose inventive capacity was enhanced, art being no longer considered simply a technical or manual skill, as was the case in the past. With Giotto a new era was born. The frescoes of the church of San Francesco d'Assisi (1300) comprise twenty-eight squares located under the windows, where Giotto portrayed the most popular episodes of St Francis's life. Each painting is a complete story.

[xxxvi] ***Scrovegni Chapel in Padua*** - The frescoes of the Scrovegni Chapel in Padua (1310) recall Gothic sculptures, creating the illusion of depth on a flat surface. The banker Rico of the Scrovegni family called Giotto to decorate the walls of the family chapel between 1303 and 1310.

// Humanism[xxxvii]

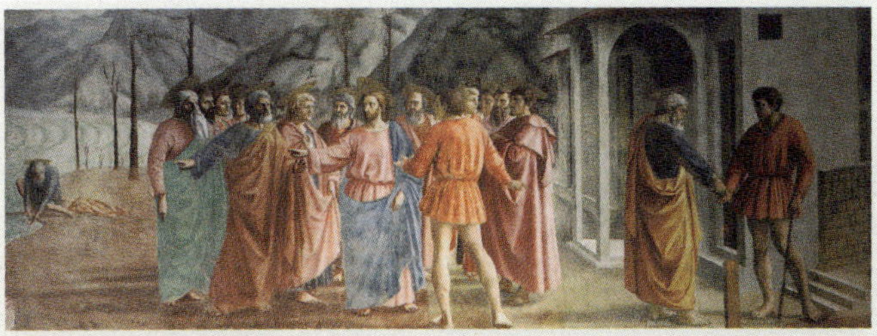

Brancacci Chapel in Santa Maria del Carmine [xxxviii]

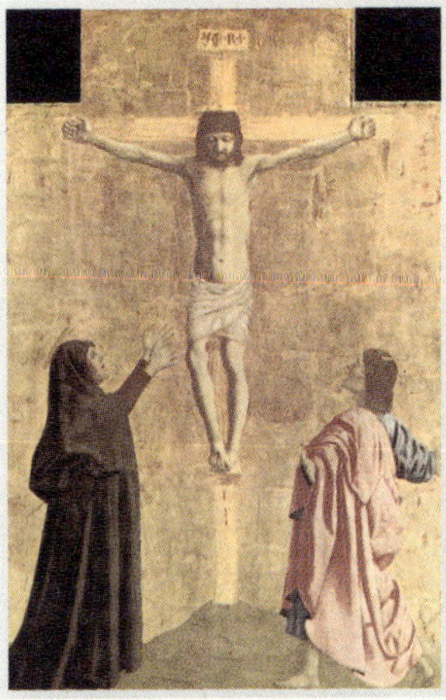

Polyptych of Misericordia: Crucifixion [xxxix]

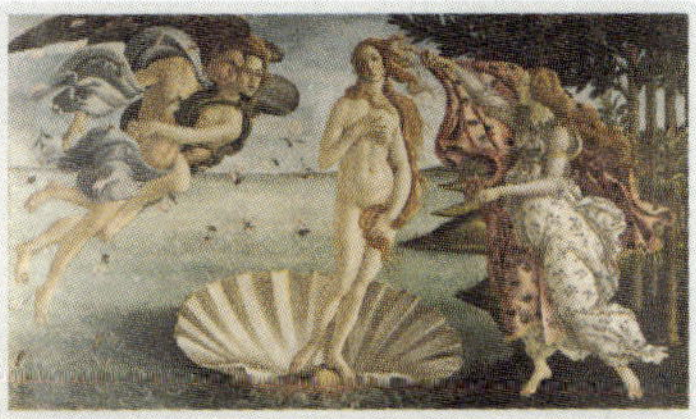

The Birth of Venus [xl]

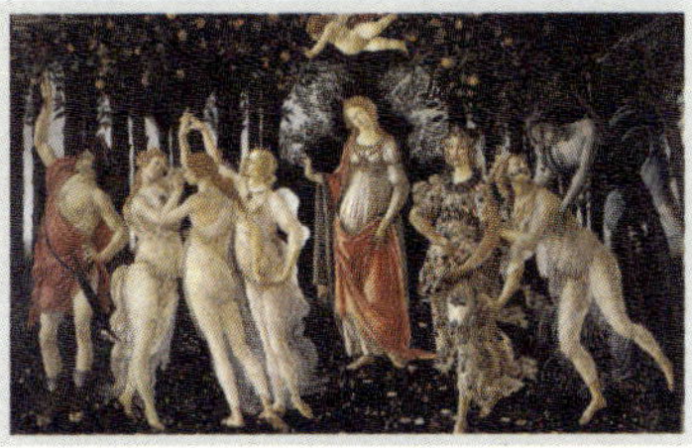

Primavera [xli]

[xxxvii] Characteristic elements of **Humanist** and Renaissance paintings include the use of perspective, the placement of figures in a real space, the centrality of the human figure (represented realistically both in the anatomical structure and in the character's expression) and the use of light (which highlights the plastic values of shapes, often interpreted purely volumetrically).

[xxxviii] ***Brancacci Chapel in Santa Maria del Carmine*** - Masaccio (1401–1428) was the artist who most revolutionized painting during this era, developing a sober, severe figurative language, and favouring figurative psychological realism in the rendering of the characters. In the frescoes of the Brancacci Chapel in Santa Maria del Carmine (Florence, 1427) the melodramatic episodes are concentrated in action, with few decorative digressions.

[xxxix] ***Polyptych of Misericordia: Crucifixion*** - In this painting of 1426, we see that the traditional image of Christ between the Madonna and St John is charged with the drama of the desperate gesture of Mary Magdalene, who raises her arms towards Christ. The mute cry of pain from Mary is considered to be the highest expression of drama in painting after Giotto.

[xl] ***The Birth of Venus*** - In Sandro Boticelli's *The Birth of Venus* (1486), the nudity of Venus (a symbol of an ideal beauty) recalls the concept of the rebirth of the soul. The goddess is born from sea-foam on a shell, inspired by mythology and classical poetry. Venus here is not only the representation of the beauty of love, but of the birth of humanity, that is, the virtue which, according to Neoplatonic culture, is produced by the union of spirit with matter. The nudity of the goddess could also be seen as an exaltation of the purity and the simplicity of the soul. From a religious angle, Venus could be the soul of the believer who is reborn through the water of baptism; the shell could be the baptismal font.

[xli] ***Primavera*** - In Botticelli's *Primavera* (1482), Venus is depicted at the centre of the composition, surrounded by Safilius, Flora, Mercury and the three graces. Here one can recognize the double meaning, natural and intellectual, of the creative capacity of Venus, or love—the maximum force of the universe according to Neoplatonic conceptions.

// Renaissance [xlii]

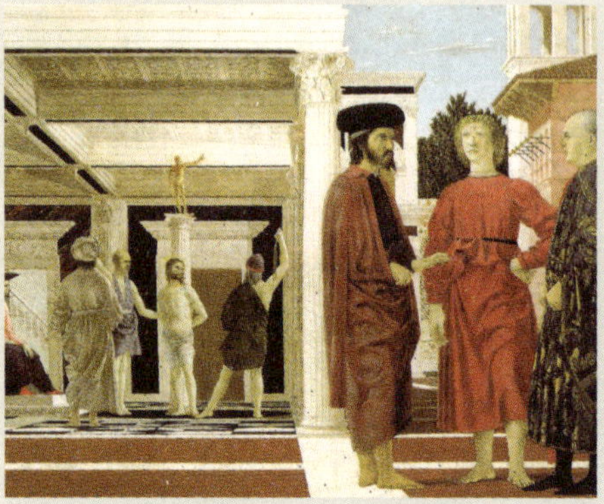

The Flagellation of Christ [xliii]

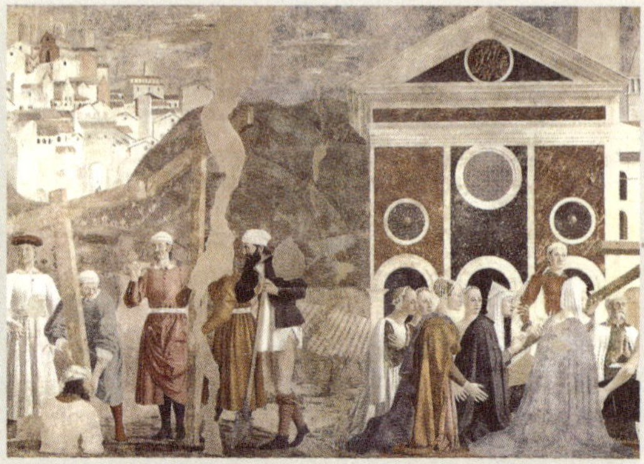

The Legend of the True Cross [xliv]

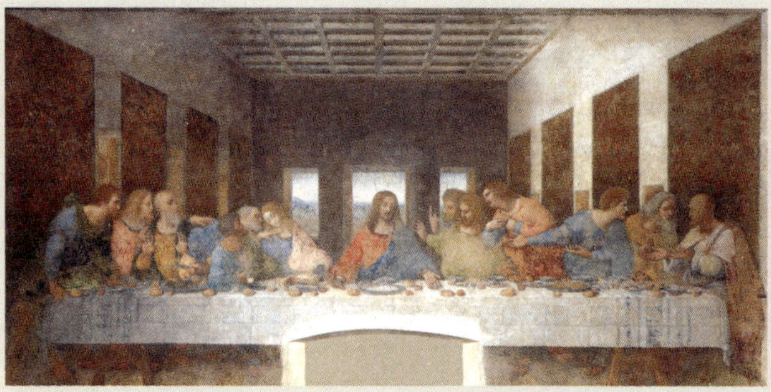

The Cenacle [xlv]

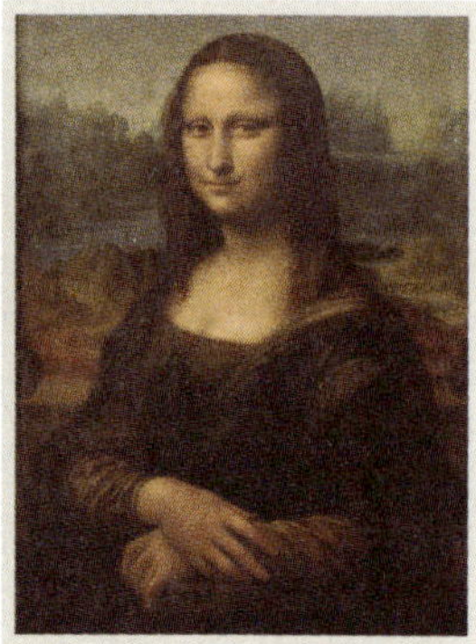

Mona Lisa [xlvi]

[xlii] It was in art that the spirit of the **Renaissance** achieved its sharpest formulation. Art came to be seen as a branch of knowledge, valuable in its own right and capable of providing man with images of God and His creations as well as insights into man's position in the universe. In the hands of men such as Leonardo da Vinci, it was even a science, a means of exploring nature and a record of discoveries. Art was to be based on the observation of the visible world and practised according to mathematical principles of balance, harmony and perspective, which were developed at this time.

[xliii] ***The Flagellation of Christ*** - Piero della Francesca's art arises from his direct observation of nature. In his paintings, he displays the 'Leonardesque nuance', consisting of a gradual passage from one chromatic tone to the other so that the play of light and shadow gives volume and a sense of depth to the compositions. The painting appears divided into two parts—the figures in the foreground paying no attention to the suffering of Christ in the background—demonstrating the possibility of bringing together two historical moments. The use of geometric perspective rigour is very important, together with a static impassibility of the characters and the brightness of the colours.

[xliv] ***The Legend of the True Cross*** - Francesca's *The Legend of the True Cross* or *The History of the True Cross* is a sequence of frescoes that constitute one of the major works of Renaissance art. It represents several major biblical events: including the death of Adam, the story of King Solomon's meeting with the Queen of Sheba, and the Annunciation.

[xlv] ***The Cenacle*** - Also called *The Last Supper* (1497), this is one of the masterpieces of Leonardo da Vinci.
The scene, in which Jesus announces that he will be betrayed by one of his disciples, is taken from the Gospel of John. The moment that *Leonardo* chooses to portray is when Jesus says, 'One of you will betray me.' It is a work in tempera and oil, and was patronized by the Duke of Milan.

[xlvi] ***Mona Lisa*** - This famous portrait is another example of Leonardesque naturalism, found in the fading of colours

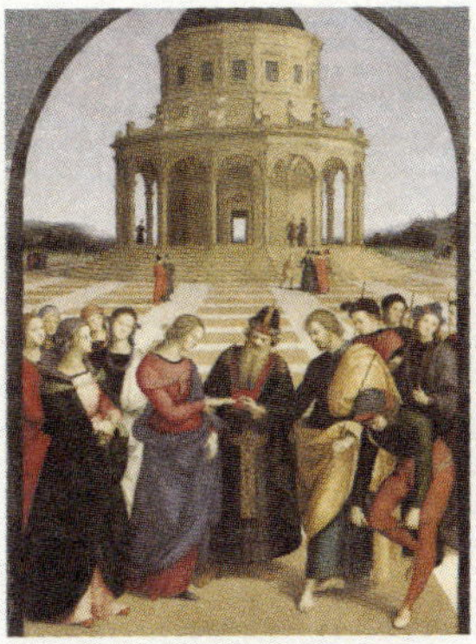

The Marriage of the Virgin [xlvii]

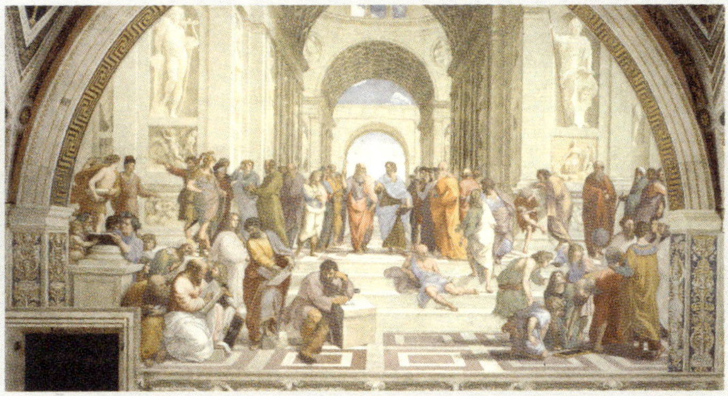

The School of Athens [xlviii]

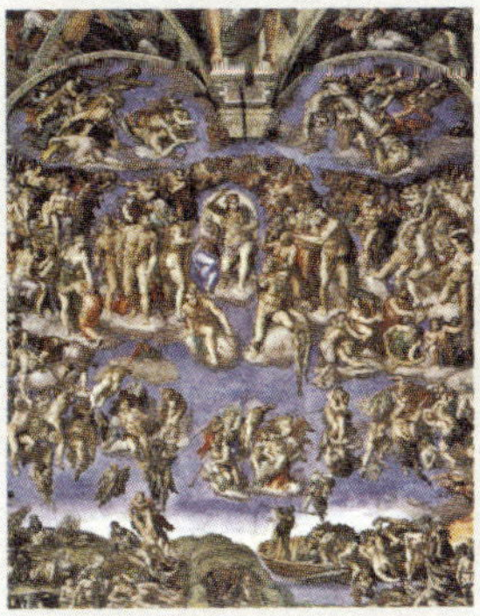

The Last Judgment [xlix]

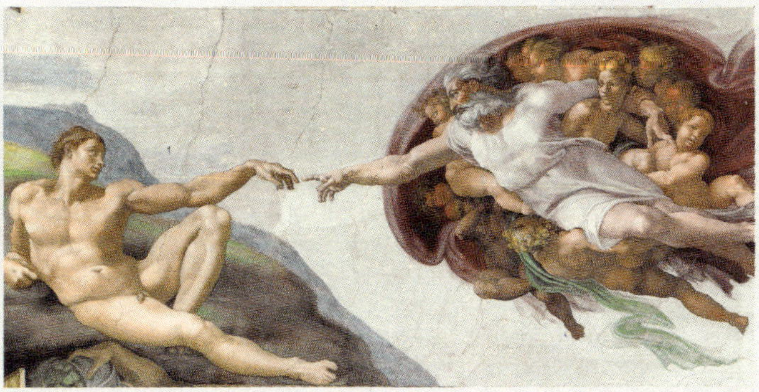

The Creation of Adam [l]

and tones and in the calibrated chiaroscuro of the composition. The painting shows a woman with a pensive expression and a slight smile, providing a strong expression of the intimate essence of the human person; a mirror of the soul. Da Vinci rejected the traditional technique of painting, which did not allow for alterations. Experimenting with his technique, he worked on dry plaster using colours similar to those he used on boards. The result was that the colour began to fade even while he was still working on the piece.

[xlvii] ***The Marriage of the Virgin*** - In the paintings of Raffaello Sanzio, classic architectural structures are embellished with dense decoration in stucco fresco, inspired by the style of the Roman caves from the Domus area. Raphael's drawing is expressed, above all, in painting, where he manages to achieve his ideal of formal perfection—chromatic balance and an expressive sweetness of faces and limbs. *The Marriage of the Virgin* (1504), composed for one of the last altarpieces made for the church of the city of Castello, was the first work dated and signed by the artist.

[xlviii] ***The School of Athens*** - This painting (1509–1511) is one of the greatest masterpieces of the Renaissance. We see an imaginary Classical building and the philosophers of antiquity as they discuss their thoughts.

[xlix] ***The Last Judgment*** - One of the greatest works of Michelangelo was the frescoes on the ceiling of the Sistine Chapel. The frescoes consist of nine central panels showing the stories of Genesis. *The Last Judgment* (1541) is a painting on the back wall of the Sistine Chapel, which depicts a mass of figures swirling around the central figure of Christ. The dramatic and terrible character of the apocalyptic scene seems to reflect the crisis of Renaissance values.

[l] ***The Creation of Adam*** - This Michelangelo painting (1512) illustrates the biblical creation narrative from the *Book of Genesis* (in which God gives life to Adam, the first man).

// Baroque Painting [li]

// 1800s [liv]

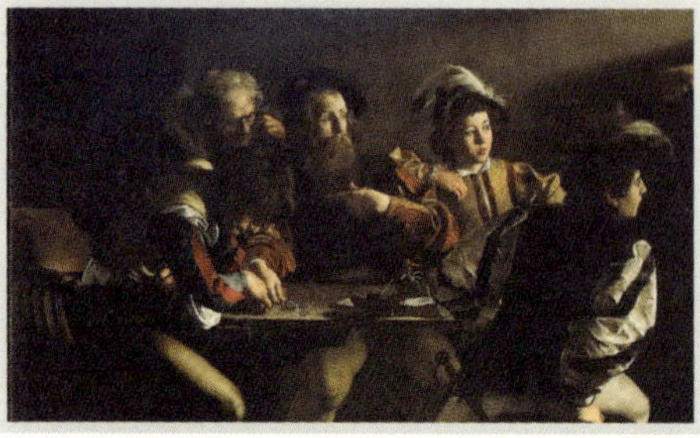

The Calling of St Matthew [lii]

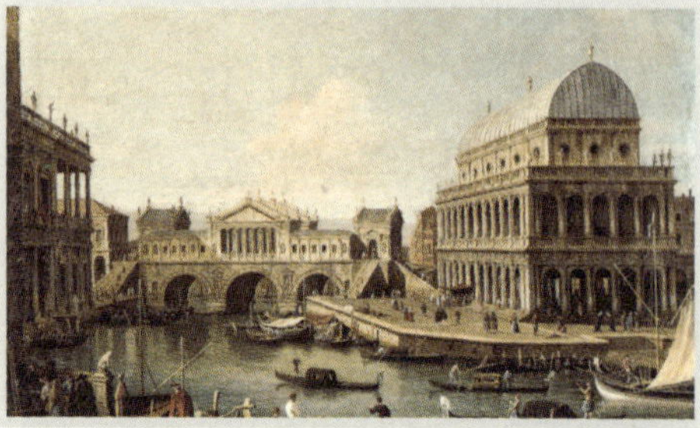

Capriccio with Palladian Buildings [lv]

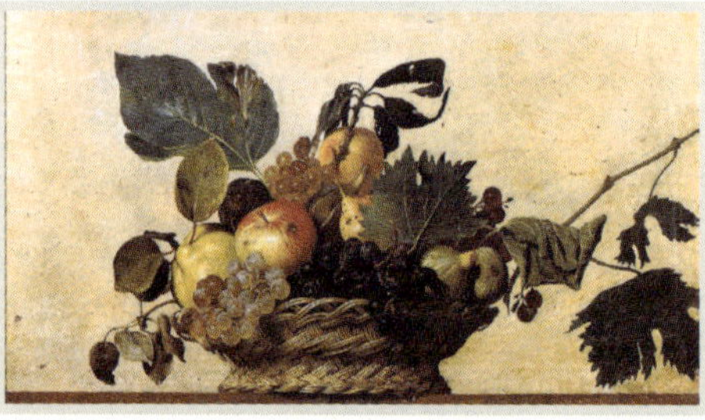

Basket of Fruit [liii]

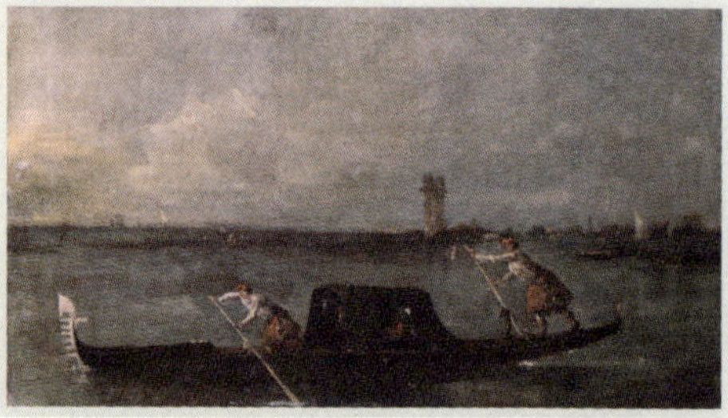

Gondolas on a Lagoon near Mestre [lvi]

[li] **Baroque Paintings** - The renaissance perspective ordered and limited space, whilst the new Baroque perspective opened infinite spaces and freed the energy of movement.
[lii] ***The Calling of St Matthew*** - This painting (Caravaggio, 1600) illustrates an episode from the Gospel in which the light of God's grace descends on all humans, giving everyone a chance of salvation. The scene takes place in a shabby, dark environment, but the light of the sacred, the divine grace which descends into the darkness of sin, lights the scene. The presence of the two figures represents the belief that spiritual salvation is obtained through the word of God (Christ) and the mediation of the Church (Peter).
[liii] ***Basket of Fruit*** - In this painting (Caravaggio, 1596), objects are represented as they are in reality, without trying to beautify nature. The arrangement of the basket is based on an almost miraculous balance—the leaves are still, but there is an impression that everything could move at any moment.
[liv] In the 18th century -the **1800s**- we witness the transition from Baroque forms to the Rococo style, where the most accomplished results can be found in Venetian painting. Venetian painting placed itself with authority among the major European artistic expressions of the century, and can thus be considered one of the great manifestations of the Italian artistic tradition.
[lv] ***Capriccio with Palladian Buildings*** - Antonio Canaletto enhanced his work (1756) with the original feature of the including monuments belonging to other places; this makes his scenes look as if they have undergone photographic editing.
[lvi] ***Gondolas on a Lagoon near Mestre*** - In this work (1793) Francesco Guardi sensitively interpreted the nuances of International Rococo in a personal, original manner, as an expression of the state of mind. The genre, known as Vedutismo, occupied a prominent place in 18th century Italian art. The forerunners of this style were the great decorators of the palace of the papacy in previous centuries. These painters were in charge of representing and celebrating historical, political and religious events, and setting them against the backdrop of the urban landscape of the city where the events had taken place.

// Romanticism [lvii]

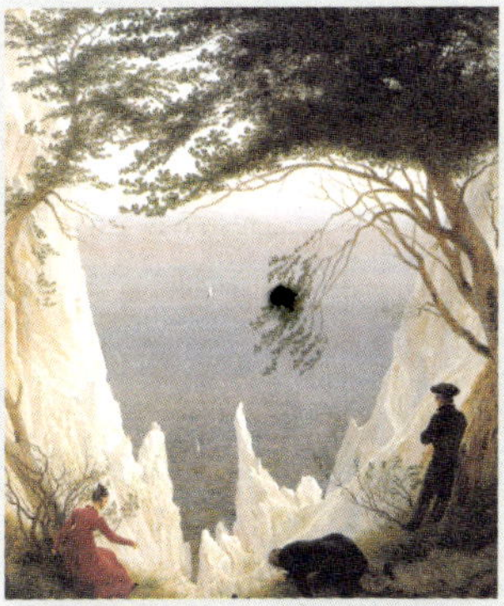

Chalk Cliffs on Rügen [lviii]

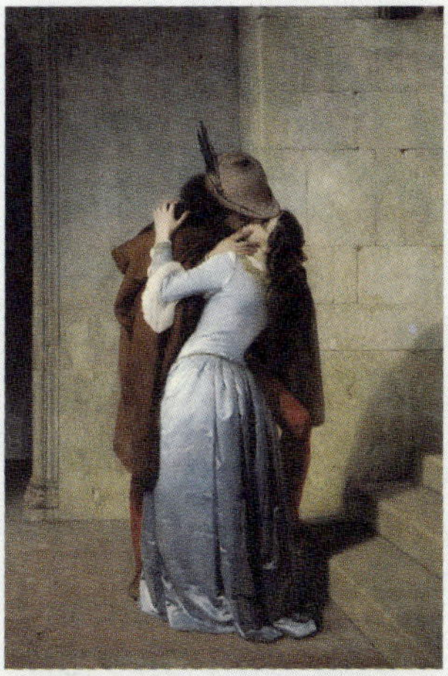

The Kiss [lx]

// The Historical Romance [lix]

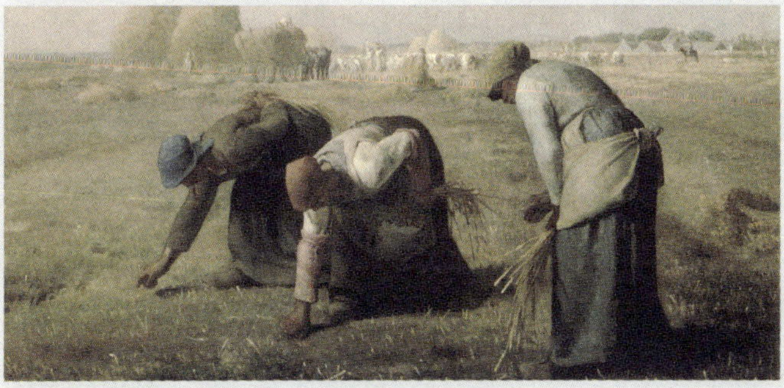

The Gleaner [lxii]

// Realism and Naturalism [lxi]

[lvii] Against the uniformity of the culture imposed by the Napoleonic period, each of the different European states searched for value in their own history. So, when the Romanticism style spread throughout Europe, it was characterized by an emphasis on human values, sentiment and love for one's country. Painting was the most important innovative form of art during this period and was based on the great historical themes, with preference for the moments of popular patriotic struggle. It embraced the representation of landscapes. Romantic paintings were more communicative than the Neoclassical style—the artist wanted to express feelings and emotions, his brush strokes were fluid, the colours alive, the contours less defined and the contrast of the light often dramatic.

[lviii] ***Chalk Cliffs on Rügen*** - In this painting (1818) David Freidrich portrayed nature and nocturnal atmospheres, which were corpuscular, melancholic and in connection with the idea of death.

[lix] Also in Italy around 1820, a reaction against the academic Neoclassicism resulted in adherence to the **Historical Romance** - a connection of the literary trends to the emerging political events.

[lx] ***The Kiss***(1859), painted by Francesco Hayez, shows a passionate encounter between a couple from the Middle Ages.

[lxi] The term **'Realism'** was often used to describe works in which the representation of objects and figures was so faithful to the truth that it could sometimes become unpleasant, especially when considered in relation to the beauty of Classicism. Realist art often featured subjects from the lower social classes and denoted a strong social criticism, with the movement openly placing itself at odds with the idealistic painting style. In the 18th century - 1800s - we witness the transition from Baroque forms to Rococo style, where the most accomplished results can be found in Venetian painting. Venetian painting placed itself with authority among the major European artistic expressions of the century, and can thus be considered one of the great manifestations of the Italian Artistic tradition. We must also keep in mind that in the domain of art, during the 1800s, several trends coexisted. The first of these was Neoclassicism, which was a decorative trend (as opposed to the Baroque), trying to reach a formal perfection through the inspiration of models from Classical Greece.

[lxii] ***The Gleaner*** - Jean-François Millet (1857) depicts three peasant women gleaning a field of stray stalks of wheat after the harvest. The painting is famous for featuring, in a sympathetic way, what were then the lowest ranks of rural society. However, the work was received poorly by the French upper-classes.

// Photographic Portraits

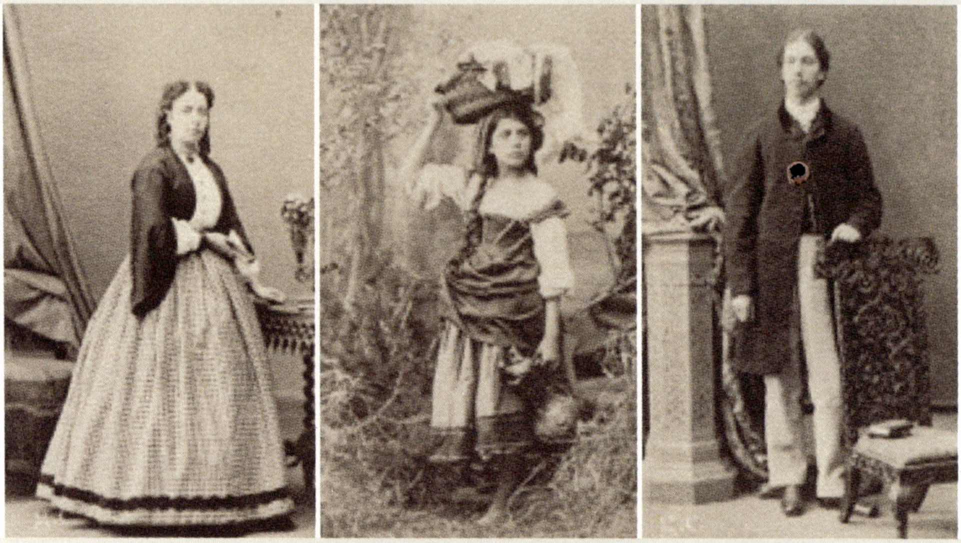

Portrait of a Woman (left), *Venetian Girl, 1871* (centre) and *Portrait of a Man Standing* (right) - photographed by Antonio Sorgato [lxiii]

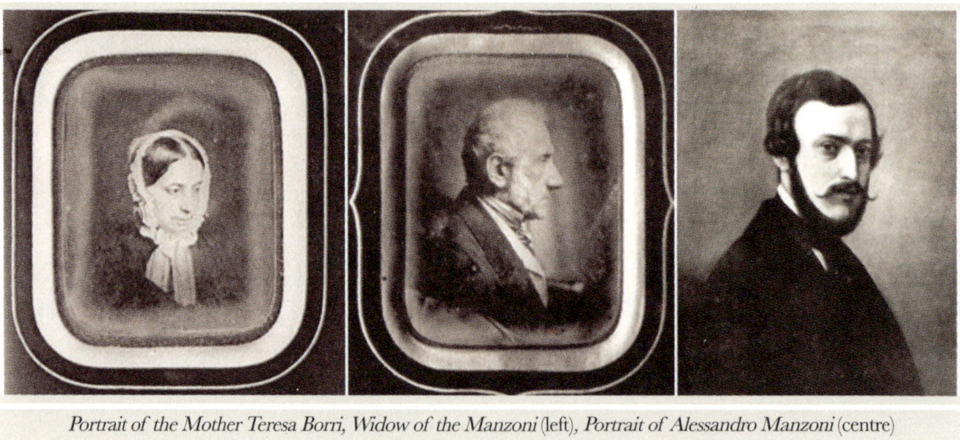

Portrait of the Mother Teresa Borri, Widow of the Manzoni (left), *Portrait of Alessandro Manzoni* (centre) and *Stefano Stampa* [lxiv] *in a Portrait of Carlo Gerosa* (right) - photographed by Stefano Stampa in 1851–1852

These posed portraits reveal the potential of the camera to capture realistic representations with greater speed and ease than the traditional painted portrait.

[lxiii] **Antonio Sorgato** became one of the most famous daguerreotypist portraitists in Venice. The daguerreotype process of printing was the first feasible method of creating permanent images with a camera.

[lxiv] **Stefano Stampa** (real name Giuseppe Stefano), was an Italian 1800s nobleman. Born with an innate predisposition for figurative art, he studied in Massimo d'Azeglio's studio and in that of Francesco Hayez himself. Stefano Stampa was a photographer and writer - his most important work was certainly the very long account of Alessandro Manzoni's

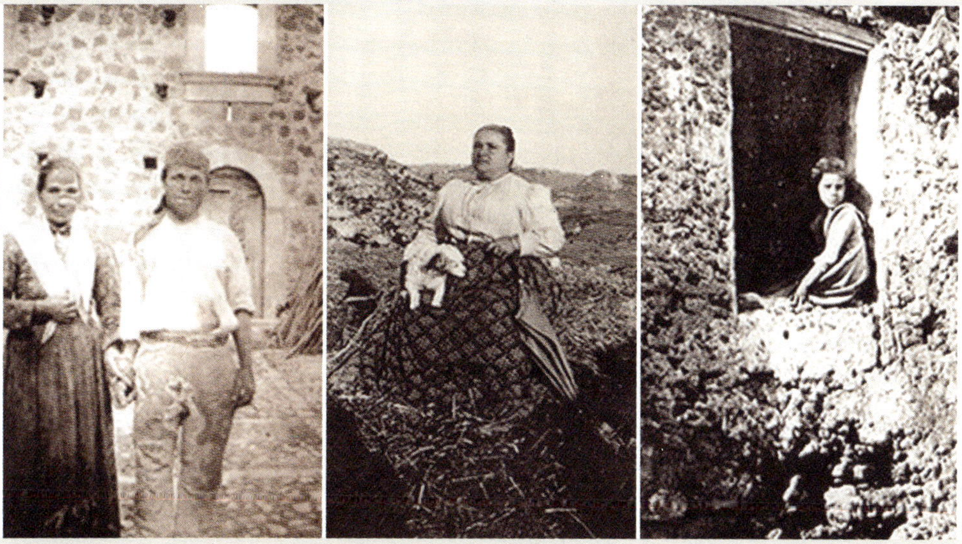

Portrait of Mr and Mrs Pisasale, servers of Verga family, 1897 (left), *Donna Lida Verga, the sister-in-law of Giovanni Verga, 1897* (centre) and *Little Girl in a House, 1911* (right) - photographed by Giovanni Verga [lxv]

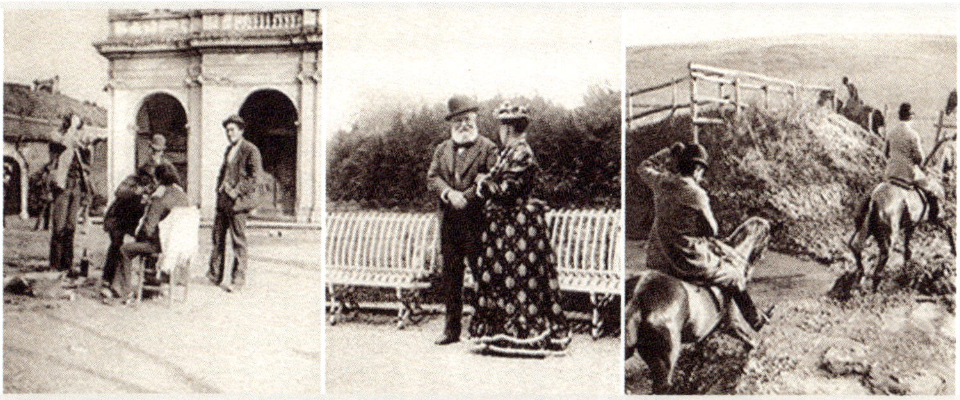

Barber outside Santa Bibiana Church, 1890, Rome (left), *Princess Mathilde Bonaparte and Charles Gounod, 1893* (centre) and *Riders Wading Through Water, 1895* (right) - photographed by Giuseppe Primoli, Italy [lxvi]

life and thought he was in fact the son in law of Manzoni entitled 'Alessandro Manzoni':his family, his friends (Ulrico Hoepli, 1885).

[lxv] **Giovanni Verga** was not only the father of Italian Realist writing, but also a photographer. His photos show simple and modest images of the daily life of the people of Sicily.

[lxvi] **Primoli** shot more than 10,000 photographs during the end of 19th century.

// Photographic Portraits

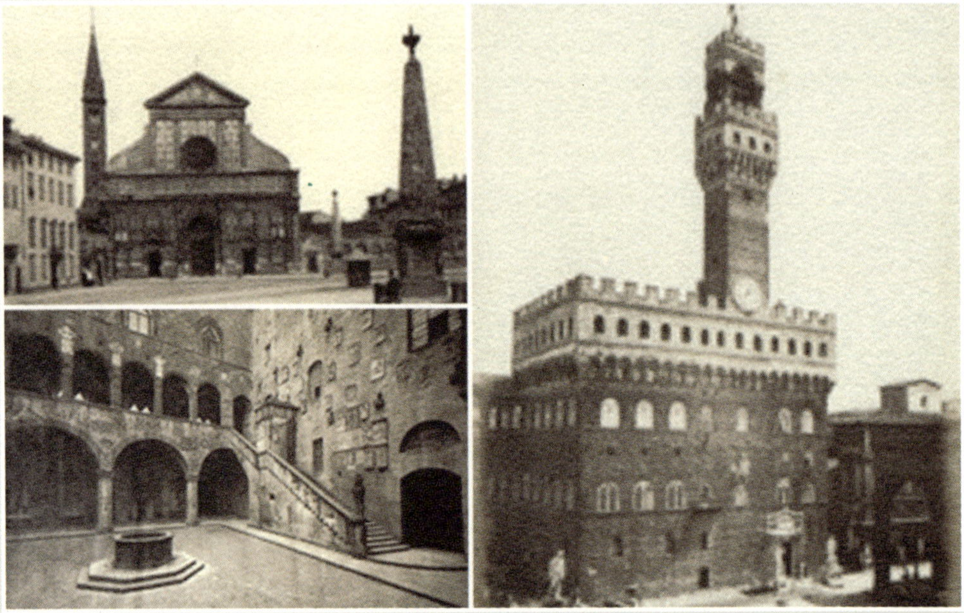

The facade of the Maria Novella Church, 1850s (top left), *Bargello Court, 1880* (bottom left), and *the Sala dei Clinque-cento (Plazzo Vecchio), 1850s* (right) [lxvii] *- photographed and printed by the Alinari brothers, Florence, Italy*

// Photography and Futurism

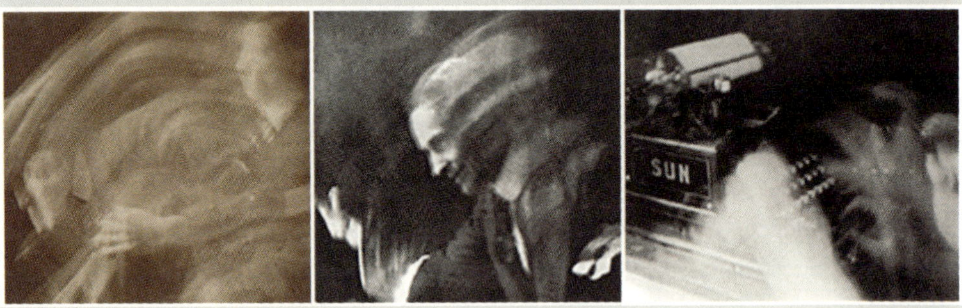

Change of Position, 1911 (left), *The Bow, 1911* (centre), and *The Typist, 1913* (right)
- photographed by Anton Giulio Bragaglia [lxviii]

[lxvii] The title of the image **Sala dei Clinque-cento** refers to the impressive chamber inside, which has a length of 52m (170ft) and a breadth of 23m (75ft). It was built in 1494 by Simone del Pollaiolo, commissioned by Savonarola.
[lxviii] **Anton Giulio Bragaglia** was a pioneer of Italian Futurist photography. 'Futurist Photodynamism' was a major theoretical achievement, which consisted of a forty-seven-page essay. It also included sixty-seven photographic plates, which were further divided into forty-five numbered sections.

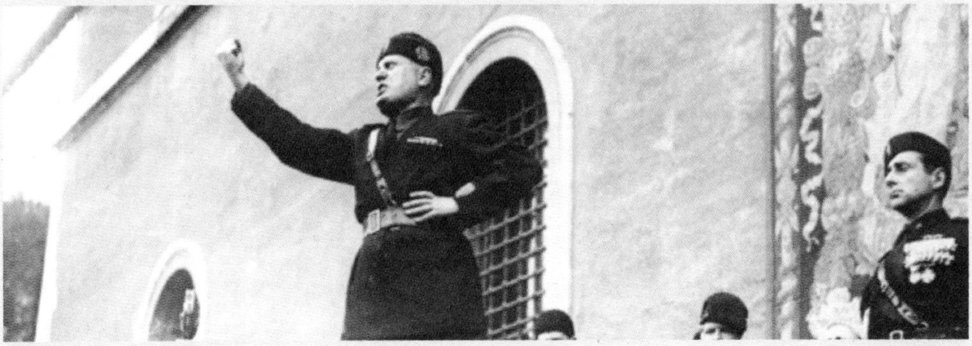

Italian fascist leader Benito Mussolini making a fist during a speech in 1935.

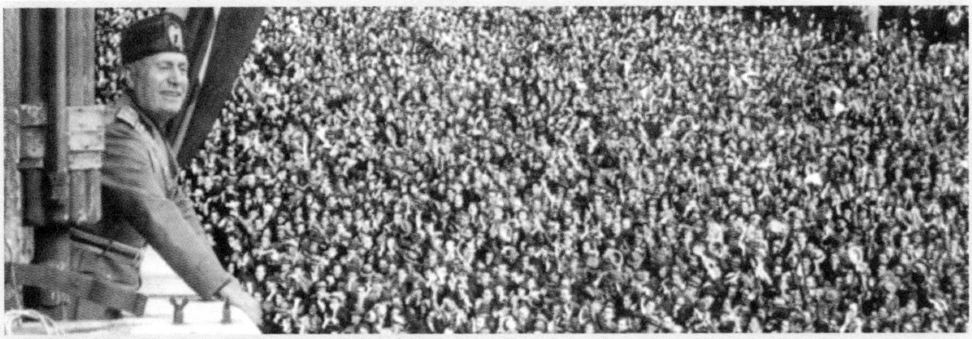

Benito Mussolini speaking to the crowds from the balcony of the Palazzo Venezia, Rome, Italy, in the late 1930s.

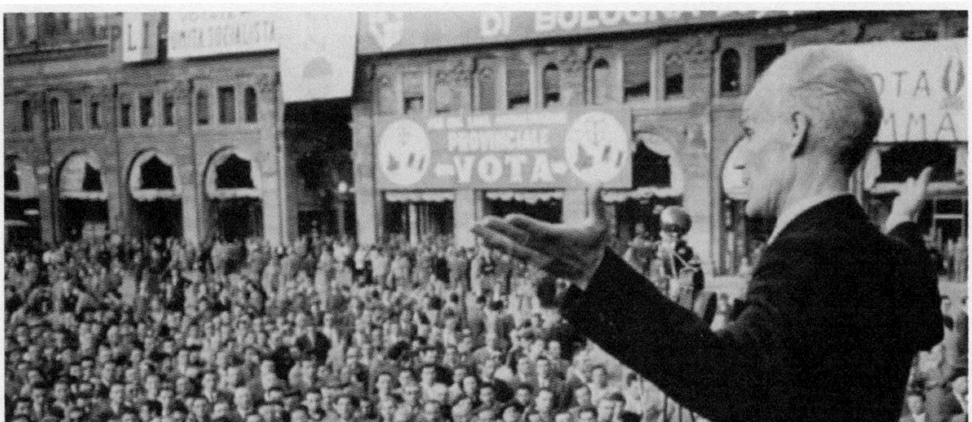

Neo-Fascist leader Augusto De Marsanich giving a speech at Piazza Maggiore, Bologna, Italy, in 1950 during the Italian elections.

// Impressionism

In the 19th century, a group of French painters began a new movement named 'Impressionism', characterised by a tendency to work outside rather than inside a studio, and with attention focused on the play of light in the painting and the inclusion of 'ordinary' people as subject matter.

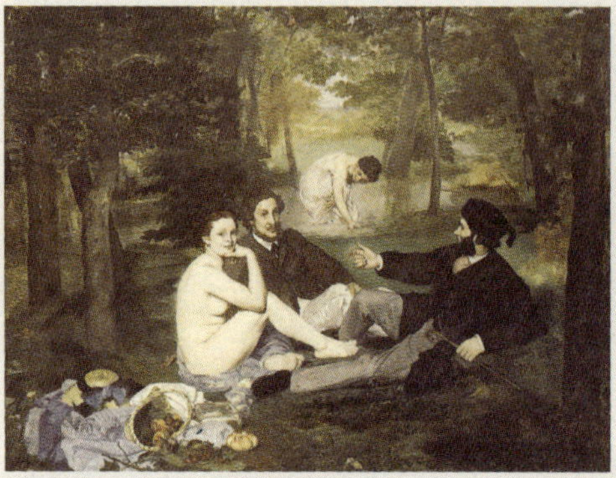

Le Déjeuner sur l'herbe [lxix]

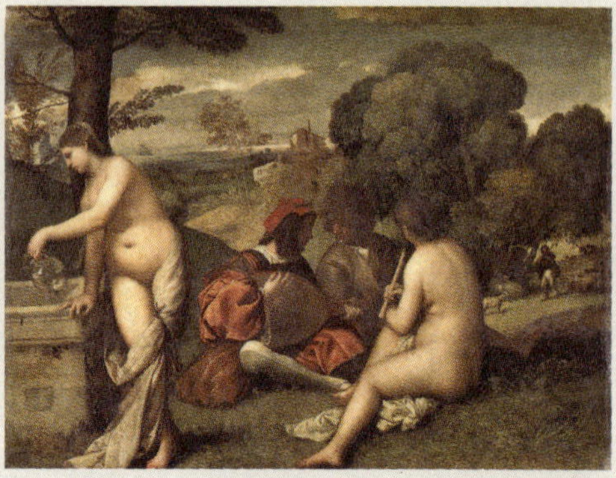

The Pastoral Concert

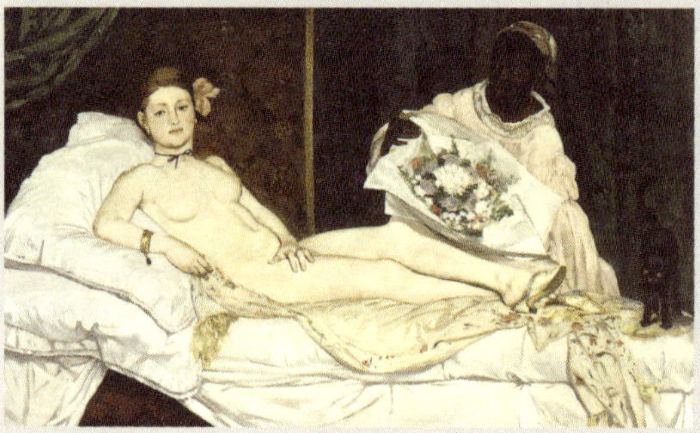

Olypmia [lxx]

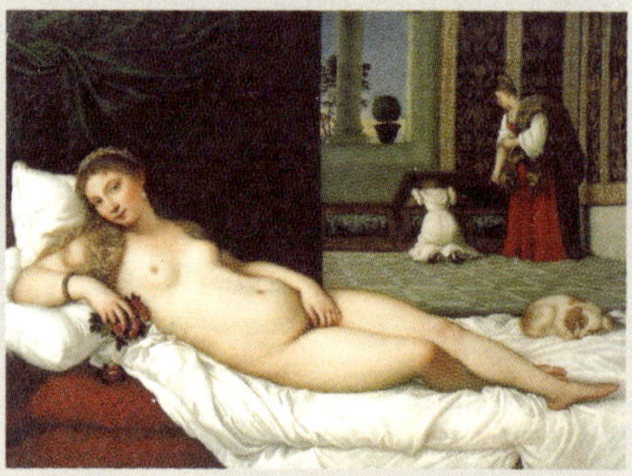

Venus of Urbino [lxxi]

[lxix] ***Le Déjeuner sur l'herbe*** - This is an oil painting by Edouard Manet, created 1862–1863. Manet is said to have been inspired by *The Pastoral Concert by Giorgione (or Titian)*, Louvre, Paris. Some critics propose that the modern art movement began with this work by Manet. It became notorious owing to its depiction of one nude woman and one scantily clad woman with two fully dressed males. A subsequent Manet painting *Olympia*, similarly aroused a brief scandal when it was exhibited at the Paris Salon in 1865.
[lxx] ***Olympia*** - This painting, said to be inspired by Titian's *Venus of Urbino*, by Manet features a nude woman reclining upon a chaise lounge, with a small black cat at her feet and a black female servant behind her holding a bouquet of flowers. In using a contemporary subject (and not Venus), Manet mocked that tradition and dared to suggest that the Classical past held no relevance for the modern industrial present.
[lxxi] ***Venus of Urbino*** - Titian completed this in 1538 for the Duke of Urbino Guidobaldo II Della Rovere. It was a gift from the Duke to his young wife. The painting represents the allegory of marriage, and was a 'teaching' model to the young Giulia.

// Post-Impressionism

By the end of the 19th century a movement against Impressionism had began—termed 'Post-Impressionism'. This movement consciously rejected the earlier emphasis on the realistic representation of light and colour. The emphasis moved towards abstract forms and symbolic meaning.

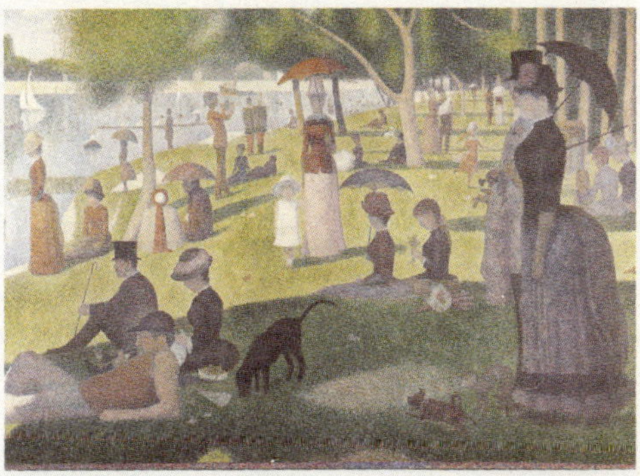

A Sunday Afternoon on the Island of La Grande Jatte [lxxii]

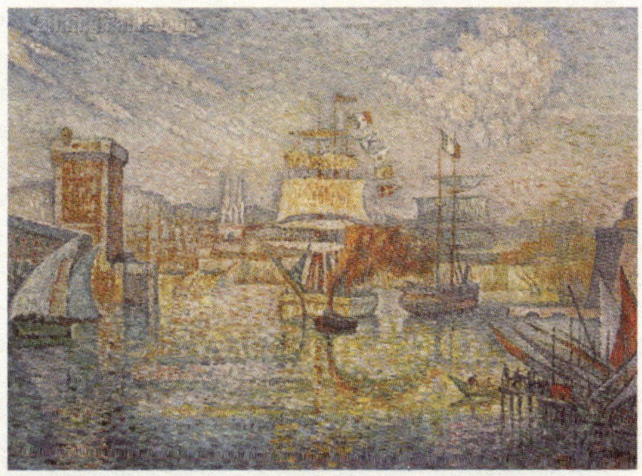

The Entrance to the Port of Marseilles [lxxiii]

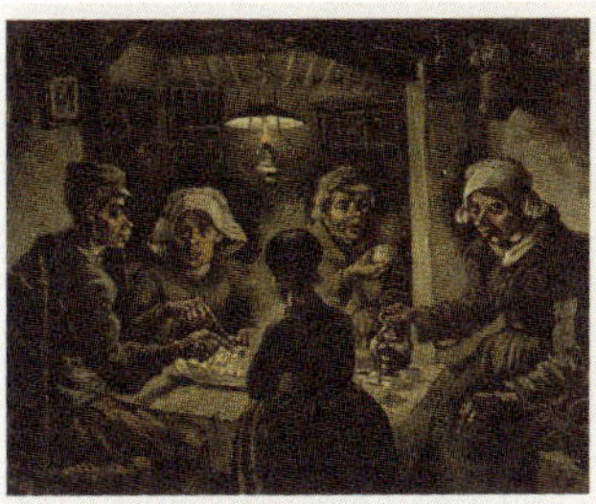

The Potato Eaters [lxxiv]

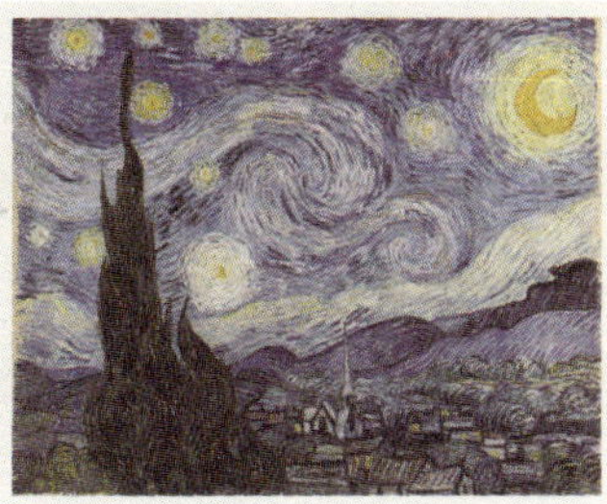

Starry Night [lxxv]

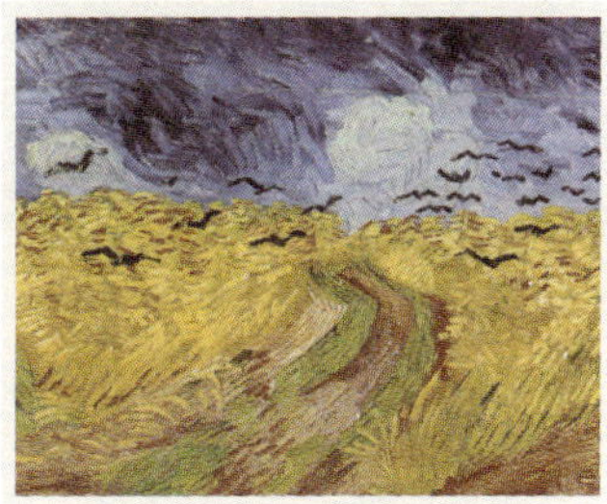

Wheatfield with Crows [lxxvi]

lxxii ***A Sunday Afternoon on the Island of La Grande Jatte*** - This painting (1884) is regarded as an iconic part of Western culture and is viewed as one of the most pivotal works of art ever put on canvas. It depicts a popular retreat for the Parisian middle and upper classes in the 19th century. As a painter, Georges Seurat wanted to make a difference and with *La Grande Jatte* he succeeded. It took him two years to finish the work.

lxxiii ***The Entrance to the Port of Marseilles*** - Marseilles is the third-largest city in France and the country's largest port. It holds a strategic location on the Mediterranean Sea. In this painting (1911) we see the dazzling effect of the 'play of hues'. The rectangular strokes of unmixed pigment, arranged like tiles in a mosaic, are Paul Signac's variation on the innovative painting method pioneered by Seurat.

lxxiv ***The Potato Eaters*** - This is considered to be one of the earliest masterpieces of Van Gogh. It was painted while he was living amongst the peasants and labourers in Nuenen in the Netherlands. Van Gogh tried to depict the people and their lives truthfully. His goal was to paint human figures that did not appear to be awkward, but rather existing naturally.

lxxv ***Starry Night*** - Van Gogh's magnum opus (1889) was based on his direct observations, as well as his imagination, memories, and emotions. It depicted the view outside his sanatorium room window at night. The artist was aware that his *Starry Night* composition was somewhat surreal and stylized. In a letter to his brother, he even referred to his 'exaggerations in terms of composition'.

lxxvi ***Wheatfield with Crows*** - This painting (1890) stands out as one of Van Gogh's most powerful and fiercely debated paintings. It is said to be his final painting. The menacing sky, the crows and the dead-end path are said to refer to the end of his life approaching. But this is just a persistent myth. This is a tranquil painting in which compositional and rhythmic effects contribute to the sense of peace as much as the light and colour do.

// Expressionism

A modernist movement which began in the domains of poetry and painting, Expressionist art conveyed emotion and sought to provoke certain moods in the viewer.

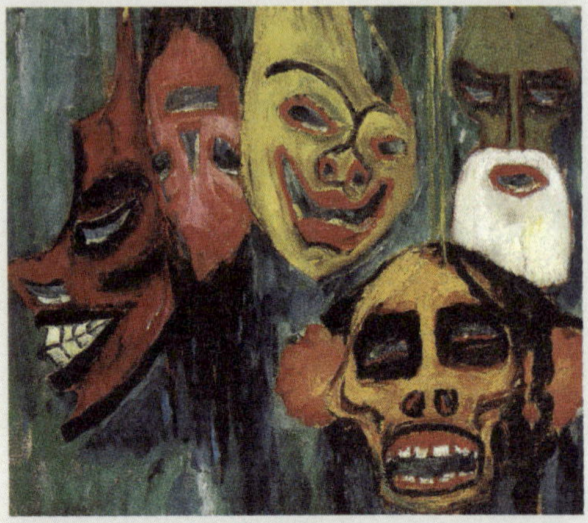

Masks [lxxvii]

// Expressionism in Italy

Although Expressionism began in Germany, the movement soon spread to neighbouring countries, including Italy. Italian Expressionist artwork was characterized by the use of strong colours and bold shapes.

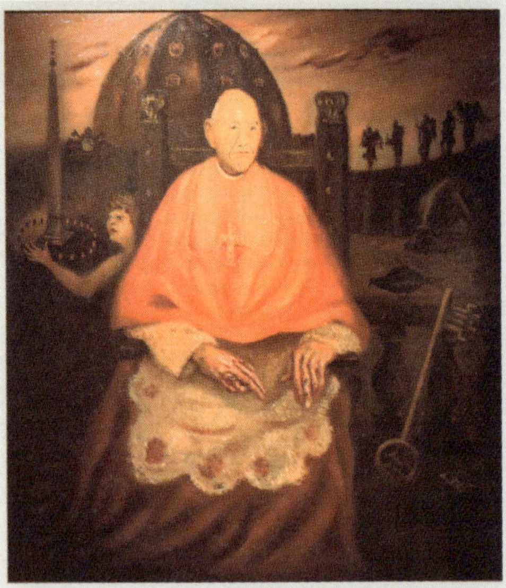

The Cardinal Dean [lxxviii]

[lxxvii] ***Masks*** - This was painted in 1911 as a reflection of Emil Nolde's growing interest in non-Western cultures. Nolde, the oldest member of Die Brücke, often included masks in his art as a symbol of alienation and disconnect. Studying the masks at the Berlin Museum of Ethnology, Nolde was able to capture a variety of cultures, all on one canvas, with carnival masks at the centre.

[lxxviii] ***The Cardinal Dean*** - This painting by Gino Bonichi is also known as *Scipione* (Rome, 1930). The surreal atmosphere of this portrait evokes the end of the world.

// Cubism

Often credited to Pablo Picasso and Georges Braque, Cubism was a revolutionary style of abstract painting which emerged at the start of the 20th century.

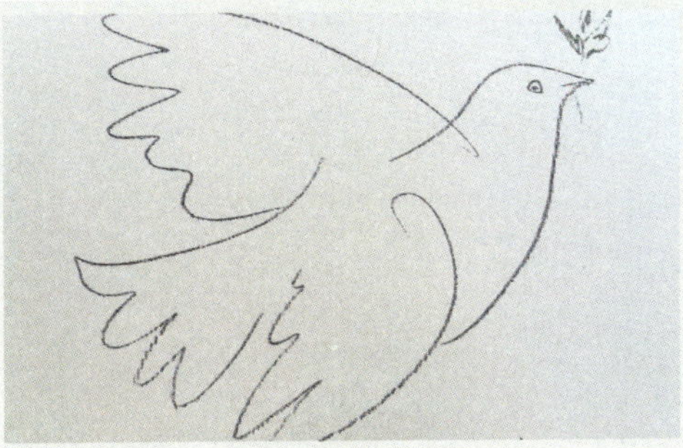

Blue Dove [lxxix]

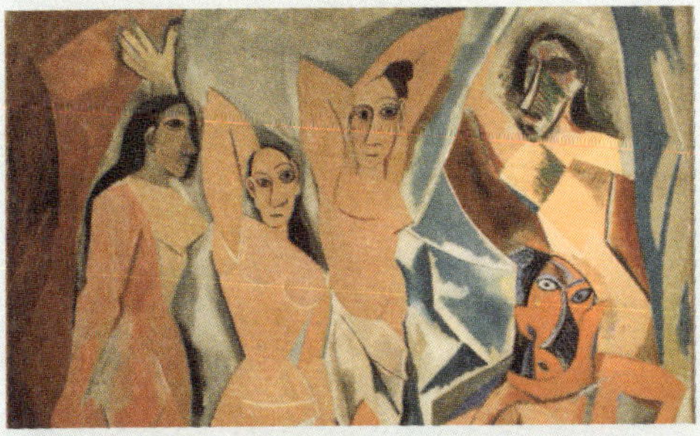

Les Demoiselles d'Avignon [lxxx]

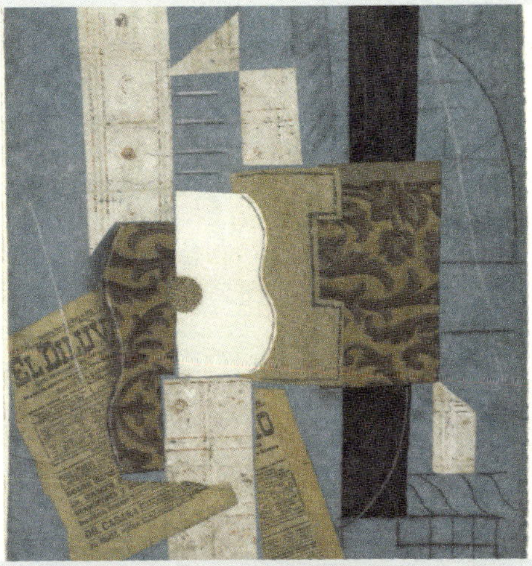

Guitar [lxxxi]

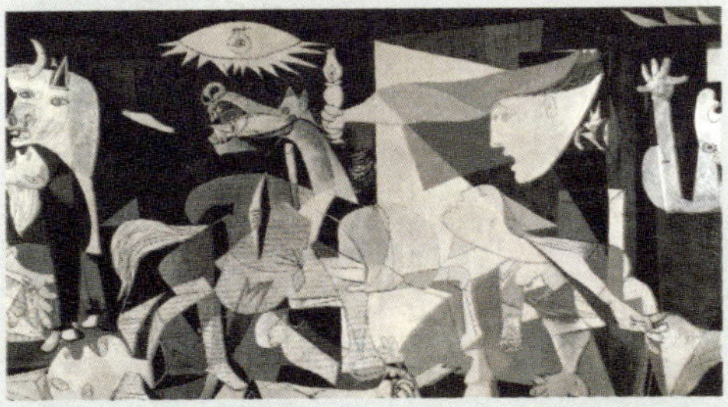

Guernica [lxxxii]

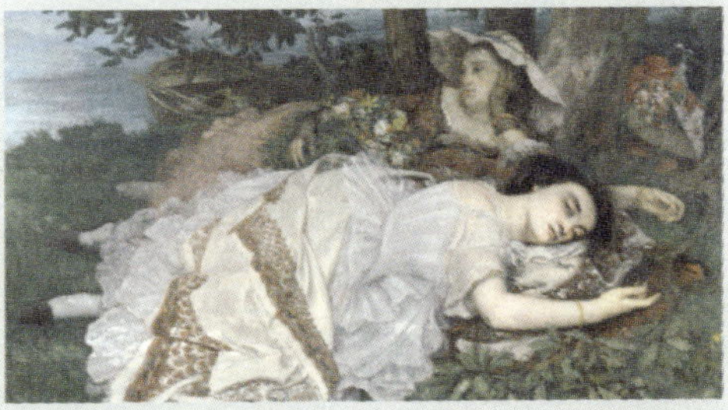

Young Ladies on the Banks of the Seine [lxxxiii]

[lxxix] ***Blue Dove*** - This is a drawing (Picasso, 1961) that symbolized peace.

[lxxx] ***Les Demoiselles d'Avignon*** - Picasso's Rose period, marked by the use of oranges and pinks, lasted from 1904 to 1906. In *Les Demoiselles d'Avignon* (1907), Picasso addresses the problems of volume, making this the work with which he equates the birth of Cubism. *Les Demoiselles d'Avignon* is traditionally seen as Picasso's pivotal first step towards the new Cubist style, a step that established him as the leader of avant-garde art in Paris. The picture is like a cinematic close-up. The five women, each over seven feet tall, are shockingly present, and it seems a force is pressing them to the surface of the picture.

[lxxxi] ***Guitar*** - This is a 1912 Picasso painting featuring broken, free images. It was a radical leap from the sculptural tradition of modelling (carving or moulding) to a new technique of assemblage.

[lxxxii] ***Guernica*** - This painting (1937) is a dramatic representation in white, black and grey of the massacre of Guernica. The work, which marked a fundamental stage in Picasso's artistic and political commitment, depicts a historical event while highlighting effective visual and essential emotional components.

[lxxxiii] ***Young Ladies on the Banks of the Seine*** - This painting (Courbet, 1857) marks the return to a more traditional style.

// Futurism

Pioneered by Filippo Tommaso Marinetti, Futurism was a movement launched in 1909 which sought to represent the dynamic movement of the modern world through artistic media.

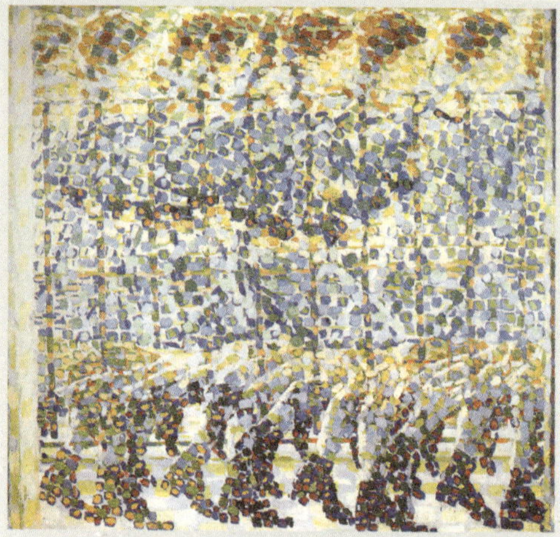

Young Girl Running on a Balcony [lxxxiv]

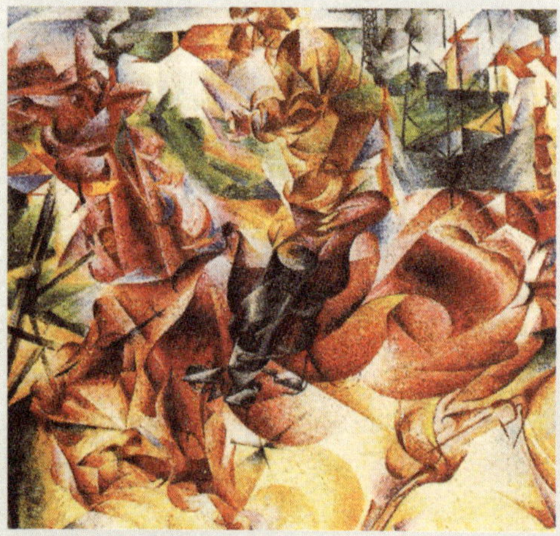

Elasticity [lxxxv]

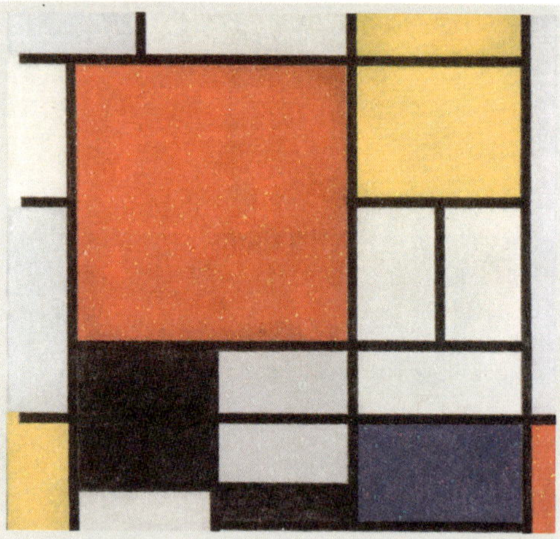

Composition with Black, Red, Gray, Yellow and Blue [lxxxvi]

[lxxxiv] ***Young Girl Running on a Balcony*** - This painting (1912) indicates Giacomo Balla's growing interests in creative nuances, which would later formally be realized as part of the Futurist movement. The artist was influenced heavily by the north Italians' use of Divisionism and the French's better-known Pointillism.

[lxxxv] ***Elasticity*** - Umberto Boccioni's *Elasticity* of 1912 focuses exclusively on the study of vigorous, sequential movements, foreign to the intellectual dynamics of Analytical Cubism. By using this Impressionist compositional technique, Boccioni implies not only that his tightly compressed subject is so dynamic that it must burst its four-sided confines, but that it is a fragment of a constantly changing visual experience. The painting depicts the pure energy of a horse and is preserved in the National Gallery of Modern and Contemporary Art in Rome. It fully expresses the artist's reflection on the theme of movement and the environment; the shape is completely replaced by the representation of action.

[lxxxvi] ***Composition with Black, Red, Gray, Yellow and Blue*** - Avoiding references to the real world and using only the primary colours (red, blue and yellow), the primary values (black, white and grey) and the primary directions (horizontal and vertical), Piet Mondrian (1921) created abstract paintings through which he sought to reveal universal harmony and order. They are preserved in the National Gallery of Modern and Contemporary Art in Rome.

// Dadaism

Dada artists sought to highlight and mock the meaninglessness of contemporary society.

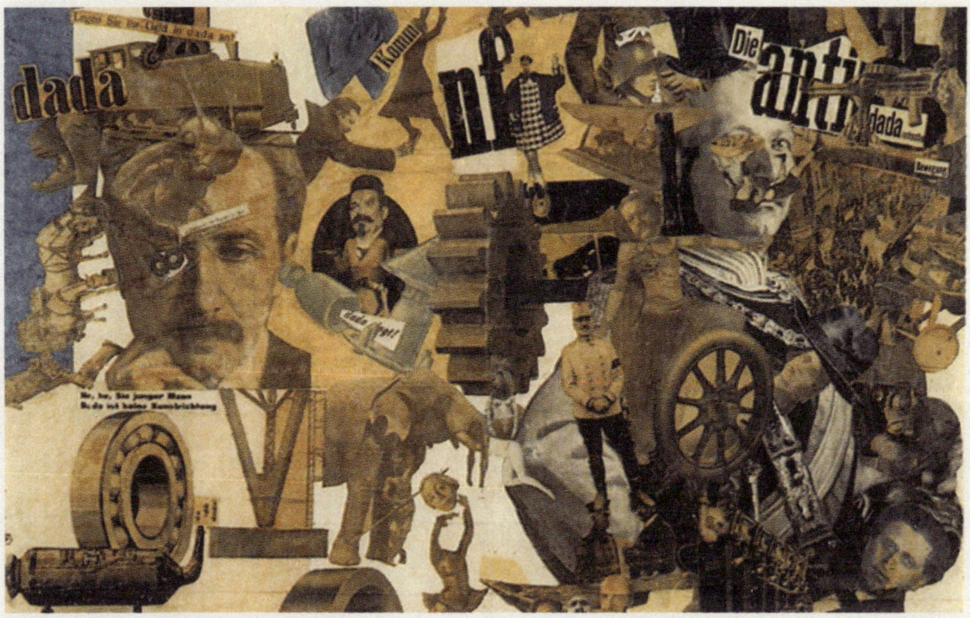

Cut with the Dada Kitchen Knife Dada through the Weimar Beer-Belly [lxxxvii]

[lxxxvii] ***Cut with the Dada Kitchen Knife Dada through the Weimar Beer-Belly*** - This collage of pasted papers (Hannah Höch, 1919) symbolizes the artist cutting through patriarchal society. The piece is a direct criticism of the failed attempt at democracy imposed by the Weimar Republic. *Cut with the Dada Kitchen Knife* is 'an explosive agglomeration of cut-up images, bang in the middle of the most well-known photograph of the seminal First International Dada Fair in 1920' (Hudson 1919).

// Metaphysical Painting

A style most often associated with the work of Italians Carlo Carrà and Giorgio de Chirico, Metaphysical painting was characterized by dream-like scenes that produced unsettling effects on the viewer.

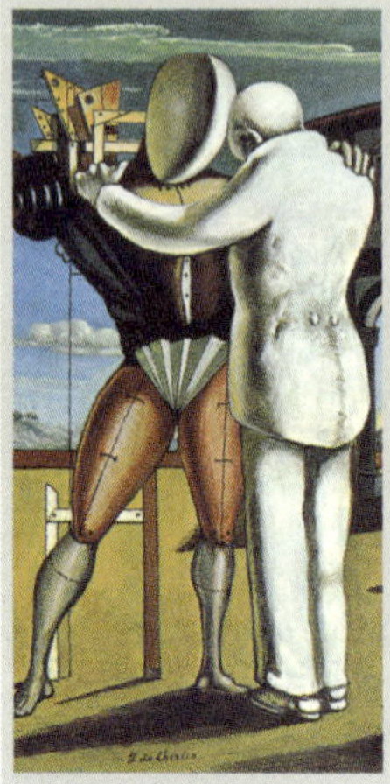

The Prodigan Son [lxxxviii]

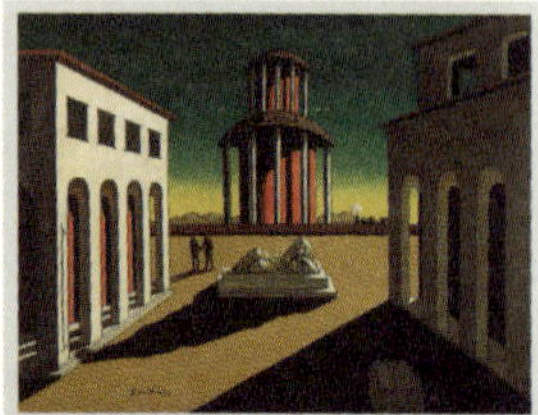

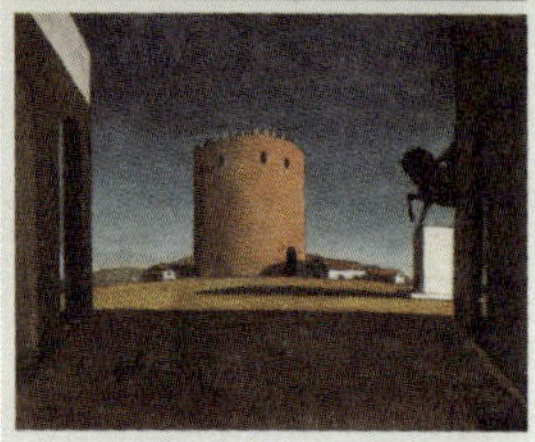

Italian Piazza (top) and The Red Tower (bottom) [lxxxix]

// Amedeo Modigliani

This Italian-Jewish sculptor and painter (1884–1920) produced simple but visually striking work, playing on the use of elongated forms and striking lines.

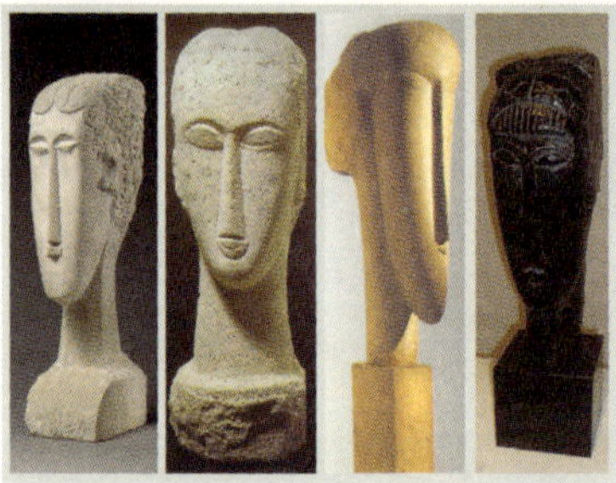

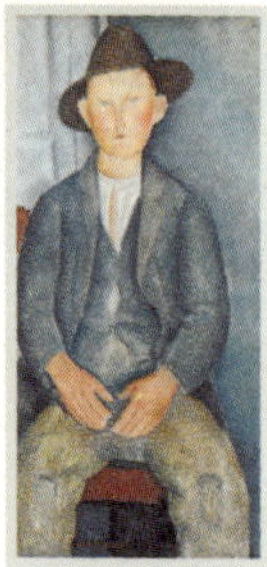

Tête (left) [xc] *and The Little Peasant (right)* [xci]

[lxxxviii] ***The Prodigal Son*** - This was painted (1922) in tempera on canvas as Giorgio de Chirico was transitioning from the Metaphysical style of his earlier works to the Neoclassicism he adhered to in the 1920s. The biblical subject matter was interpreted by De Chirico as a stone effigy of a father placing his hand on the shoulder of a mannequin representing the son. It is displayed in the Museo de Novecento in Milan.

[lxxxix] ***Italian Piazza*** and ***The Red Tower*** - Painted in 1913, these are the among the first of De Chirico's paintings—striking because of their simplicity. Many of his paintings show architectural visions like buildings with porches, streets—lonely and deserted. But his visions of reality are different from the reality which the observer understands in the paintings. The light shows the actual colours of objects, while the sky features unnatural colours. The shadows contrast with the bright areas and are excessively long. The perspective is almost always deliberately deformed, thus the space has an unusual appearance. His scenes are dominated by the absence of life and absolute silence. The atmosphere of these paintings is similar to that of a dream or a vision.

[xc] ***Tête*** - One of twenty-seven known sculptures by Amedeo Modigliani, this was made between 1911 and 1912. The limestone head stands over two feet tall and depicts the head of a woman wearing a tribal mask with her hair swept back.

[xci] ***The Little Peasant*** - This is one of a small group of paintings of youths by Amedeo Modigliani (1918). The artist inscribed the work's title on the bottom right of the canvas, identifying the sitter as a 'peasant boy'. The painting has a faint chromatism and a delicate colour variation and harmony. It is located in the Tate Gallery in London.

// Surrealism

In the 1920s, the creative movement known as Surrealism was born; an experiment in unleashing the subconscious though the media of art and literature.

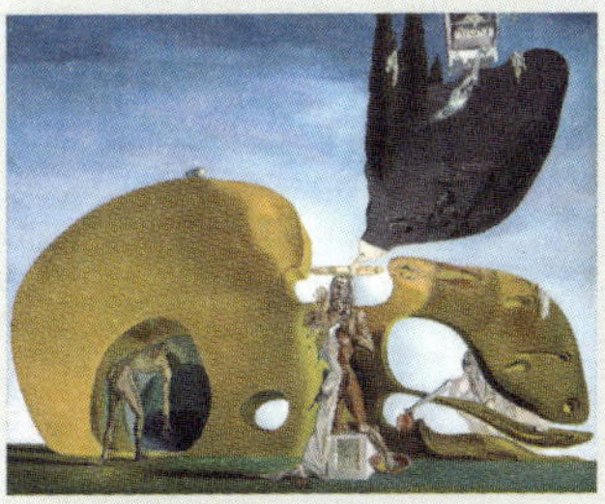

The Birth of Liquid Desires [xcii]

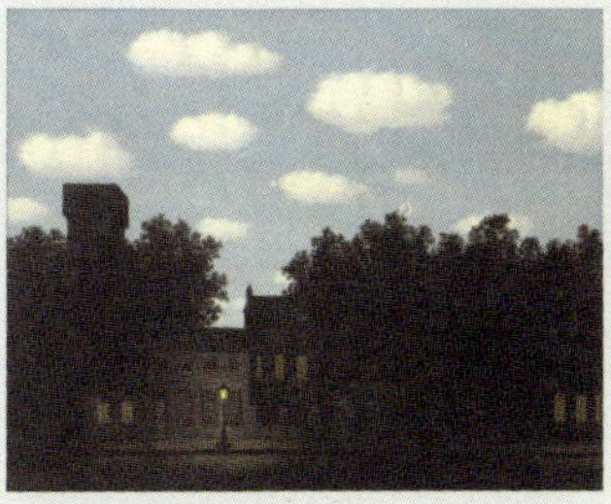

Empire of Light [xciii]

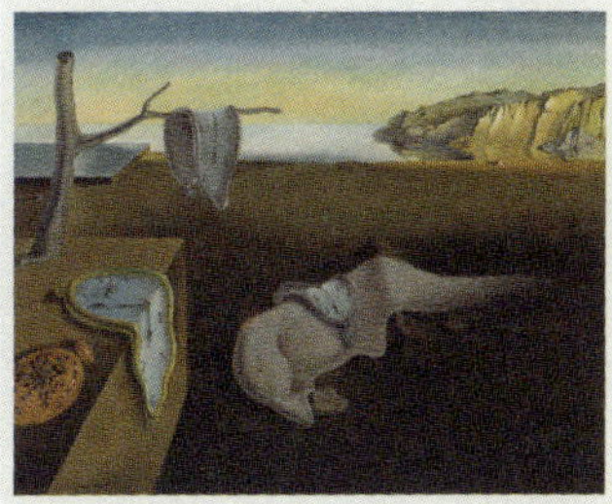

The Persistence of Memory [xciv]

// Surrealism

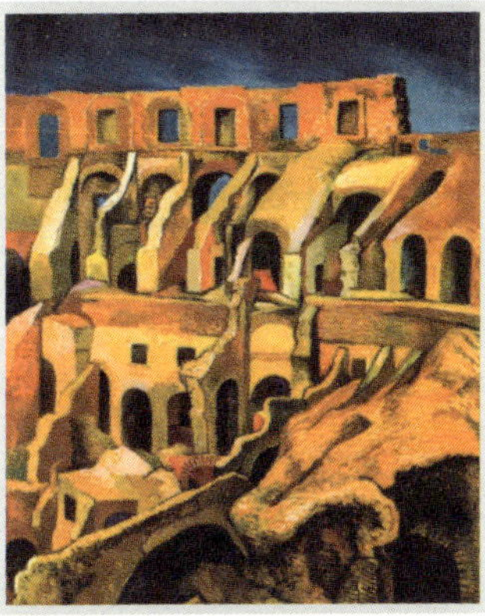

Colosseum [xcv]

Bright, neoclassical landscape scenes remained popular in Italy well into the 20th century.

[xcii] ***The Birth of Liquid Desires*** - This painting (1932) is an expression of Salvador Dali's inner mental conflict, stemming from his love for a woman ten years his senior. The painting echoes the William Tell allegory. In this case, we see the apple on the head of the victim in the allegory supplanted by a loaf of bread on the head of the figure with ambiguous sexual identity.

[xciii] ***Empire of Light*** - Numerous versions of this painting (1950) exist. It is a dark, nocturnal street scene set against a pastel-blue, light-drenched sky spotted with fluffy cumulus clouds. With no fantastic element other than the single paradoxical combination of day and night, René Magritte upsets a fundamental organizing premise of life. Sunlight, ordinarily the source of clarity, causes here the confusion and unease traditionally associated with darkness. The luminosity of the sky becomes unsettling, making the empty darkness below even more impenetrable than it would seem in the normal context.

[xciv] ***The Persistence of Memory*** - This painting by Salvador Dali is often called *Clocks* (1931). In the painting, four clocks are prominently on display in an otherwise empty desert scene. While this might seem uncanny enough, the clocks are not flat as you might expect them to be, but bent out of shape, appearing to be in the act of melting away. Clocks seems illogical or irrational, but one might be surprised by the very representational and nearly photographic quality of the painting, fitting well with Dali's own description of his art as being 'hand-painted dream photographs'. The concept of the 'dream' is integral to understanding Surrealism and plays a key role in the meaning of the art.

[xcv] ***Colosseum*** - Renato Guttuso was a Sicilian painter who moved away from informal trends and thus became the founder of Social Realism in Italy. In *Colosseum*, he attempted to create an art fundamentally new and different, an art free from figurative constraints and based on the value of the creative act itself.

2

Part Two

visual excursus

// Leonardo's Art

Leonardo da Vinci remains one of the best-known Italian artists of all time. As well as being a prolific inventor, scientist and architect, he was a creator of strikingly realistic paintings with religious themes.

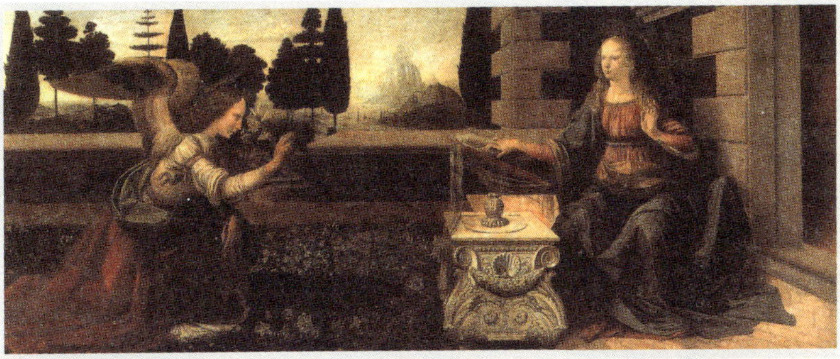

The Annunciation [xcvi]

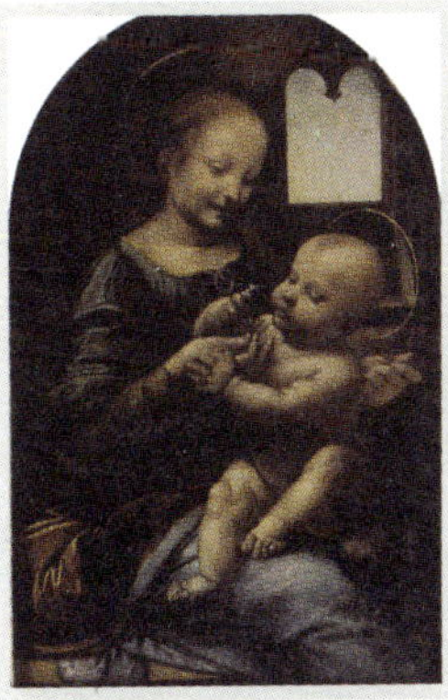

Benois Madonna [xcvii]

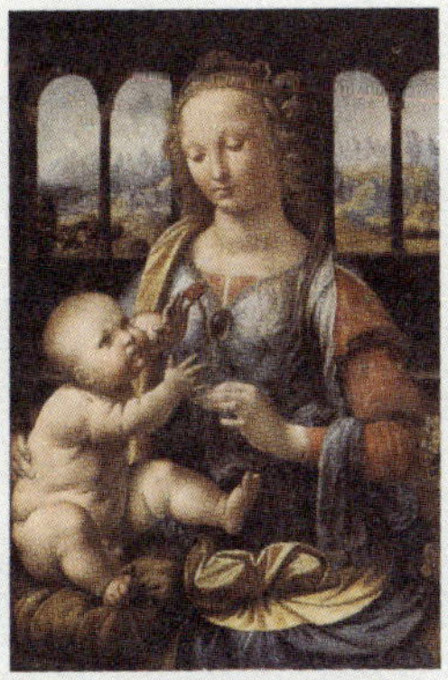

Madonna of the Carnation [xcviii]

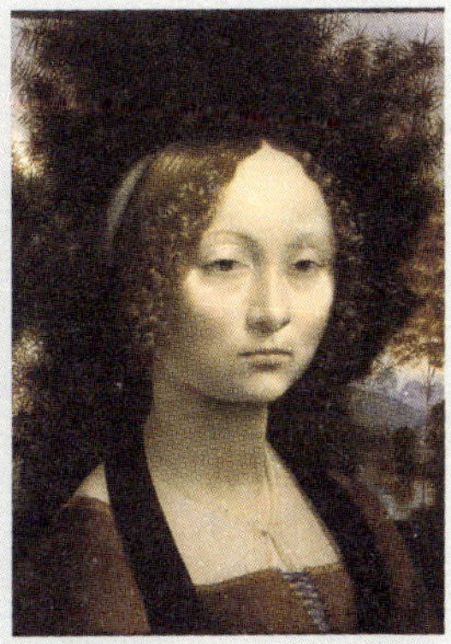

Portrait of Ginevra de' Benci [xcix]

[xcvi] ***The Annunciation*** - This is housed in the Uffizi Gallery in Florence, Italy. The composition by Leonardo da Vinci and Andrea del Verrocchio (1472–1475) follows a centuries-old model—the angel on the left, the Virgin on the right and a lectern in between, the whole depicted in an architectural setting that opens out to a landscape. The kneeling angel is magnificently youthful, with a high forehead, stylized wings, rich clothing and a lily. The Virgin, who has been surprised while reading, raises her hand in a gesture of astonishment and displays a fine-featured face, which some have described as cold. Her pose, with knees evenly spread and covered with drapery, gives her a strong monumental character.

[xcvii] ***Benois Madonna*** - During the very early years, Leonardo favoured the subject of the Madonna and the Child. He produced several paintings on this theme, along with a number of sketches and a large number of drawings. His works showed mother and child in precious, private moments and focused on the emotions between them—Leonardo aimed to make the subjects look natural. This painting, *Benois Madonna* (1478), was named after the 19th-century artist Leon Benois, who sold it to the Hermitage in Leningrad at the beginning of the century.

[xcviii] ***Madonna of the Carnation*** - Here Jesus reaches out awkwardly for the flower held delicately in Mary's fingers. Like all infants, he looks unable to control his movements as he attempts to grasp the symbol of Passion. Dating from 1478–1480, this painting, also known as the *Munich Madonna* or the *Madonna with the Vase* (due to the vase of flowers sitting beside her), is usually considered one of Leonardo's first autonomous works.

[xcix] ***Portrait of Ginevra de' Benci*** - Unlike Leonardo's other portraits of women, the lady in this painting (1474–1478) looks sulky, unforgiving and haughty. This is emphasized by the slightly smaller cast of one eye, making her appear withdrawn. Her left eye seems to gaze directly at us while the right looks beyond to some invisible point. Like other Florentine women of the period, Ginevra has shaved her eyebrows (this is also obvious in the *Mona Lisa*). Maybe her expression indicates she was not entirely happy about her forthcoming marriage. In later life, she was to go into self-inflicted exile in an attempt to recover from a severe illness. She was also tormented by an ill-fated love affair.

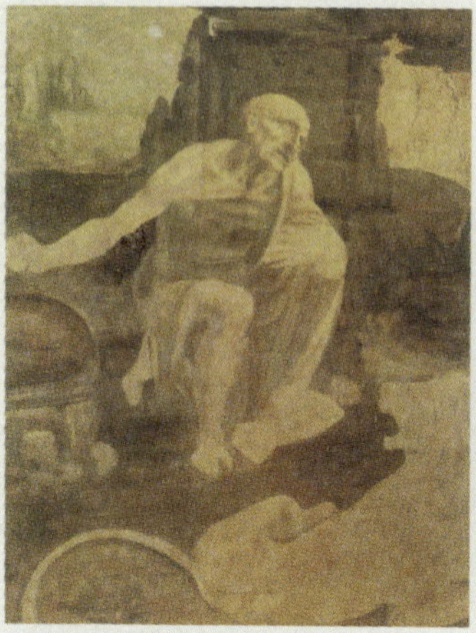

Saint Jerome in the Wilderness [c]

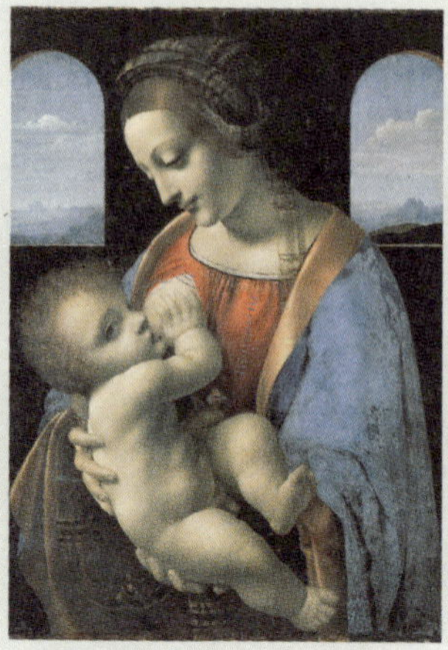

Madonna Litta [ci]

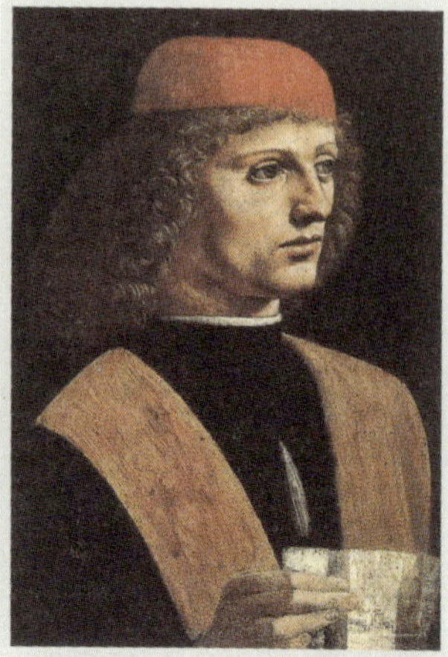

Portrait of a Musician [cii]

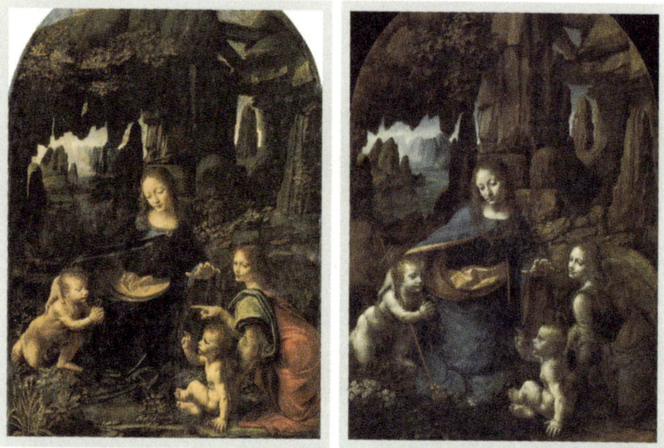

The Virgin of the Rocks [ciii]; *Louvre version (left) London version (right)*

[c] ***Saint Jerome in the Wilderness*** - This painting (1480) depicts Saint Jerome during his retreat to the Syrian desert, where he lived the life of a hermit. The saint kneels in a rocky landscape, gazing towards a crucifix, which can be discerned faintly sketched at the extreme right of the painting. In Jerome's right hand he holds a rock, with which he is traditionally shown beating his chest in penance. At his feet is the lion which became a loyal companion after he extracted a thorn from its paw. The lion, the stone and the cardinal's hat are the traditional attributes of the saint.
[ci] ***Madonna Litta*** - This painting (1490) depicts the Virgin Mary breastfeeding the Christ child, a devotional subject known as the Madonna lactans. The figures are set in a dark interior with two arched openings, as in Leonardo's earlier *Madonna of the Carnation*, and a mountainous landscape in aerial perspective can be seen beyond. In his left-hand, Christ holds a goldfinch, which is symbolic of his future Passion. *Madonna Litta* passed from the hands of the Vicontis family into the Litta family of Milan and thus the painting takes its name from them.
[cii] ***Portrait of a Musician*** - The man in the painting (1485) was at one time thought to be Franchino Gaffurio, who was the master of music at Milan Cathedral. However, others think the man is anonymous. The piece of paper he holds is at least one part of a musical score—it has notes written on it. The painting was restored and repainted; Leonardo probably left the portrait unfinished (but close to completion).
[ciii] ***The Virgin of the Rocks (The Madonna of the Rocks)*** - This is the name used for two of da Vinci's paintings (1483-86). Both paintings show the Madonna and Christ Child with the infant John the Baptist and an angel, and they have identical compositions except for two significant details—the gaze and the right hand of the angel. There are also many minor ways in which the works differ, including the colours, the lighting and the flora. In the *Virgin of the Rocks*, the laws are nature's but the final creation Leonardo's. And here he defies nature in many ways, cutting across previous

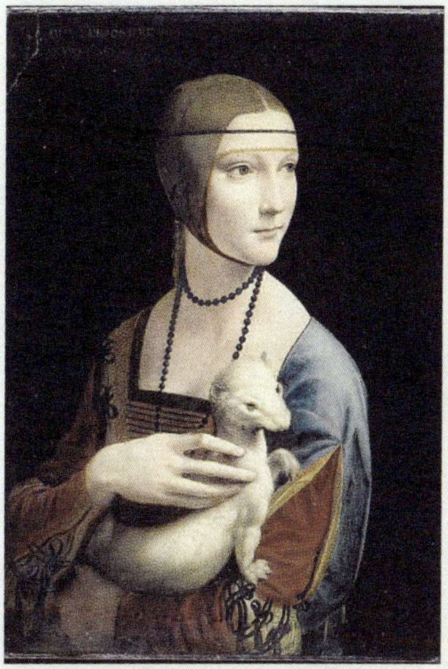

Lady with an Ermine [civ]

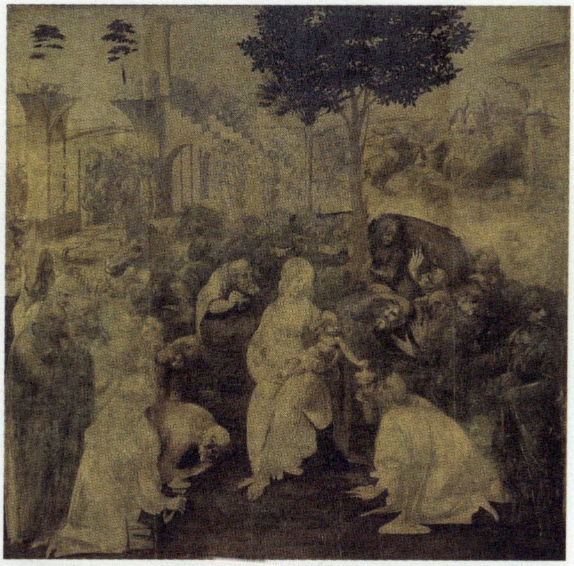

The Adoration of the Magi [cv]

artistic assumptions. The result is organic rather than intellectual. One painting usually hangs in the Louvre, Paris and the other in the National Gallery, London.

[civ] ***Lady with an Ermine*** - This portrait (1489–90) shows signs of having been heavily retouched. The entire background was darkened, the dress below the ermine was retouched and a transparent veil worn by the woman was repainted to match the colour of her hair. The result of this last retouching gives the appearance that her hair reaches below her chin. Yet another change was the addition of dark shadows between the fingers of her right hand—a close look at the bottom two fingers reveals that they are quite inferior to the others after an unknown restorer repainted them. An object of the greatest rarity, the *Lady with an Ermine* is a captivating image of exquisite elegance, which reveals the artistic genius of Leonardo da Vinci's incomparable creative mind.

[cv] ***The Adoration of the Magi*** - The Virgin Mary and Child are depicted in the foreground and form a triangular shape with the Magi kneeling in adoration. Behind them is a semicircle of accompanying figures, including what may be a self-portrait of the young Leonardo (on the far right). In the background on the left is the ruin of a pagan building, on which workmen can be seen, apparently repairing it. On the right are men on horseback, fighting, and a sketch of a rocky landscape. *The Adoration of the Magi* (1481) is perhaps one of Leonardo da Vinci's strangest and most fertile compositions. By combining the figures of pleading old men and armed horsemen, he transformed a banal biblical subject into a scene from human history. At the same time, he took the technique of non finito to its extreme. The figures and architectural elements, boldly delineated and filled out in earth colours, on the five boards which make up this panel, anticipate the type of sketch work that would characterize Modern art. This picture is remarkable for its extreme concentration and power.

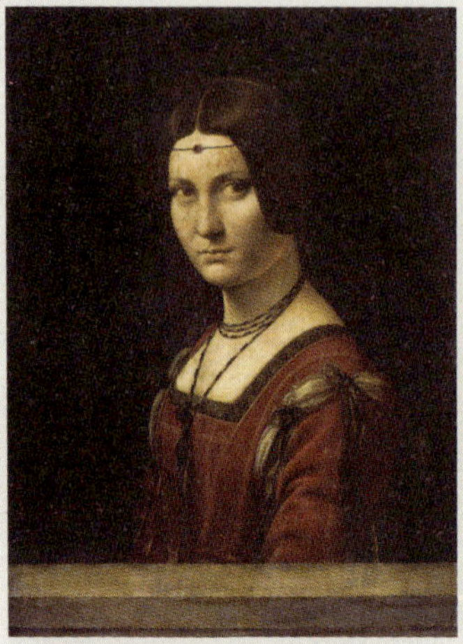

La Belle Ferronniere [cvi]

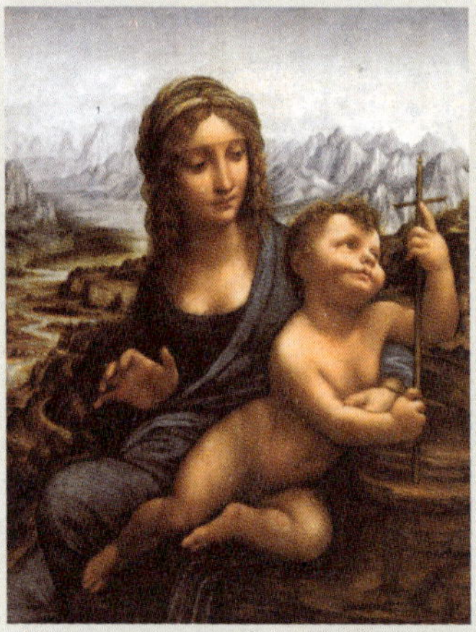

The Madonna of the Yarnwinder [cvii]

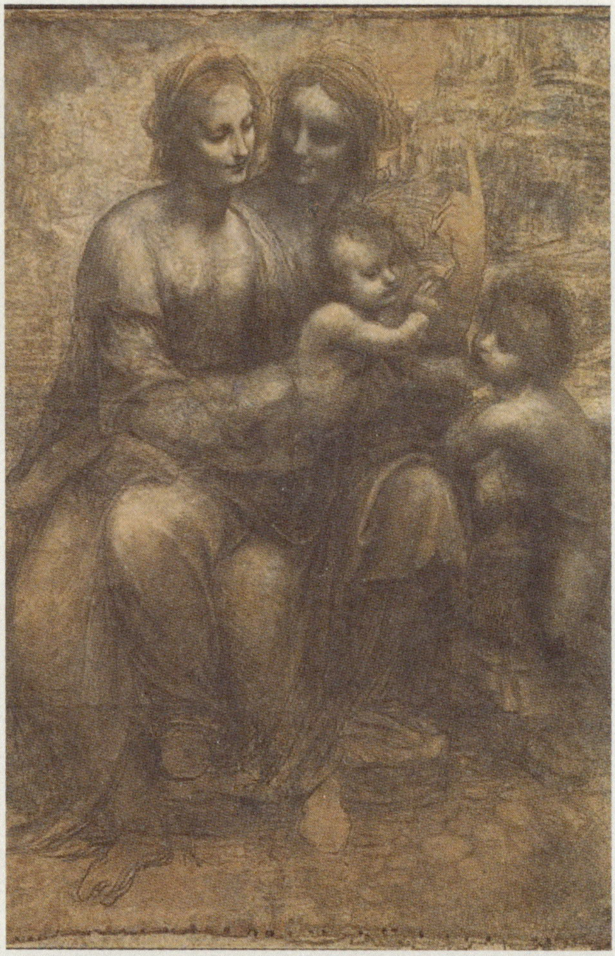

The Virgin and Child with St Anne and St John the Baptist [cviii]

[cvi] ***La Belle Ferronniere*** - This portrait (1490–1496) of a lady is usually attributed to Leonardo da Vinci and is currently displayed in the Abu Dhabi Louvre. It is also known as *Portrait of an Unknown Woman*. The painting's title, given as early as the 17th century, identifies the sitter as the wife or the daughter of an ironmonger (a ferronnier), and was said to be discreetly alluding to a reputed mistress of Francis I of France, married to a certain Le Ferron. The tale is a romantic legend of revenge, in which the aggrieved husband intentionally infects himself with syphilis, which he passes to the king through infecting his wife. Created around 1495, this painting may also take its name from the ferronniere the sitter wears around her brow—a common Lombard fashion.

[cvii] ***The Madonna of the Yarnwinder*** (The Lansdowne Madonna) - This painting (1499 or later) shows the Virgin Mary seated with the Christ child, who gazes at a yarnwinder (used to collect spun yarn). The yarnwinder serves both as a symbol of Mary's domesticity and as a foreshadow of the cross on which Christ will be crucified. It appears that Mary wants to pull the child away from the symbol of his future, but even she is powerless to prevent the crucifixion, which is a part of his destiny. The painting's dynamic composition and implied narrative was highly influential on later High Renaissance depictions of the Madonna and Child by artists such as Raphael and Andrea del Sarto.

[cviii] ***The Virgin and Child with St Anne and St John the Baptist*** - The subject of this drawing (c. 1499–1500 or c. 1506–1508) is a combination of two themes popular in Florentine paintings of the 15th century—the Virgin and Child with St Anne and St John the Baptist, and the Virgin and Child with St Anne. The drawing is notable for its complex

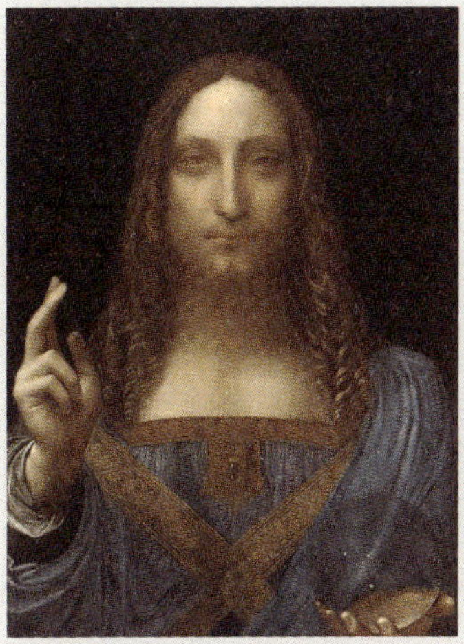

Salvator Mundi [cix]

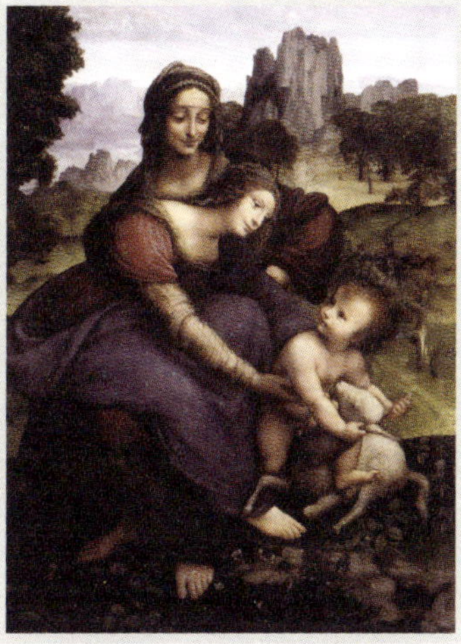

The Virgin and Child with St Anne [cx]

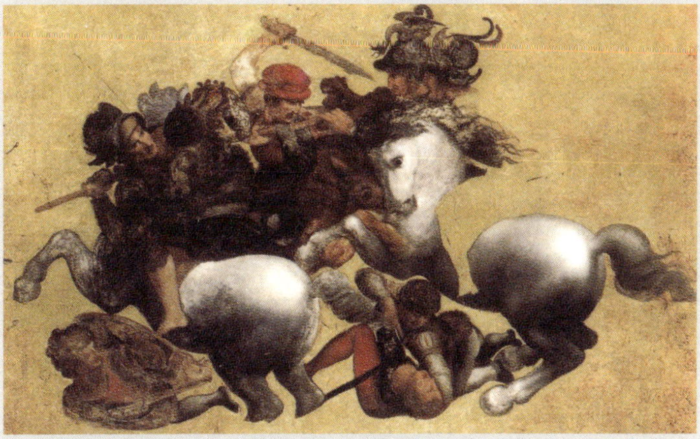

The Battle of Anghiari [cxi]

composition, demonstrating the alternation in the positioning of figures which first featured in Leonardo's work in the *Benois Madonna*. While the lower halves of their bodies turn away in sinuous movement, the faces of the two women turn towards each other, mirroring each other's features. The delineation between the upper bodies is unclear, suggesting that the heads are part of the same body.

[cix] ***Salvator Mundi*** - This representation of Jesus (c. 1500) shows him in a Renaissance dress, making the sign of the cross with his right hand while holding a transparent rock-crystal orb in his left hand. This signals his role as Salvator Mundi (Latin for 'Saviour of the World') and master of the cosmos, the orb representing the crystalline sphere of the heavens as it was perceived during the Renaissance.

[cx] ***The Virgin and Child with St Anne*** - This painting (c. 1503) was commissioned as the high altarpiece for the Church of Santissima Annunziata in Florence. It depicts St Anne, her daughter the Virgin Mary and the infant Jesus. Christ is shown grappling with a sacrificial lamb, symbolizing his Passion, while the Virgin tries to restrain him.

[cxi] ***The Battle of Anghiari*** - This painting (1505) is at times referred to as *The Lost Leonardo* and some commentators believe that there is more of it still hidden beneath later frescoes in the Hall of Five Hundred (Salone dei Cinquecento) in the Palazzo Vecchio, Florence. Its central scene depicts three men riding raging warhorses, engaged in a battle for the possession of a standard.

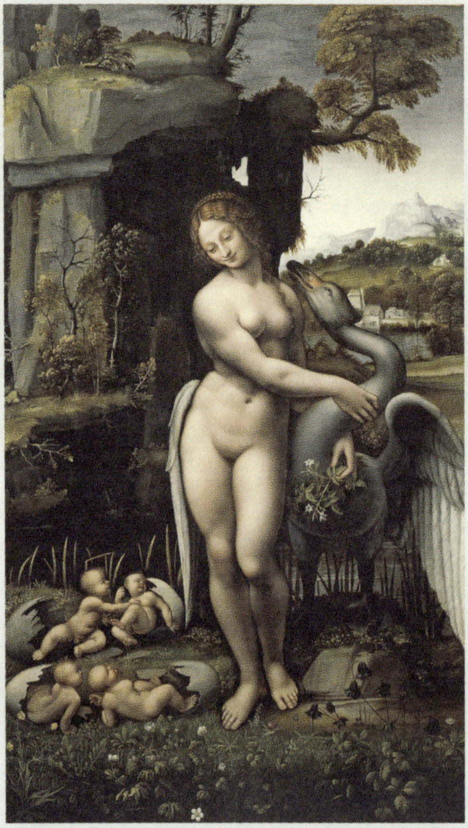

Leda and the Swan cxii

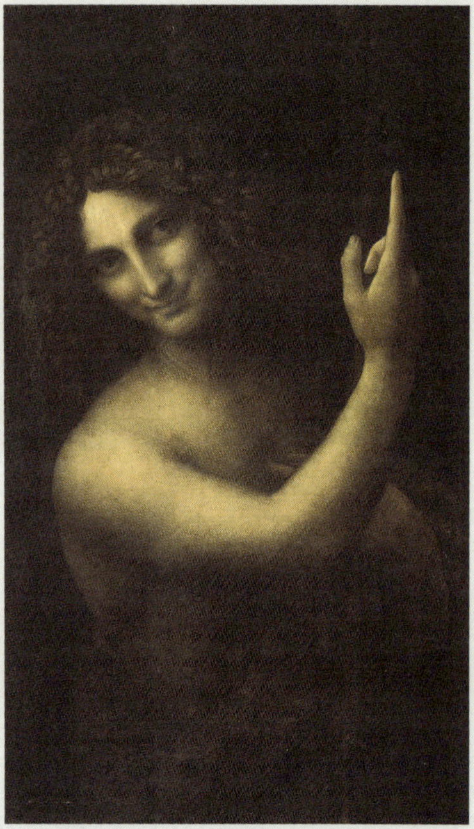

St John the Baptist cxiii

cxii ***Leda and the Swan*** - Leonardo was very absorbed with the theme of Leda during the time he was working on the *Mona Lisa*, and while in Milan he made many sketches of the swans in the moat around the Castello. When the picture (c. 1504–1508) was in the royal collection in Fontainebleau in 1625, it was described by Cassiano del Pozzo as 'a standing figure of Leda almost entirely naked, with the swan by her, and two eggs, from whose broken shells come forth four babies. This work, although somewhat dry in style, is exquisitely finished, and the landscape and the plant life are rendered with the greatest diligence.'

cxiii ***St John the Baptist*** - The pointing gesture of St John the Baptist towards the heavens suggests the importance of salvation through baptism, which John the Baptist represents. The work (1513–1516) is often referenced by later painters, especially those from the late Renaissance and Mannerist schools. The inclusion of a gesture similar to John's would increase the importance of a work with a religious theme.

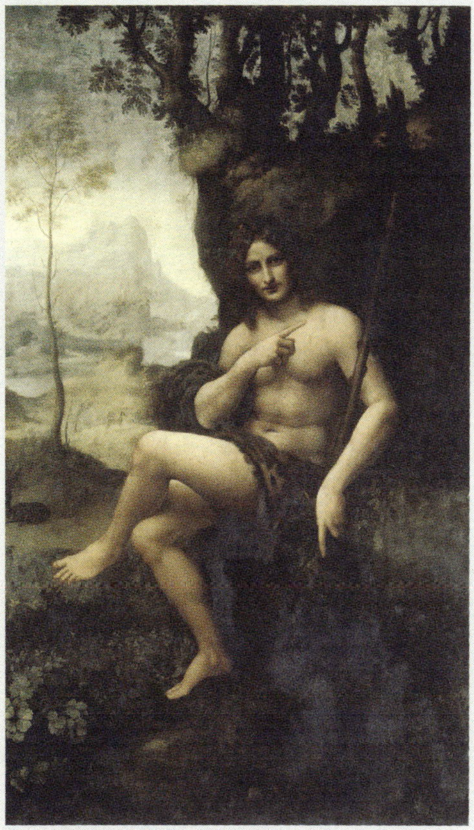

Bacchus [cxiv]

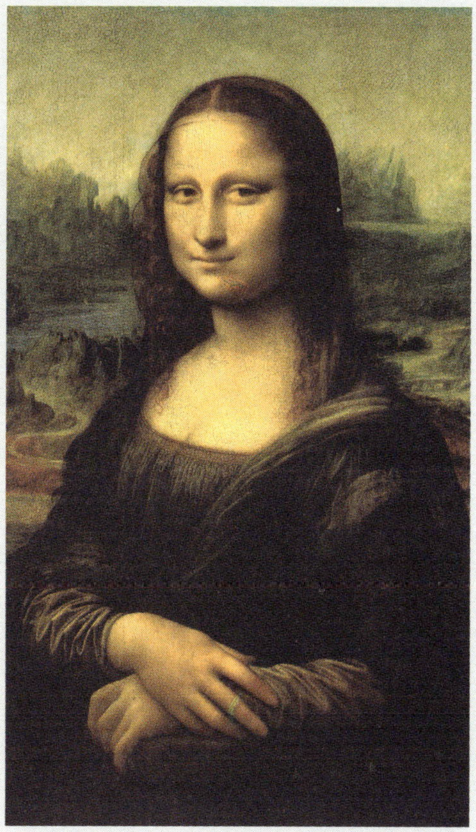

Mona Lisa [cxv]

[cxiv] ***Bacchus*** - Formerly known as St John the Baptist, this picture (1510–1515) was on display in the Musée du Louvre, Paris, France. It is based on a drawing by Da Vinci and shows a male figure with a garlanded head, wearing a leopard skin and seated in an idyllic landscape. The figure points with his right hand to his left, and with his left hand he grasps his thyrsus (a staff or spear tipped with an ornament like a pine cone, carried by Bacchus and his followers) and points down to the earth.

[cxv] ***Mona Lisa*** - This famous portrait (c. 1503–1506, perhaps continuing until c. 1517) is of La Gioconda, the wife of Francesco del Giocondo. The lady is dressed in the contemporary Florentine fashion and is seated in a mountainous landscape. Her enigmatic expression, which seems both alluring and aloof, has given the portrait universal fame. The *Mona Lisa* is also one of the most valuable paintings in the world.

// Mandalas

// Tibetan Tradition

Mandalas can be found across cultures and in civilizations throughout history. The term can be applied to any diagram or pattern that represents the cosmos in a microcosm.

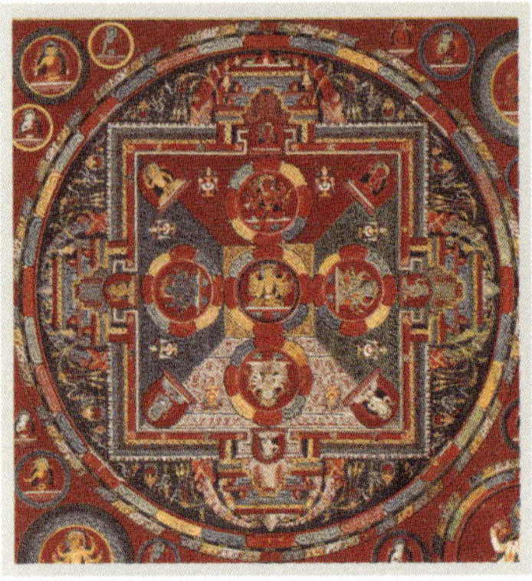

The Tibetan Mandala [cxvi]

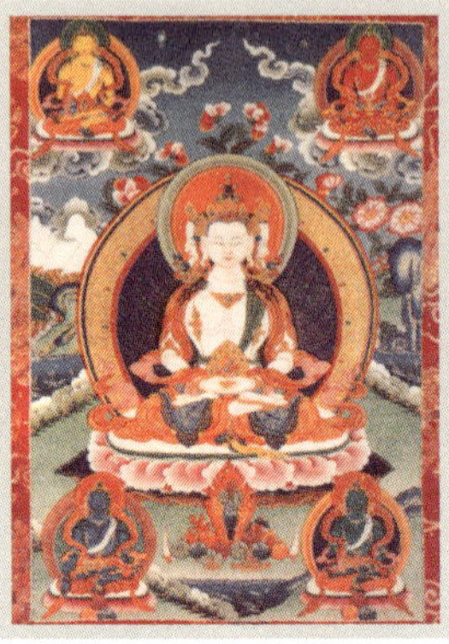

Five Dhyani Buddha [cxvii]

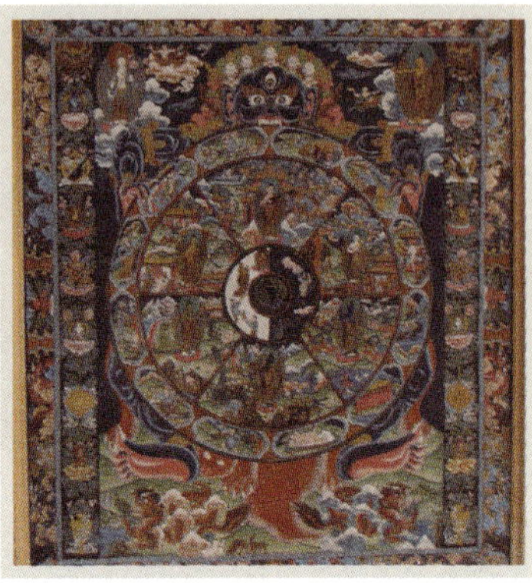

Bhavacakra [cxviii]

[cxvi] ***The Tibetan Mandala*** - The frame, decorated with a garland of flowers or of lotus petals, refers to the heart of the practitioner, who must be full of love and pure devotion in order to aspire to enter the palace of the Mandala. This central palace, also called the building of consecration, is surrounded and protected by a high wall. In the walls, four doors, called torana, open in the direction of the cardinal points and are guarded by fierce deities. The construction is almost always symmetrical and houses a Buddha or another deity, who protects the Dharma (meaning order, balance, harmony).

The colours of the clothes, the positions of the body and the hands, the gestures with which the figures show themselves to the practitioner, are not random. Each element is inserted into the Mandala to represent a particular area of the psyche, an attitude to be internalized.

[cxvii] ***Five Dhyani Buddha*** - In the Mandalas used by the Vajrayana Buddhists, it is very common to see the five Dhyani Buddhas. According to the tradition of Tantric Buddhism, the five Dhyani Buddha were born as the emanation of Adi Buddha ('adi' from the Sanskrit, 'the first' or 'the primordial') who, in the great emptiness preceding time and space, created them for the desire to be able to contemplate oneself.

Also called the five Buddhas of meditation, their names are—Vairocana, Akshobhya, Ratnasambhava, Amitabha and Amoghasiddi. Each Dhyani Buddha, his partner and all the elements related to him (symbols, animals, colours, gestures of hands and bodies, etc.) are not random, but constitute a set of powerful symbols and archetypes that serve to arouse profound transformations in the practitioner's mind. If, on the one hand, they stimulate the emergence of any negative tendencies, on the other, they induce the meditator to refer to the specific Buddha who possesses, and therefore can bestow, the qualities necessary to overcome them.

[cxviii] ***Bhavacakra*** - One of the most widespread Mandalas in Buddhism depicts a six-spoke wheel (the Wheel of Life or Samsara), which displays the six dimensions through which the existence of beings (connected to the Wheel of Samsara—the continuous cycle of deaths and rebirths) takes place.

At the centre we see three images—a red rooster (a symbol of attachment), a green snake (which refers to the concept of aversion) and a black pig (which depicts ignorance). These three animals chase one another on the Mandalic stage, biting one another's tails, in an endless round dance. This means that these three worldly drives are inextricably linked to one another and are precisely the ones who set the Wheel of Samsara in motion in a dimension in which imbalance, duality and conflict reign. The Wheel of Samsara is controlled by Mahakala, who, after holding it tightly between his claws and teeth, swallows it and spits is out in an endless continuum.

Six worlds are represented—the heavens (positioned at the top), the underworld (positioned below), the demons (to the right), the priests (beneath the demons), the men (to the left) and the animals (below the men).

Each world is a stage of the Buddhist life cycle and has its own colours, characteristics, symbolic characters and objects. The six worlds are also associated with the syllables of the most famous mantra of the Buddhist tradition, the *Om Mani Padme Hum*, which represents the sonorous condensation of the power of compassion of the bodhisattva Avalokiteshvara. The worlds are visited and assisted by the Dhyani Buddha, who dispenses all kinds of graces and beneficial qualities as support and help to those who are still trapped in the Wheel of Samsara.

In the rim of the wheel there are a series of symbolic images which help the meditator to become aware of all the possible poisons that can pollute the mind and to remind him that all phenomena are interdependent.

In some of these cases, as in many other rituals, the construction and the use of the mandala and the yantra are combined with the recitation of one or more mantras (as if the mantra were the vital breath, prana, which gives life and energy to the symbolic diagram). In fact, this operation, called divinity through the mantra, is called pranapratishtha, which, in the tantric field, is used not only for the activation of the mandalic diagrams but also for the installation of murti, the sacred statues. The mantra, in fact, has the power to protect and free the mind—mantra comes from two Sanskrit words—manas (mind) and trayati (free). However, for the mantra to take effect, it is necessary to have faith, to believe that its repetition has the strength to awaken or strengthen already present energies, even if in the form of a seed, in the human soul.

The Mandala, however, is not just a graphic representation that performs certain tasks. It has always been used in the field of architecture as a symbol that expresses the structure of the universe according to divine principles. In this sense, the temples belonging to any religion or era are built in such a way that their fundamental elements are representations of the constituent elements of the universe.

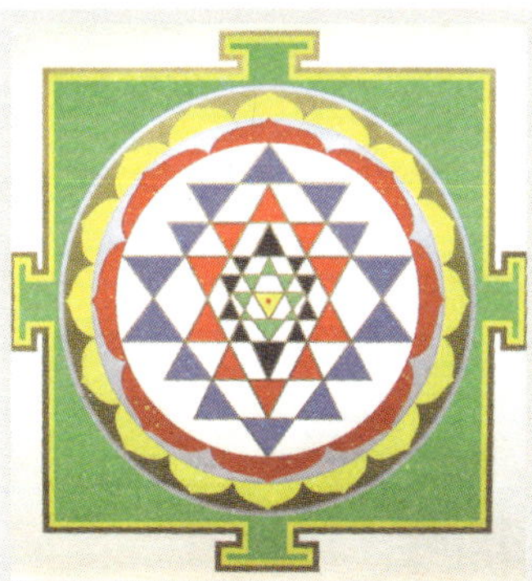

Yantra with Bindu [cxix]

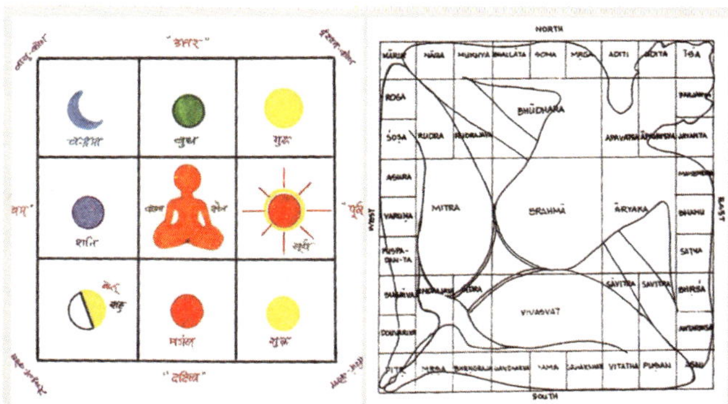

Vastu Shastra [cxx]

[cxix] ***Yantra with Bindu*** - Yantra refers to any device or instrument, but in the tantric context, the word refers to a diagram with precise characteristics which has the capacity to generate psychic or mental experiences in the subject who observes it. The yantra is primarily made up of geometric shapes in which letters of the Sanskrit alphabet are inscribed. Immense concentration and attention must be exercised by those tracing a yantra. The performance of a yantra becomes, rather than an artistic expression, a real ritual.
The first geometric element, which occupies the central point from which the whole structure of the yantra radiates, is the bindu—the symbol of the undifferentiated One, in which Shiva and Shakti are still fully involved in the eternal cosmic embrace. Another element constituting the yantra is the circle, which has its own dimension and circumscribes a sacred space. It hints at the circularity of time and the unfolding of the universe from the emptiness of its centre. The third geometric figure is the square. It symbolizes the earth element, evoking the concept of stability, justice and divine perfection in the material world. The last geometric figure in the yantra is the triangle. If the vertex is pointing upwards, it symbolizes fire and is connected with the male element (Shiva); if the vertex is facing downwards it represents water and is connected with the female principle (Shakti). The downward vertex is also a symbol of the One that bends back to humanity, while the upward vertex symbolizes the effort of the human who tries to ascend towards the divine.
The four T-shaped doors that give access to the central diagram (placed in the same direction as the four cardinal points) symbolize the possibility (or the need) to move from the human to the spiritual dimensions.
[cxx] ***Vastu Shastra*** -Vastu Shastra is the ancient mystic science of interior design to promote health and happiness. The crucial elements (Water, Air, Fire, Earth and Space) must be coordinated in building architecture and decoration to ensure prosperity.

// Christian Tradition

The Gothic architecture of Chartres Cathedral in France presents a symbology very close to that of Hinduism and the Eastern world, making frequent use of Mandala-style patterns. An excellent example is the Rose window on the facade of the building. At that time of its construction in the Middle Ages, Chatres was an important cultural centre. The magnificent cathedral is an excellent example of the typically tantric tendency to integrate humans with the divine. The numerous beautiful windows of the cathedral were probably designed to convey the message that God is Light, and that every living creature is an emanation of this light, receiving and transmitting the divine illumination according to its capacity and degree of evolution.

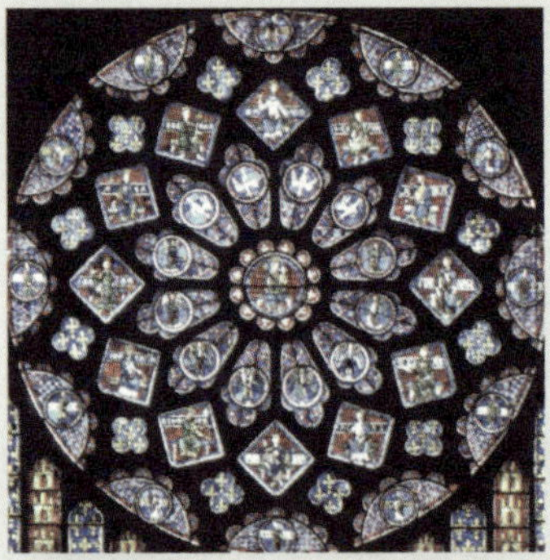

Rose window of the Cathedral of Troy, 1160–1180

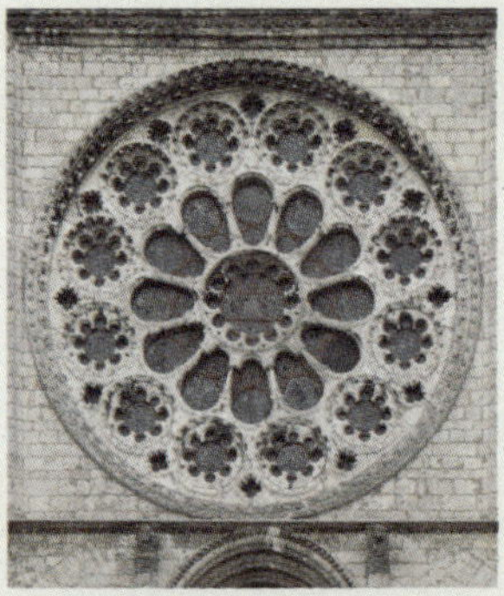

Rose window of the Cathedral of Chartres, 1194–1220

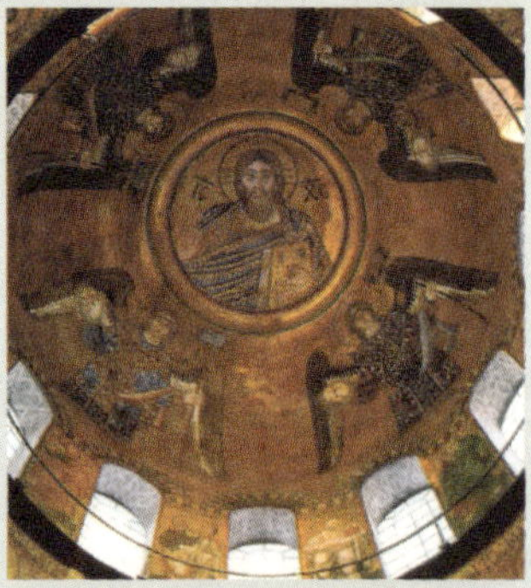

Mosaics of St. Sophia Cathedral, Kiev, 11th century

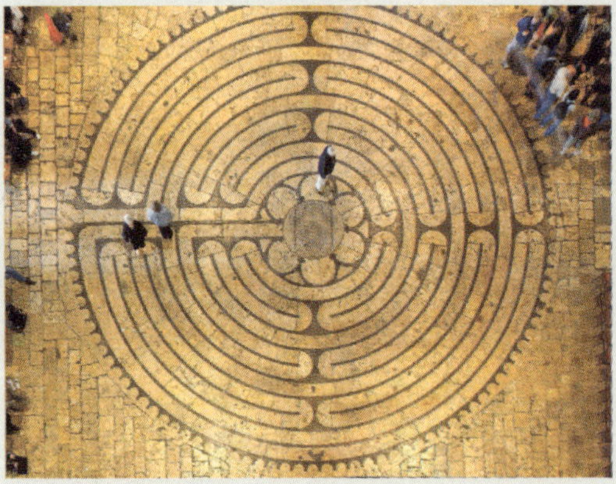

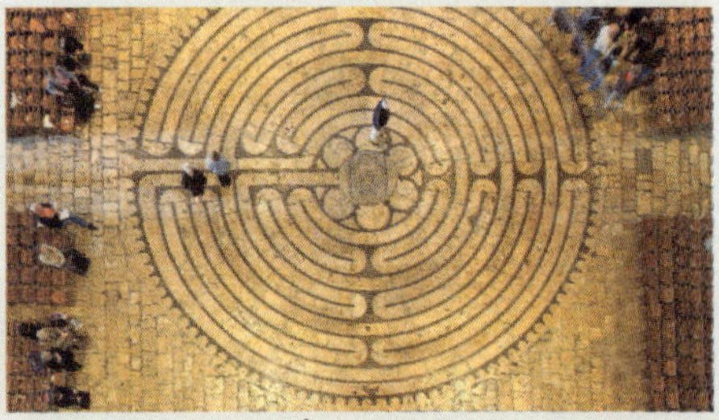

The Labyrinth of Cathedral of Chartres (France) mostly constructed between 1194 and 1220 [cxxi]

[cxxi] ***Cathedral of Chartres*** - On the floor of the Chartres Cathedral there is a circular labyrinth with a diameter of 12.87m. The labyrinth has always symbolized a tortuous inner journey from the profane exterior to the sacred centre. It is a space of constraint, where we must avoid being overwhelmed by the disruptive forces for our spirit to evolve and rise to a higher level. Thus, the labyrinth offers us exactly the same journey of the Mandala, and at the same time provides us with a faithful image of the universe as humans perceive it—constant wandering, forced choices and multiple alternative paths. Reaching the centre of the maze demands an abandonment of the typical ideas and conventions. We must be guided by our inner voice, in a state of total trust and abandonment. Perhaps it is for this inherent sacredness that the labyrinth became a central feature of many churches from the 12th century onwards.

// Everyday Life

Our everyday life is full of Mandala-style images. There are numerous symbols that at first sight might seem insignificant (such as snowflakes or shells) but are waiting to be discovered and interpreted. They can help us to understand that we need to return to the centre of ourselves, to regain our true essence, our most authentic nature, that is, our divine origin.

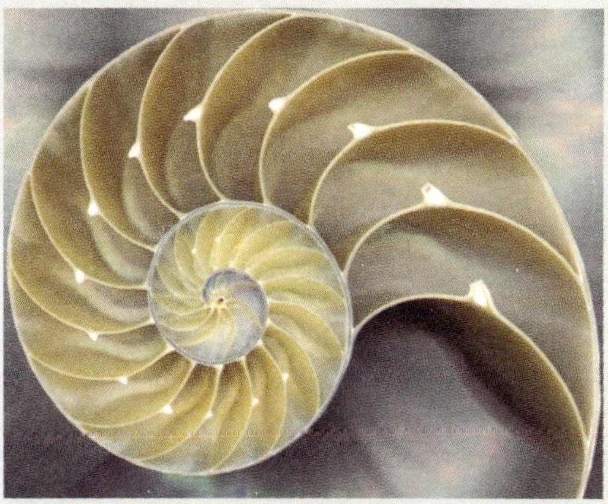

Shell

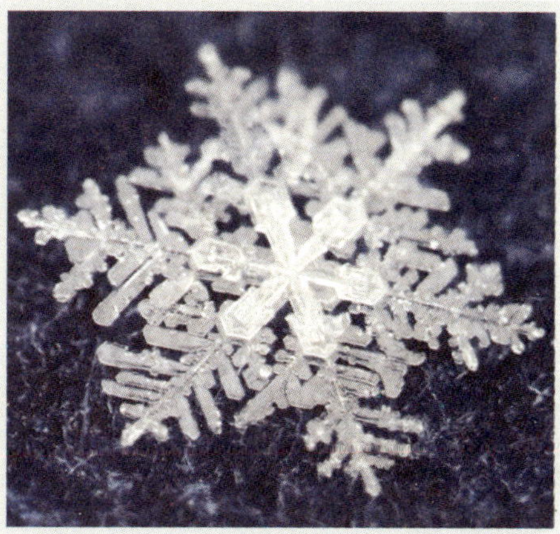

Geometric Art of Snowflakes

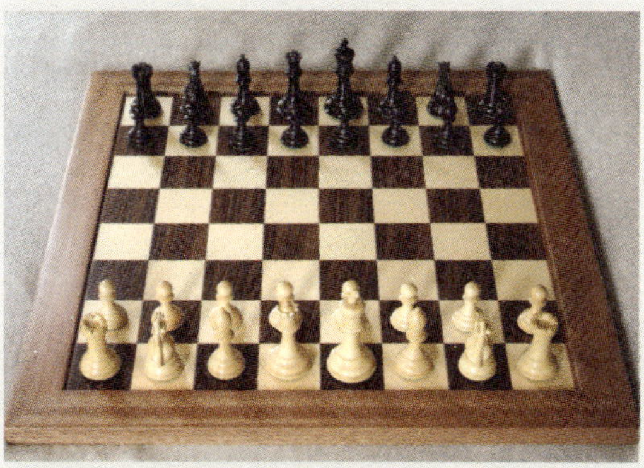

Chessboard [cxxii]

[cxxii] ***Chessboard*** - A good example is that of the chessboard and chess itself—a centuries-old game that has barely altered even as it has spread around the world. A traditional chessboard is a typical sixty-four-square Mandala, and is constituted of four sub-squares arranged around a hypothetical, invisible central point—the bindu.

// Art, Traditional Mandalas and Drawings of Jung's Patients: A Comparison

// The Circle

The circle is often represented as a seed of life endowed with great symbolic meaning. The spiritual interior of humans, according to an ancient tradition, also has a spherical shape.

The quadrature of the circle is the archetype of totality and the scheme for all images of God. In Plato's *Timaeus*, '1, 2, 3—and where is, dear Timaeus, the fourth?' The continuous reference to the number four corresponds to the four cardinal points, which are historically often represented as four divinities.

Individual Mandalas try to express this essential inner reference point. Their object is the self, which includes the totality of the psyche, the consciousness and the unconscious. Often, the individual mandalas have a division into two halves, one light and the other dark. The centre is often symbolized by a new star or represented by the sun—a beaming nucleus of light in the ocean of the sky. The image describes the appearance of the self, which emerges as an ordered star from chaos.

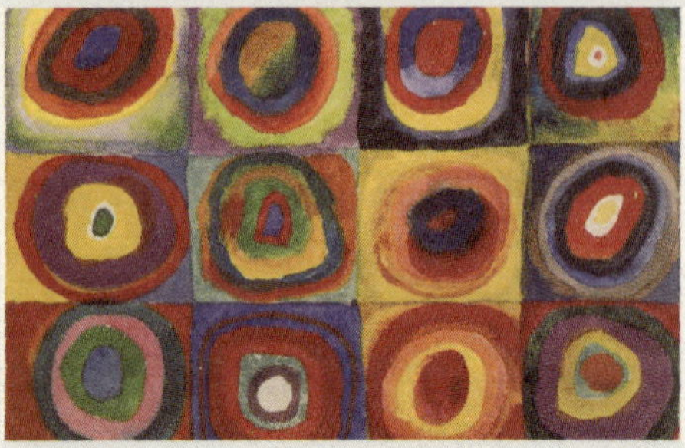

Colour Study: Squares with Concentric Rings [cxxiii]

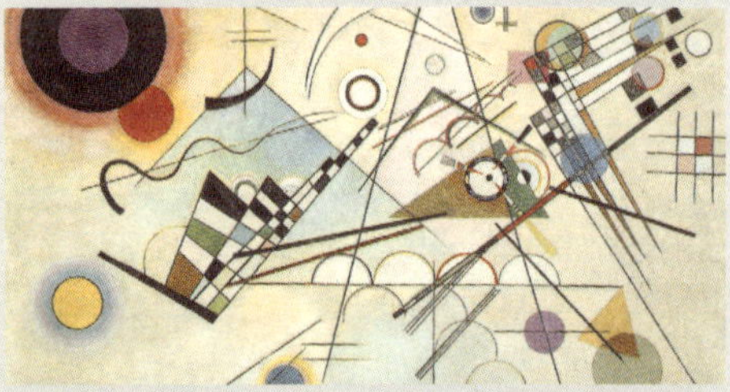

Komposition 8 - Composition 8 [cxxiv]

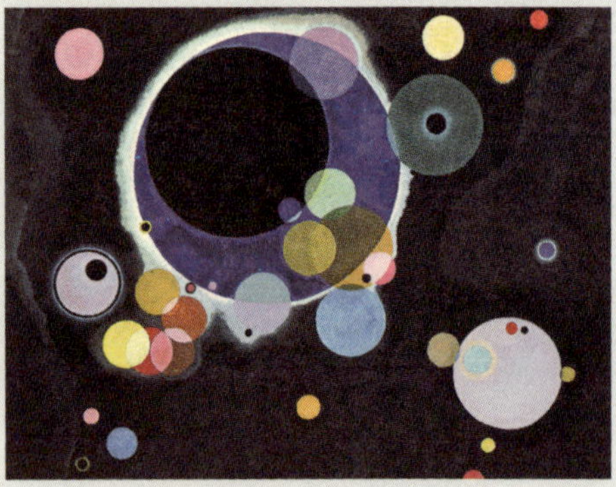

Einige Kreise - Several Circles [cxxv]

[cxxiii] ***Colour Study: Squares with Concentric Rings*** - This painting (Vasily Kandinsky, 1913) was created as a small study on how different colour combinations are observed from the creative perspective of the painter. For Kandinsky, colour was the soul of the picture. He was unique in the sense that he had synaesthesia—he could 'hear' colours and 'see' sounds.

[cxxiv] ***Composition 8*** - In this piece (Vasily Kandinsky, 1923), the circles, triangles and linear elements interact with one another. The importance of circles in this piece foreshadowed many of Kandinsky's future works. He regarded this painting as the biggest achievement of the post-war era.

[cxxv] ***Several Circles*** – This was painted by Vasily Kandinsk in 1926. 'The circle is the synthesis of the greatest oppositions. It combines the concentric and the eccentric in a single form and in equilibrium. Of the three primary forms,

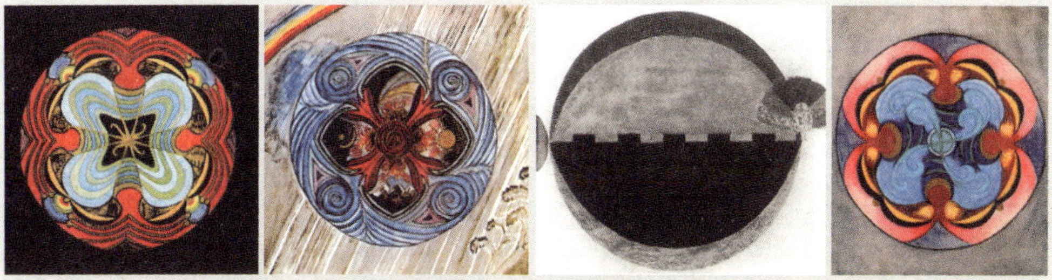

Mandalas Created by Carl Jung's Patients

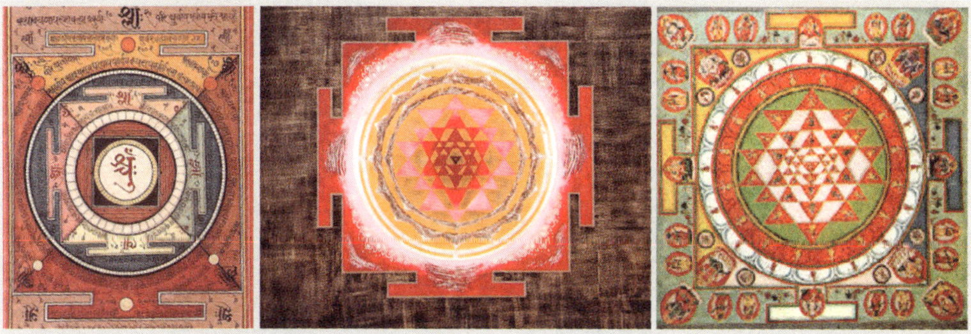

Hindu Yantras

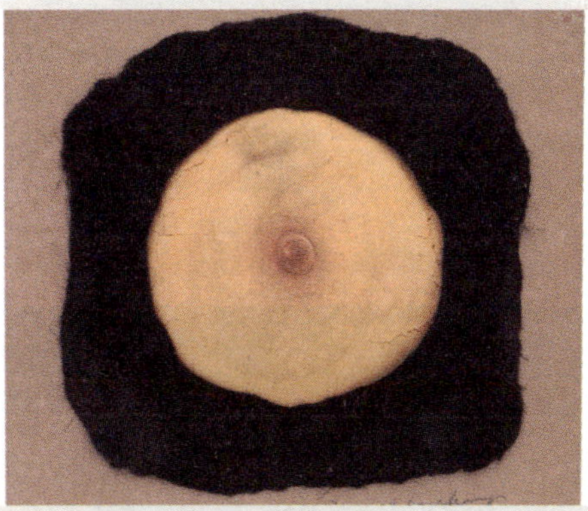

Priere de Toucher - Please Touch [cxxvi]

it points most clearly to the fourth dimension.' Vasily Kandinsky to Will Grohmann, 12 October 1930, quoted in Angelica Zander Rudenstine, *The Guggenheim Museum: Paintings 1880–1945*, vol. 1, p. 310.

[cxxvi] ***Priere de Toucher (Please Touch)*** - This was designed by Marcel Duchamp in 1947 for the cover of the catalogue *Le Surréalisme* en 1947. Duchamp collaborated with painter Enrico Donati in the design and production. Donati purchased 999 pre-fabricated foam and rubber breasts (known as 'falsies') from a warehouse in Brooklyn, New York, and Duchamp utilized the sexual tension of this erotic object. On the back of the catalogue it read 'please touch', provoking the viewer to experience the art tactically. This daring use of mischievous surrealism had a lasting effect on European tastes and aesthetics.

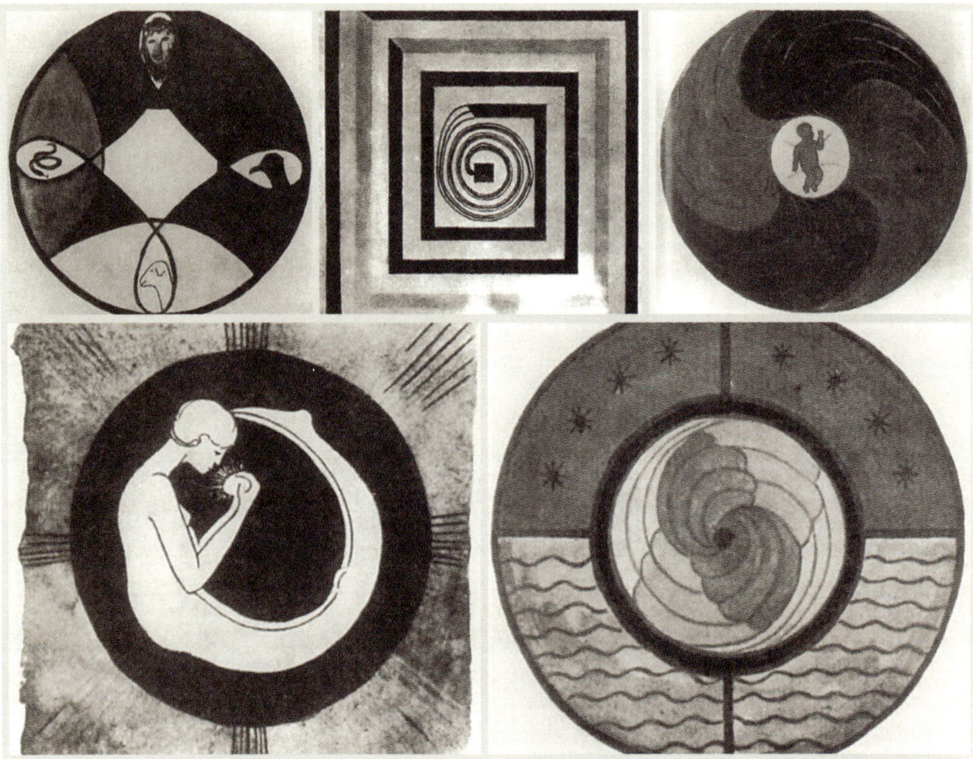

Mandalas Created by Carl Jung's Patients

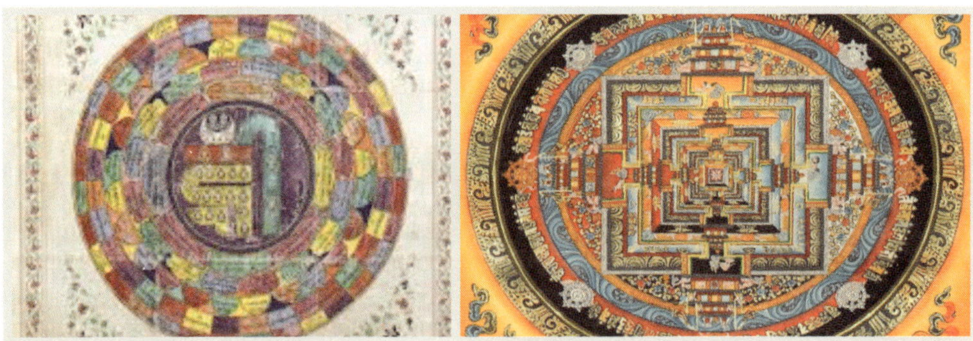

Hindu and Tibetan Mandalas

//The Eye

The eye represents awareness or understanding of the self.

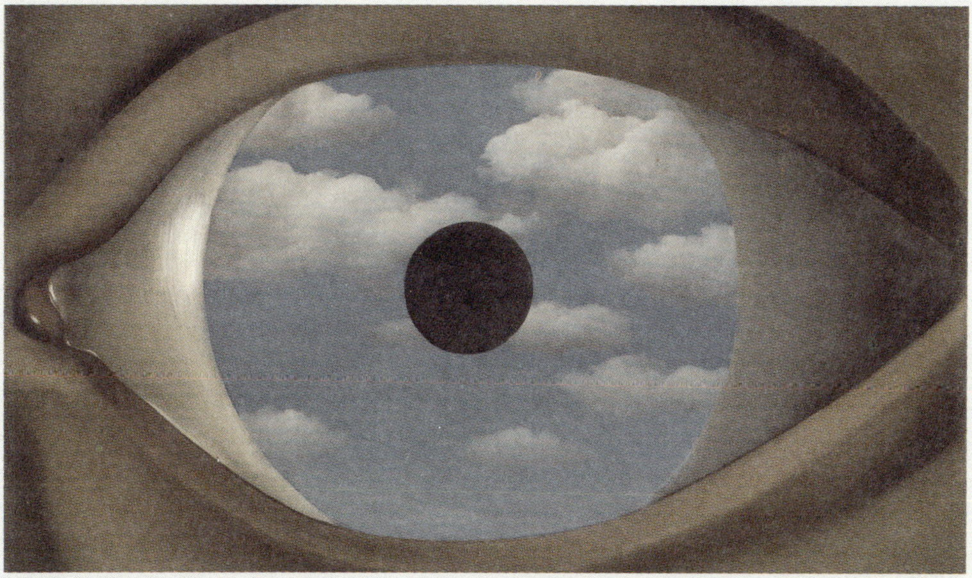

Le Faux Miroir - (The False Mirror) [cxxvii]

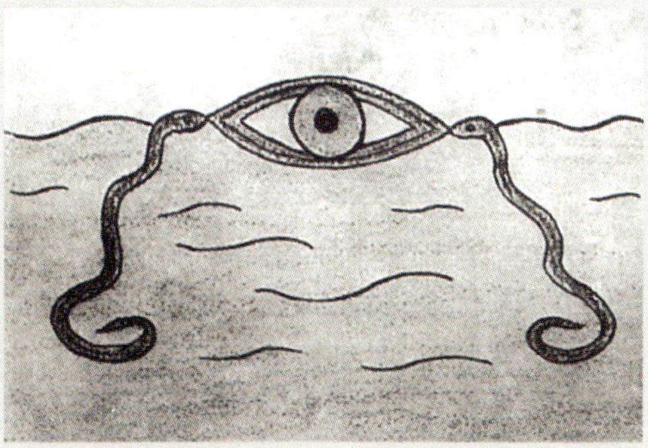

Mandala Created by Carl Jung's Patients

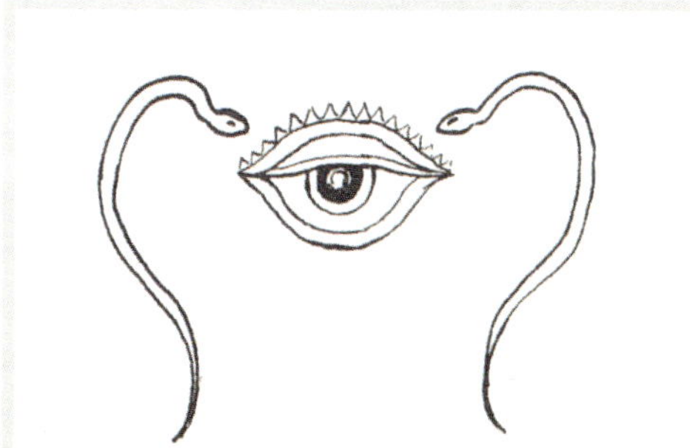

Roman mosaic of a floor in Moknine, Tunis. It is a symbol to protect against the evil eye.

[cxxvii] ***Le Faux Miroir (The False Mirror)*** - This painting (René Magritte, Paris, 1929) shows a huge eye without eyelashes. A blue clouded sky fills the iris and a black disk represents the pupil. The viewer is looking at the painting as though looking through a window, yet the eye is seen and seeing at the same time.

// The Tree: Axis Mundi

The plant represents growth, similar to the green sprout depicted in the chakra diagram of the Kundalini system (which indicates Shiva). The shoot denotes the centre, the masculine, whereas the flower represents the feminine, that is to say, the germination or birth. As the plant represents growth, so the flower denotes the unfolding, the development, starting from a centre. The Buddha is represented as germinated in the lotus. In medieval times, Mary was also represented as a chalice of a flower into which Christ descends like a bird.

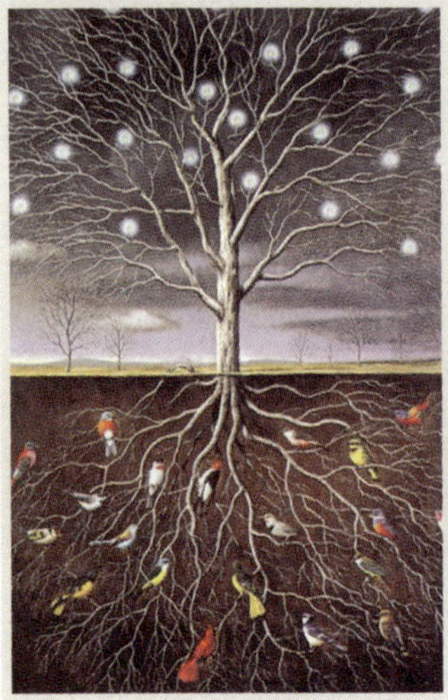

Requiem for Birds [cxxviii]

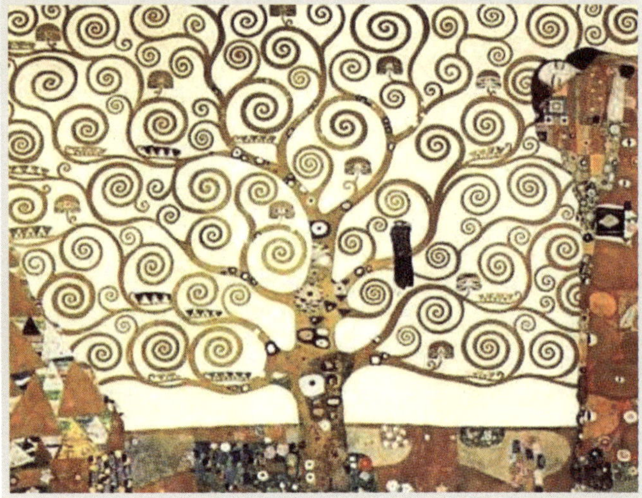

The Tree of Life [cxxix]

[cxxviii] ***Requiem for Birds***- This painting is another good example of Rafal Olbinski's unique and suprising style with Surrealist elements.

[cxxix] ***The Tree of Life*** - This was the only landscape painting (1905) made by Gustav Klimt in his prime years. He painted the twisted and twirling branches with long vines and fragile threads to depict the complexity of life. The black bird in the middle represents the fact that anything which has a beginning will eventually end. The painting encourages the viewer to spend more time with the painting while wondering about all of its meanings.

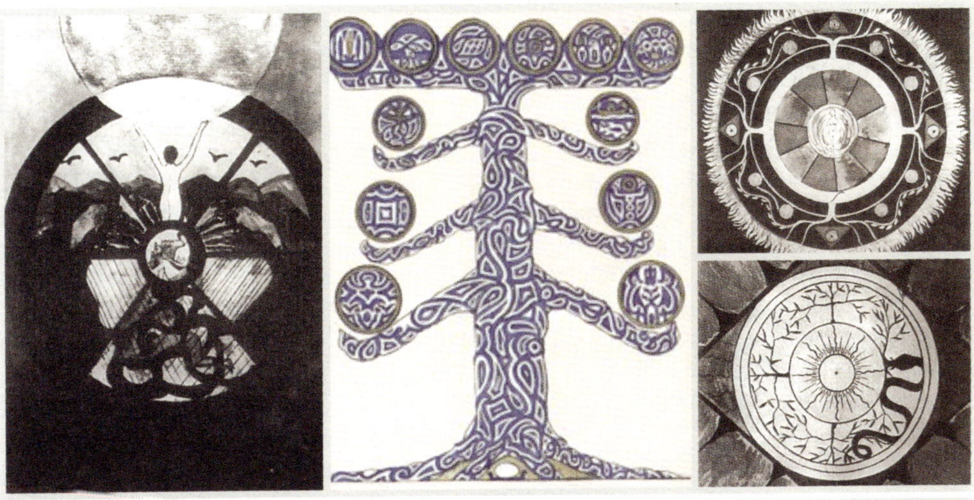

Mandalas Created by Carl Jung's Patients

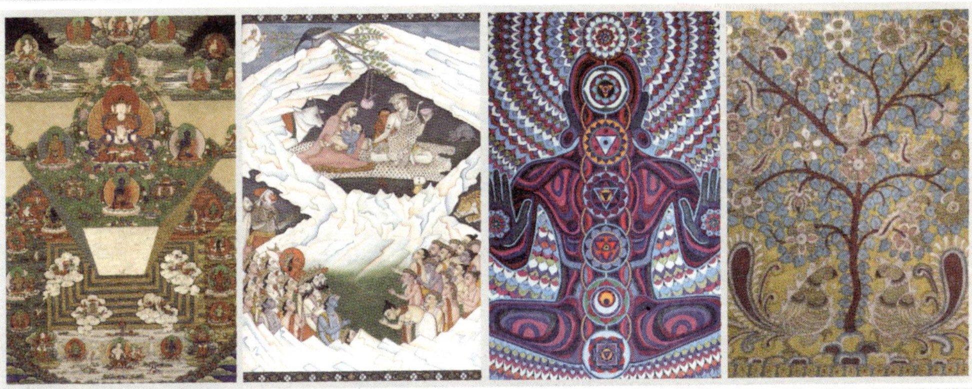

Hindu and Tibetan Mandalas

// The Flowers

In Western paintings, roses are the equivalent of the lotus flower. The lotus, padma, represents the female womb. The Buddha and other Indian deities are often represented as seated on the lotus flower. The flowers are mostly arranged in groups of four petals, signifying the quaternity of the circle, the union of opposites. The rose is often represented as a wheel, or even as a mural crest, where nothing can come out from the inside and nothing can enter from the outside.

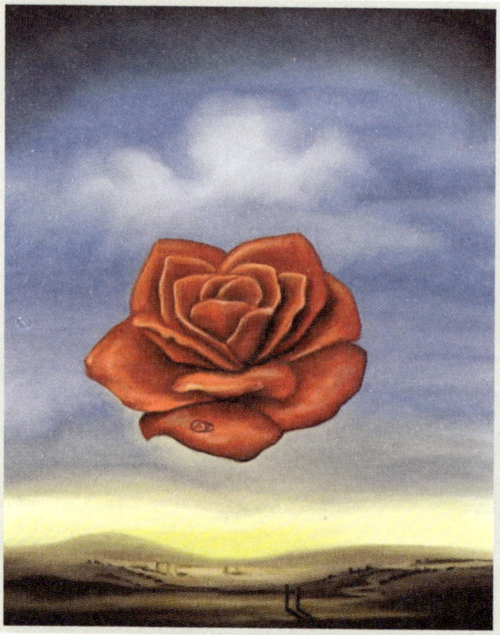

Rose Meditative [cxxx]

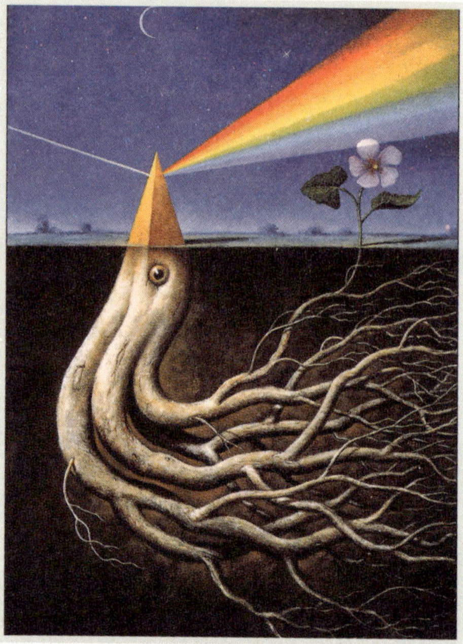

Marshmallow [cxxxi]

[cxxx] ***Rose Meditative*** - Salvador Dali often used roses in his paintings. For him, a rose was a symbol of female desires. In this image (1958), the big red rose is hovering in the sky, suggestive of the Om symbol. Dali said, 'In the Surrealist period I wanted to create the iconography of the interior world and the world of the marvellous, of my father Freud. Today the exterior world, and that of physics, has transcended the one of psychology. My father is Dr Heisenberg.' It is unclear how this piece fits into either the paranoiac method or the nuclear mysticism practices.

[cxxxi] ***Marshmallow*** - Oblinski was born in Kielce, Poland, in 1945. He graduated in architecture from the Warsaw Politechnical School before dedicating himself to painting and design. He received more than 150 awards for his achievements in arts. He also received gold and silver awards from the Society of Illustrators in New York and Los Angeles. But his biggest achievement was when the president of the Republic of Poland gave him the highest award in the field of arts, the Gold Medal. *Marshmallow* is a typicaly example of Oblinski's unique, Surrealist style.

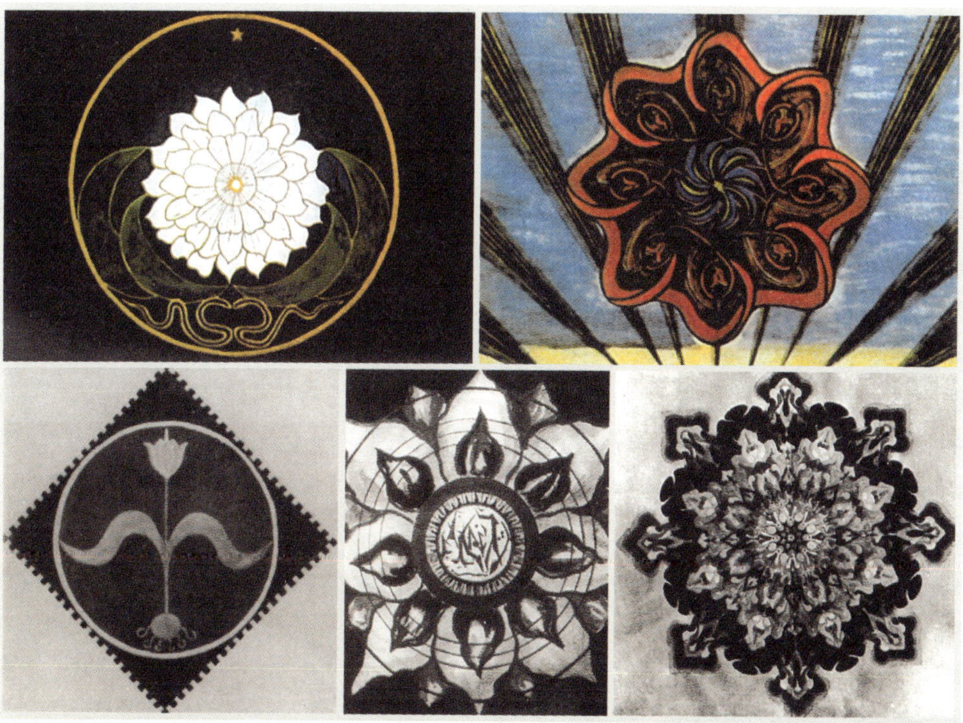

Mandalas Created by Carl Jung's Patients

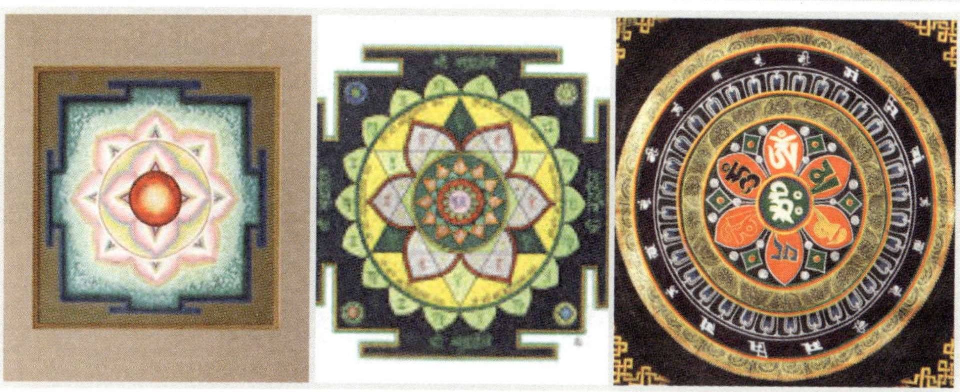

Hindu and Tibetan Mandalas

// The Meeting of the Two Creative Energies

The motif of the vase or the vessel is an expression of the content, just as Shakti represents the realization of Shiva. The self is androgynous and therefore consists of a united masculine and feminine principle.

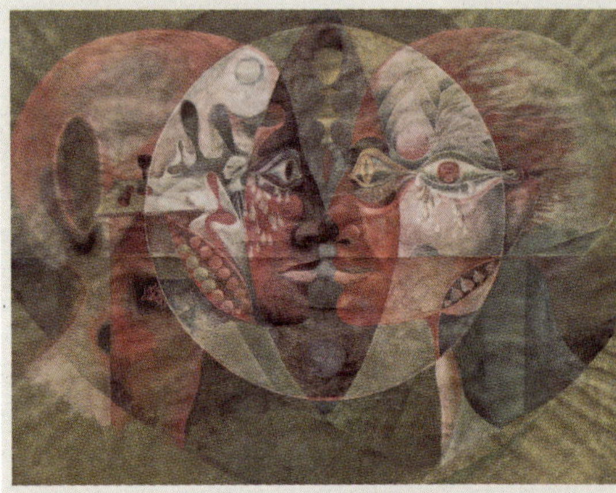

Voyage for Two [cxxxii]

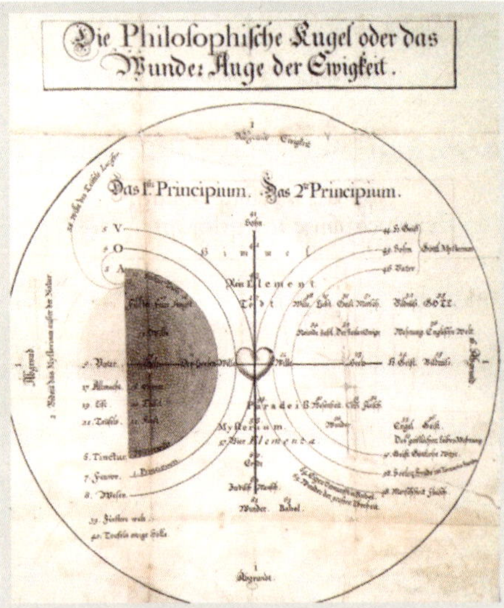

Viertzig Fragen von der Seele [cxxxiii]

[cxxxii] ***Voyage for Two*** - In this painting (Leo Kenney, 1953), a pair of heads are joined together in a mystical circular union. At the centre there is a chalice, which represents a vessel for their communication with each other. The painting is the portrayal of their combined spiritual journeys.

[cxxxiii] ***Viertzig Fragen von der Seele*** (Forty Questions Concerning the Soul) - This is the figure of the Mandala reproduced from the text by Jacob Bohme entitled '*Viertzig Fragen von der Seele*' (1620), in the English edition of 1647. The two semicircles are opposed, rather than closed in a ring. The quaternity (the Father God, the Holy Spirit, the Son, the

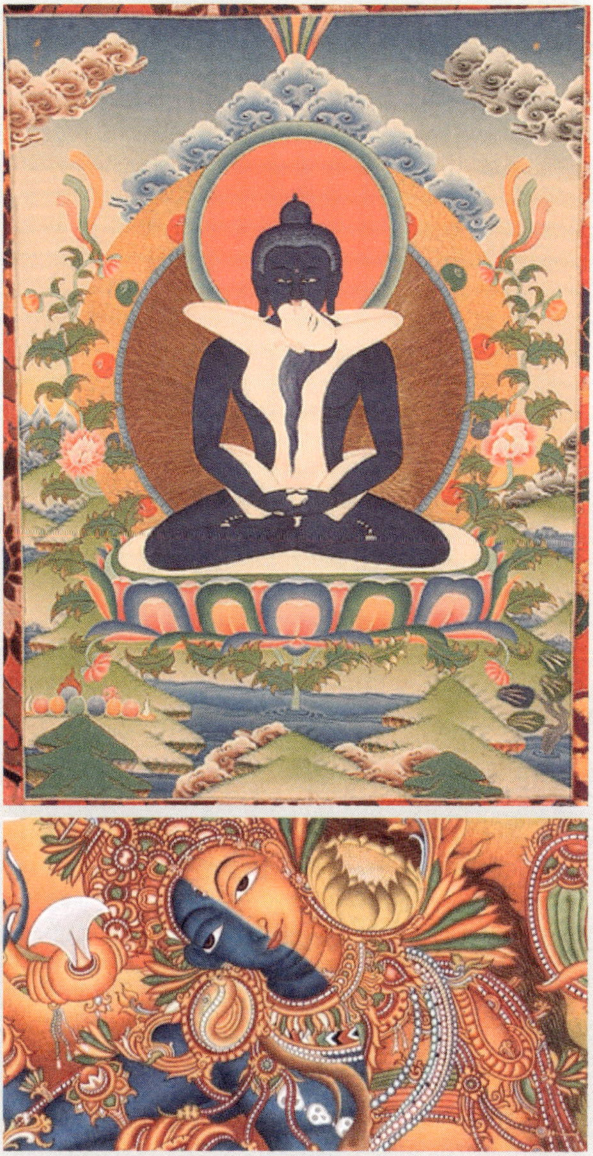

Hindu and Tibetan Mandalas

earthly human), that perhaps is also the duality of the feminine and the masculine, is united together in the heart, that is, in the middle. Bohme tells us, 'This heart, when mitigated by the four qualities or the four spirits, then the powers of the four spirits rise up to the light, they become alive and they love the light, that is, they welcome it in itself, and they become impregnated with it.' (*Aurora*, 11.16, page 144). His Mandala represents, at the same time, the image of God. This is not accidental, because the Indian philosophy, which, more than any other, develops the idea of the self (atman), makes no distinction of principle between the human essence and the divine one.

// The Animals

Generally arranged in the four cardinal positions, animals can be used to denote the instinctive forces of the unconscious—which in the Mandala, merge into unity. It is common to see a peacock (an alternative for the phoenix). The peacock is an ancient symbol of rebirth and resurrection, as according to a legend, from the ashes of the stake where the bird Sementa is burnt, a worm is formed, from which the bird rises. In the alchemical process, the dragon is transformed into an eagle, a peacock and a phoenix. We also often see phoenix or peacock symbols on Christian sarcophagi.

// The Snakes

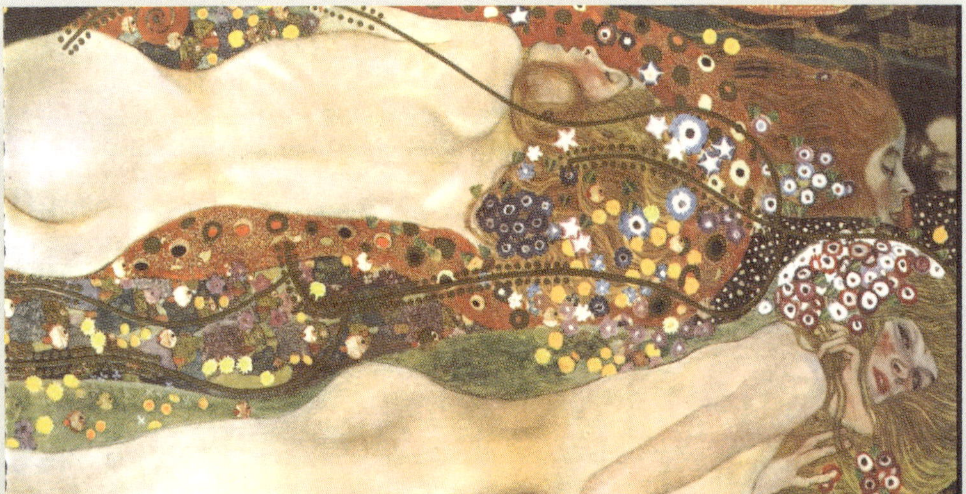

Wasserschlangen II [cxxxiv]

In art, the snake, as a terrestrial and spiritual being, symbolizes the unconscious. Often, the snake is presented wrapped around a straight rod and identifies the awakening or the activation of nature. This rod may be identified as the spinal cord. Kundalini, also called serpentine, is the snake that in human philosophy lies in hibernation in the lower sacrum, the base of the body trunk.

[cxxxiv] ***Wasserschlangen II*** (Water Serpents II) - With this piece (1904), Gustav Klimt returned to painting sensual women in water. By painting the women as underwater creatures, he was able to fluently show the untapped complexities of humans. It also gave him the opportunity to show the female body in a feminine and erotic manner without fearing censorship.

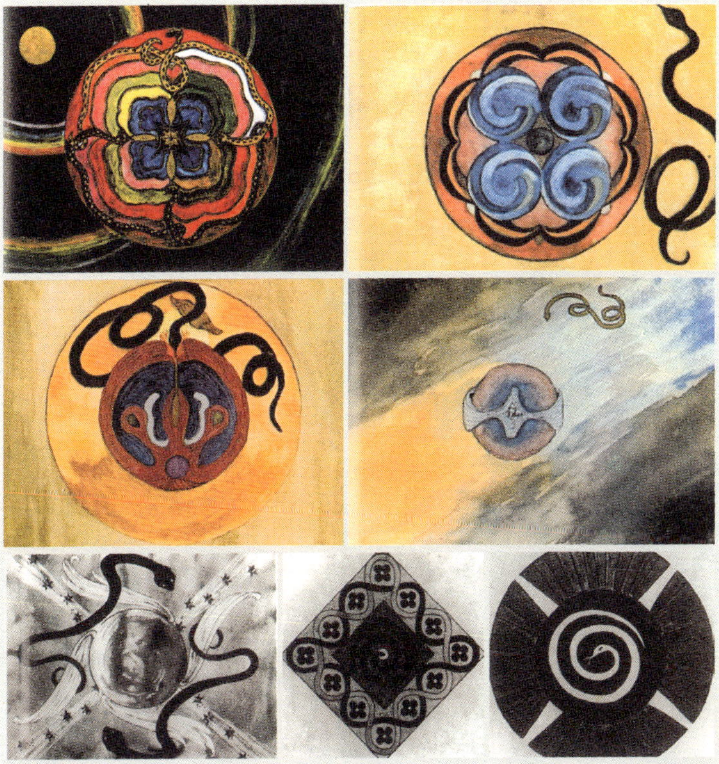

Mandalas Created by Carl Jung's Patients

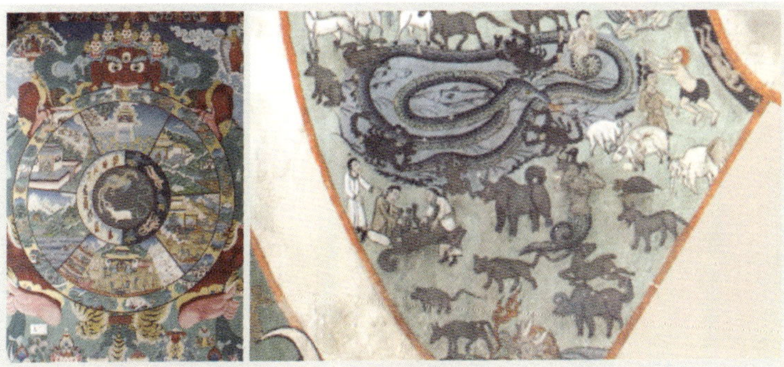

Tibetan Mandalas

Both the fish and the snake are symbolic of Christ and the devil at the same time. In the sea of the unconscious, there is a vortex within which a pearl must be formed. The snake usually represents the unconscious, while the fish mostly represents the pearl. The creatures correspond to two different degrees of evolution—the snake represents a more primitive and instinctual state of the fish and the fish has a stronger authority than that of the snake.

// The Fish

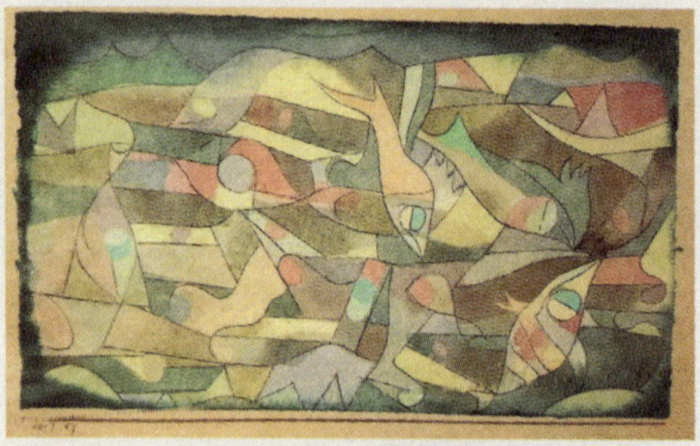

Spielende Fische [cxxxv]

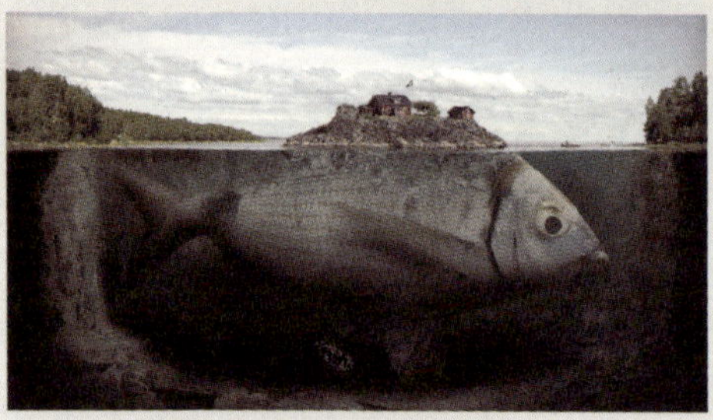

Fishy Island [cxxxvi]

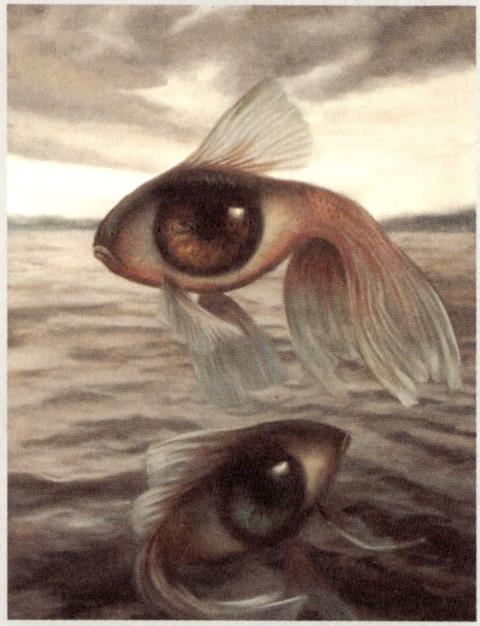

Fisheye - Vincent Cacciotti

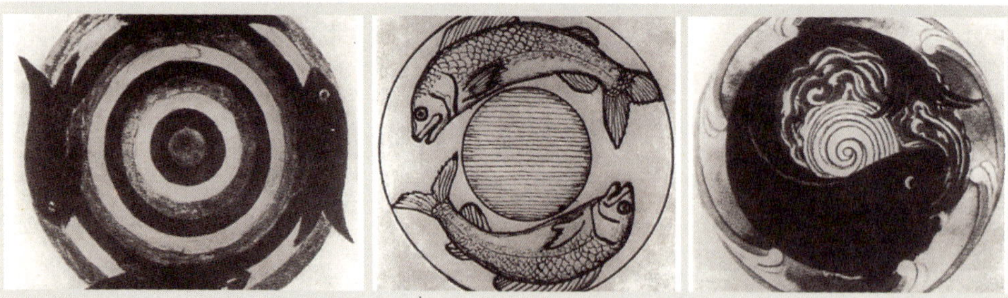

Mandalas Created by Carl Jung's Patients

[cxxxv] ***Spielende Fische*** (Playing Fish) - Paul Klee was greatly influenced by the art movements of Expressionism, Cubism and Surrealism. Klee's lectures on colour, 'Writings on Form and Design', are considered as important as Leonardo da Vinci's, '*A Treatise on Painting*'. This painting reflects his childlike perspective and his dry comical side.
[cxxxvi] ***Fishy Island*** - This photo (2009) is a combination of photos taken at six different places. Eric Johansson had to wait for permission to photograph some of the locations to get the perfect shot.

// Fire

The motif of fire can have two connotations—the erotic fire of greed and desire, and the fire of love, which flares up from the most intimate self, moulds the destiny of the person and helps the self translate destiny into reality. Fire also expresses an intense process of transformation—all that fire consumes rises towards the other, towards the dwelling of the gods. In the Mandalas created by Jung's patients shown here, lightning is born from the torment inflicted by fire and a flaming demon throws itself into the night in the direction of a star. Fire thus can mean the transition from a chaotic state to an ordered and safer state.

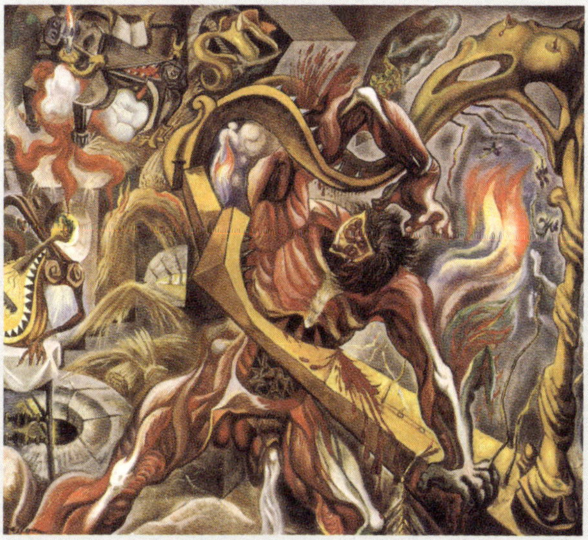

In the Tower of Fire [cxxxvii]

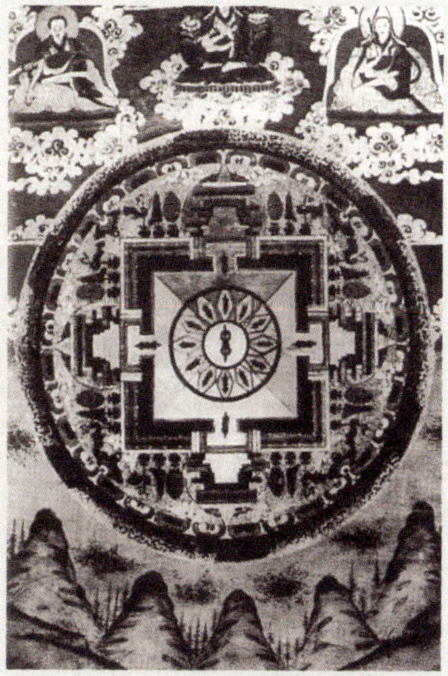

Tibetan Mandala

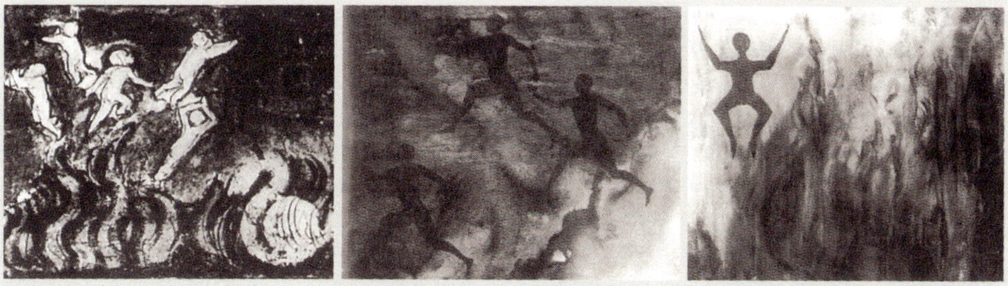

Mandalas Created by Carl Jung's Patients

[cxxxvii] ***In the Tower of Fire*** - In this image (1938), André Masson used a lot of lines and dark bloody colours to evoke the emotions of anger and fear in the viewer. The intention was to represent all the emotions that were conjured up during a nightmare.

// About Jung's Patients

I could show many more images from various parts of the world, and it would amaze us to see how these symbols are governed by the same basic laws that can be observed in individual Mandalas. [154]

All the featured Mandalas created by Carl Jung's patients are original products—their authors had no contact or influence with cultures which have the Mandalic tradition. Furthermore, despite all external differences and regardless of the temporal spatial origin, substantial conformity is found between Mandalas. This leads us to conclude that, beyond the consciousness, there exists in every individual an unconscious disposition to produce symbols that are the same (or at least similar). The individual is generally unaware of this disposition—Jung called it the 'collective unconscious'—and as its basis it has certain primordial images or archetypes. Penetrating a little deeper below the surface of the unconscious, we come across historical layers that continue to exist and act within every human being. This process is not conscious, but comes from an instinctual impulse.

That these mandalic images have considerable therapeutic effects is an empirically established fact. They represent an attempt to grasp irreconcilable contrasts and overcome irreducible divisions.

'It is as if I saw everything from a window overlooking eternity,' said one patient.

The unconscious has a tendency to introduce certain images into art, as if using the patient's pictorial inexperience to insinuate its own traces. The classic motifs are usually flower, star, circle, fence and the city plan with neighbourhoods and the citadel. With the series of images explored in this book, I hope to have been able to give the reader an idea of symbolism. I did not intend to go beyond a superficial review of the empirical material. Instead, I aimed to make only a series of parallelisms. I arranged these images, painted by inexperienced hands, close to the works that the avant-gardes produced, and close to the real Mandalas that both Hinduism and Tibetan Buddhism have cultivated for centuries. I did this to reveal the similarities which connect the new works of art of the 20th century with the designs of European patients, who had never had a relationship with these cultures. We could see all these paintings as yantra in the Indian sense—instruments of meditation, immersion, concentration and realization of an inner experience. Their purpose is to produce an interior order—a safe haven and a place of internal reconciliation and totality.

Finally, after describing and explaining the intent of this work, we have reached the last stage. We have charted out a path of interconnection between the evolution of art—from clear shapes to forms and colours which are no longer contained in well-marked parts. We have framed this transition within the epoch of the evolution and development of philosophy with psychology. I hoped to explore my thesis without referring to a great deal of reading material. I did not intend to analyse a historical period, but to enable an unrestricted interpretation of information until a final idea is reached.

In this conclusion, however, I feel the need to explain my own reading of this historical

[154] C.G. Jung, *Simbolismo del mandala*

period. We started with an excursus, which showed how, for centuries, the intent of art was to represent reality. Art was a mirror of the values conveyed in the era in which it came to be, but art was also subjected to strict rules that aimed to standardize the representation of the visible world. It was only later that artists were free to adopt the perception of the real world as an illusion, as being and not being, formed by the separation of opposites, something that seems concrete and real, but, by its very nature, is in continuous transformation and always different from itself at every moment. It is real only when it is seen in its entirety, in the unification of what it contains, what it does not contain, what it apparently is and what it is apparently lacking.

In the case of the Indian subcontinent, we must understand that it is not only a different place but a different world.[155] Its culture is one of the oldest in existence, one of the few that have survived over 3,000 years, with only minor interference from other cultures. It is a culture with a primordial and eternal faith which does not change (sanātana), a land where time passes along a cosmological line in which the act of creation took only a day of the life of Brahma,[156] a day which corresponds to 430 million years. It is a place where division is absent, and even between gods and humans there is a continuation. It is a place where Aristotle's idea, that the opposite cannot be linked together, is unthinkable. In India, sentences such as 'it is impossible that the same thing belongs and not belongs to the same thing at the same time and in the same respect',[157] or 'the most certain of all basic principles is that contradictory propositions are not true simultaneously'[158] are not only refused, but are also wrong. Here, duality is at the same time non-duality—the universe itself is created through the feminine and masculine energies combined[159] an expansionist male principle (Shiva[160], a centrifugal force) with its opposite, a feminine contraction principle (Shakti[161], a centipetal force). The creation starts when Shiva—Shiva-bindu[162] —appears joined with his feminine part[163], in this case two sides of the same energy, which if balanced, produce the circular motion that is able to bring about the superior being (brahman[164]).

[155] In this part of the world, the social developments of the past two millennia have left many parts untouched—thousand-year-old gods are still alive here, together with the traditional clothes and systems of worship.
[156] Brahma is the first god in the Hindu triumvirate, or trimurti. The triumvirate consists of three gods that are responsible for the creation, upkeep and destruction of the world.
[157] Aristotle, *Metaphysics*, Book IV, 3, 1005b:19–20
[158] ivi, (1011b13–14).
[159] The terminological problem is the establishment of the full meaning of the terms, which includes the relation to the opposite of its normal understanding. Each meaning is the negation of itself until it touches a supreme non-duality (the masculine is an aspect of the feminine, and vice versa). Based on this premise, when we use English words, we have to keep in mind that it is just a general translation of the Indian concept.
[160] Shiva is the third god in the Hindu triumvirate.
[161] Also spelled as Sakthi, this is the primordial cosmic energy and represents the dynamic forces that are thought to move through the entire universe. It embodies the active feminine energy of Shiva.
[162] Bindu corresponds to the transcendental point of light—the light of the consciousness.
[163] In the symbolism of yoga kundalini, Shakti is represented as a snake, folded three times around Shiva, who is represented as a penis.
[164] This information comes from the *Vedas*—a collection of hymns and other religious texts composed in India between about 1500 BC and 1000 BC. They include elements such as liturgical material as well as mythological accounts, poems, prayers and formulas considered to be sacred. The creation story is known as the Cosmic Principle and is featured in the *Upanishads*—a collection of texts of religious and philosophical nature, written in India probably between 800 BC and 500 BC.

Keeping these concepts in mind, we continue with the study of the history of Italian art. At the end of the 1800s we saw, due to external circumstances and a need to survive, a 180-degree inversion of perspective in the art world. From the outer world and the external environment, the focus moved to the inner world of the mind and perception, and also the unconscious and invisible movements of the soul. To underline the interconnection of the various arts, we paid attention not only to the prominent figures of this period and their shifting intentions, but also to the philosophical thoughts themselves. These thoughts were increasingly directed towards the discovery of the many personal and invisible movements which took place within us, blurring the differences between philosophy and psychology. So here we are, in the 21st century—on the one hand, psychology as a discipline has really come into its own, and on the other, the forms represented in art are undergoing an involution. In this involution, the contrasts between the external and internal aspects of the figure are no longer clear—the colours are all mixed up and this gives life to a new type of art, one that is abstract, as if also representing the inner world of the unconscious.

The artistic movements that took place after the advent of photography can be seen as innovations, novelties and evolution. But the two fathers[165] of psychology termed them non-traditional arts and called them ugly. For them, the new form took away all the educational function from art.

However, as Sigmund Freud himself said, often new doctrines and tendencies do not receive credit immediately after they become operative.[166] The resolution of debates can take some time, 'so that the intellectual work of the ego overcomes all affective objections'.[167] Perhaps it is for this reason that we have not yet been able to grasp what I am about to outline. We have seen the symbolic forms and the Oriental Mandalas and, in this chapter, I have focused on the concepts that are the basis of thought in South Asia. Now I will add an explanation of what is meant by art in this part of the world and, in doing so, I will try to present to you my understanding of this picture.

In Asia, the artist (or the demiurge, the human creative force) just repeats the process of creation of the universe in a process of mimesis. The artist is Brahma, with the goal of rivalling a reflection of the universe through its product. But this is not a universe understood as an external reality, but as an internal reality (let us remember that the microcosm and the macrocosm come to intersect in this part of the world, and as the early Indian fables teach us, the universe is constituted inside us). 'The image visualized by the artist is coming from a revelation of truth of the universe.'

[165] Freud said, 'With regard to these artists, I am one of those philistines and lumaconi that he [Oscar Pfister, author of a booklet on the psychological and biological bases of Expressionist painting] puts to the pillory in its introduction.' Jung showed a certain closedness towards Contemporary art, which he found aesthetically displeasing and incapable of provoking any emotion.
[166] An example is the evolutionary theory of Darwin, which was at first rejected by his peers.
[167] James Strachey, Anna Freud, Alix Strachey and Alan Tyson, translators, 'Mourning and Melancholia', *The Standard Edition of the Complete Psychological Works of Sigmund Freud*, Volume XIV (1914–1916): On the History of the Psycho-Analytic Movement, Papers on Metapsychology and Other Works, 237–258.

The necessity for the artist to identify with his creation is a very common remark found in the canonical prescriptions (sādhana). There are rites and rituals that the artist must follow to identify in totality with the concept that he wants to express; he must purify himself through spiritual exercises and work alone. Only through meditation and a higher level of concentration will the artist be able to visualize the art piece. He will have to turn himself into a sort of clairvoyant. His gaze must not be directed towards the outside, to the real world, but towards the silence of the internal world.

In *Sukranitisara*,[168] we have seen how there is an emphasis on the importance of the contemplative act. 'When the visualization is done, the artist can start to work';[169] 'When the sample has been formulated, he realizes—on the wall—what has been visualized.'[170]

The artist can only express what is in him, and what he is. It makes no difference whether the same things have been expressed a thousand times before. There can be no property within ideas. The individual does not make them, but finds them.[171]

As has been said in previous chapters, the problem of 'originality' does not emerge, because obeying the rules[172] and being free at the same time is not impossible in India. Here, it's possible to amalgamate this opposition in the same idea of non-duality—to be loyal to the rules of the tradition doesn't mean a betrayal of the internal vision of the artist. The rules are not intended to determine the final image, but they are only an instruction of what this image is supposed to carry within it. The rules do not dictate the external shape of an artwork, but only the inner dimension of a collective and permanent reality.

The mistake was believing that the model was possible to be found in the external world, or, at worst, only in that . . . the plastic product must refer to an exclusive inner model or it won't be.[173]

The concept of art for art's sake is completely alien to Indian thought. The artist's goal is not to express himself; neither is it to create beauty. The beauty is in the topic and the topic is the beauty. Nothing is independent. Originality is not a problem; the artist must have incorporated all the rules, all the formulas and must have understood them in order to be able to add his own spirit and something new from inside his mind. A non-duality of copying and creativity is achieved with each new act. The freedom of the artist is not limited to the prescription of tradition, but creativity is developed freely from within the rules themselves.

Let him only see to it that he really takes possession of them, and his work will be

[168] One of the classic canonical scriptures.
[169] *Sukranitisara*, VII, 74, p. 116.
[170] *Sukranitisara*, I: 3, p. 158.
[171] Ananda K. Coomaraswamy, *'Understanding the Indian Art'*, *Introduction to Indian Art*, 8, p. 80.
[172] With this identification we are presented with the indissolubility of the link between human beings and divinities. Only what conforms to the rules given in the canon (sādhana) is really beautiful; what doesn't obey is not beautiful.
[173] Breton, '*The Futurist Manifesto*', 1928, p. 4.

original in the same sense that the recurrent seasons, sunrise and sunset are now, although in name they are the same. The highest purpose of Eastern art, similarly, is to reveal the same principles of life that are manifested in all their variety.[174]

I wonder if this evolution was ever anything more than a rediscovery (and not an innovation of the 20th century), unless it was intended as a novelty that abandons illusion to expose itself to a more intimate and profound truth. I wonder if those movements were just the first steps towards the rediscovery of a primordial road that other cultures discovered thousands of years ago, and if the themes of the avant-garde movements were not just the first steps towards rediscovering a language inaudible to the ears—the language of symbols, spoken by the unconscious.

I wonder if those confusing colours were perhaps the first steps towards the representation of terms, which includes the relation of the opposites within one unit.

Perhaps it was all nothing more than a re-framing of what Indian art has always known.

The truth in Indian art is that which corresponds to the universe (that dimension invisible to the eyes)—an inner universe based on forms, geometric symbols and primary colours (typical of Mandalas).

I leave the final considerations to you, but invite you to notice a string that binds together different and conflicting times and places. I will leave you with a paragraph from one of the greatest artists of abstraction of all time:

Painting in itself, that is, as 'pure painting', acts on the soul by means of its secular means—tint (colour), form, that is, distribution of planes and lines, their interrelation (movement). The object (real—man, tree, cloud) is only as an objective backbone, a resonance, an aroma of the composition. And therefore it is not necessary for this (real) object to be reproduced with precision. Inversely, imprecision reinforces only the purely pictorial composition. The contemporary (or authentically contemporary) work of art . . . invariably reflects its era. And our age is the time of the tragic clash between matter and spirit, the fall of purely material conceptions, the time of the anguished emptiness and the lack of ways out for many people—the time of the greatest problems and for some, few, for now—the presentiment, the harbinger of the path that leads to Truth. . . . Everything that apparently was so stable for eternity, everything in which knowledge lived as if it had been eternally true, suddenly revealed itself tight, crushed in some way by a relentless and saying goodbye, 'Is this really true?' Already by the brilliant hand of Nietzsche, a 'reversal of values' began, willy-nilly. And what was firmly moved. In the soul it happened like a great earthquake. And here, this tragedy and this shift, this instability and fragility of the material, is reflected in the art with the imprecision and with the dissonance. And looking at the paintings also from this point of view, once again we must not understand and not know, but only and exclusively feel with open soul. Art is the living semblance not of the intellectual sphere, but only and

[174] Ananda K. Coomaraswamy, *'Understanding the Indian Art', Introduction to Indian Art*, 8, p. 80.

exclusively of sensibility. Those who cannot feel, art will remain obscure and silent to him. Yet he will find salvation only in it.
—Wassily Wassilyevich Kandinsky[175]

[175] Wassily Wassilyevich Kandinsky was a Russian painter and art theorist. Kandinsky is generally credited as the pioneer of abstract art.

// Appendix 1
Leonardo's Legacies: Chiara Rostagno

In Leonardo da Vinci we have the perfect embodiment of the modern intellect, the highest expression of the marriage of art and science—the thinker, the poet, the wizard with whom our fascination is unrivalled. Studying his art in its incomparable variety, we find in his very caprices, to use Edgar Quinet's happy phrase with a slight modification, 'the laws of the Italian Renaissance, and the geometry of universal beauty'.[176]

1. Leonardo's legacy: the diffusion
Artist, painter, scientist, engineer, architect and city planner,[177] —the works of Leonardo da Vinci (1452–1519) include a multitude of operas, writings, studies and observations which, more than five centuries ago, were able to herald a new era in the history of art and also in science (or in the approach to knowledge). Even at that time it was clear—Leonardo da Vinci had a creative imagination and appears to have been a universal genius.[178]

Leonardo found himself faced with such a complex problem because he had taken the identity of art and science as his starting point, perhaps without initially realizing what he would encounter as he advanced further into the specific fields of investigation. He certainly never considered this problem, however, and the combination of his innate curiosity and his extraordinary capacity for the visual recording and analysis of phenomena and nature as a whole made him thirst for knowledge and overriding need.[179]

'Eye and drawing' are the tools of Leonardo's mental attitude, not only in knowing what is existing but also in the capability to define utopian ideas. The continuous swing between utopia and reality is a 'status' (a condition in Leonardo's existence) strongly related to Leonardo's life and to his works.[180]

A singular fatality has ruled the destiny of nearly all the most famous of Leonardo da Vinci's works. Two of the three most important were never completed, obstacles having arisen during his lifetime, which obliged him to leave them unfinished, namely the Sforza Monument and the wall painting of the Battle of Anghiari, while the third—the picture of the Last Supper at Milan—has suffered irremediable injury from decay and the repeated restorations to which it was recklessly subjected during the 17th and 18th centuries. Nevertheless, no other picture of the Renaissance has become so well-known and popular throng copies of every description.

If you despise painting, which is the sole imitator of all visible works of nature, you certainly despise ingenious invention that brings philosophy and subtle speculation to bear on the nature of all forms wrapped in light and shadow, places, plants, animals and flowers. And this is truly science and the genuine child of nature, for painting is born out of nature. To be more precise, we shall call it the grandchild of nature, as all visible things were brought forth by nature and these, her children, gave birth to painting.

[176] Eugène Müntz, *Leonardo da Vinci, Artist, Thinker and Man of Science*, p. 8.
[177] Richard Schofield, 'Reality and Utopia in Leonardo's Thinking about Architecture', pp. 325–331.
[178] Maria Farquhar and Ralph N. Wornum, Biographical catalogue of the principal Italian painters, with a table of the contemporary schools of Italy. Designed as a handbook to the picture gallery, p. 197.
[179] Pietro C. Marani and Maria Teresa Fiorio, 'Introduction' in Leonardo da Vinci. The Design of the World, p. 29.
[180] Fernanda Wittgens, Il Cenacolo di Leonardo da Vinci.

We shall therefore speak of it justly as the grandchild of nature and related to God. (*Treatise on Painting*, p. 12)

Leonardo da Vinci started his apprenticeship[181] at the bottega of Andrea Verrocchio[182], approximately around 1464.[183] He had the opportunity to learn a profession, despite his birth because of his 'mental powers', and he grew up during the Florentine cultural renovation of arts. Leonardo remained in Florence until 1481. From 1482 Da Vinci was in Milan at the court of the Duke Ludovico Sforza.

The magnitude of Da Vinci's legacy was immediately clear—in the middle of the 16th-century, Leonardo's works were well known all around the world. Copies of his paintings started to cross the countries and to become a virtual fountainhead of knowledge. Artists, and also people of culture and science, started to study his enormous written and artistic legacy, to visit the collections or to copy his pictorial inventions, as a crucial exercise to improve in artistic fields.

According to Leonardo, the pupil of a master must 'challenge to achieve a balance between imitating (the master's style), which should have been restricted to the formative phase, and surprising it, a point that Leonardo never failed to emphasize, as recalled by the aphorisms.'[184] He said, '*Tristo è quell discepolo che non ava[n]za il suo maestr.*' (Poor is the pupil who does not exceed his master.)

2. Leonardo's legacy: *The Last Supper* as an axis mundi

There is a painting in Milan which, for more than five centuries, is able to capture people's imaginations because of its universal language and outstanding value—Leonardo's *The Last Supper* (1494–1498). It is a masterpiece and has a timeless and unique artistic achievement due to its innumerable meanings. Magnificent and indescribable—in Leonardo's concept and execution of the absolute sense of beauty there are no conventions or limits. Perfection and imperfection find here a synthesis, or more appropriately, a balance.

He also painted . . . a most beautiful and marvellous thing; and to the heads of the Apostles he gave such majesty and beauty, that he left the head of Christ unfinished, not believing that he was able to give it that divine air which is essential to the image of Christ. This work, remaining thus all but finished, has ever been held by the Milanese in the greatest veneration, and also by strangers; for Leonardo imagined and succeeded in expressing that anxiety which had seized the Apostles in wishing to know who should betray their Master. For which reason in all their faces are seen love, fear, and wrath, or rather, sorrow, at not being able to understand the meaning of Christ; which thing excites no less marvel than the sight, in contrast to it, of obstinacy, hatred, and treachery in Judas; not to mention that every least part of the work displays an incredible diligence, seeing that even in the

[181] Marco Versiero, 'Leonardo's "Deluges": Prophesy, Legend and History', in Leonardo da Vinci. The Design of the World.
[182] Maud Cruttwell, Verrocchio.
See also: Peter Thiis Jens, Leonardo da Vinci: The Florentine years of Leonardo & Verrocchio.
[183] C.C. Bambach, ed., Leonardo da Vinci Master Draftsman, exhibition catalogue.
[184] Furio Rinaldi, 'Academia Leonardi Vinci: Leonardo's Pupils, Followers and Legacy of the Masters' Works', in Pietro C. Marani and Maria Teresa Fiorio, eds. Leonardo da Vinci: The Design of the World.

tablecloth the texture of the stuff is counterfeited in such a manner that linen itself could not seem more real.[185]

Leonardo da Vinci's *The Last Supper* was painted on the north wall in the refectory of the Dominican Friars' Convent of Santa Maria delle Grazie, in Milan. The refectory is a crucial space in the structure of a convent—it is the place of taking meals and the place of the encounter between the human time and the divine, between spiritual existence and daily life, and the many forms[186] of art such an encounter takes.[187] *The Last Supper*'s relationship with the space is so commanding that it seems it is part of the room.

The decoration of the refectory contained the mural painting of Leonardo's *The Last Supper* and the fresco of *The Crucifixion*, painted by Giovanni Donato Montorfano, and completed in 1495. Montorfano's fresco on the south wall of the refectory is an expression of 15th-century tradition and is a sort of a vision of the Calvary. The comparison with Leonardo's painting lets us understand how strong the first announcement of the 'modern manner' expressed by Da Vinci was. Two artists, two different languages and approaches in the same room give the message, which we can find also in the body of the Church of the Convent site, of coexistence between tradition and innovation.

At the mealtime it must have been a telling sight, when the tables of the Prior and Christ looked upon each other as two opposite pictures, and the monks at their places found themselves enclosed between them. And just on this account the skill of

---

[185] Giorgio Vasari, *Lives of the Most Eminent Painters Sculptors and Architects*, pp. 92–95.
It is also important to remind:
It is said that the Prior of that place kept pressing Leonardo, in a most importunate manner, to finish the work; for it seemed strange to him to see Leonardo sometimes stand half a day at a time, lost in contemplation, and he would have liked him to go on like the labourers hoeing in his garden, without ever stopping his brush. And not content with this, he complained of it to the Duke, and that so warmly, that he was constrained to send for Leonardo and delicately urged him to work, contriving nevertheless to show him that he was doing all this because of the importunity of the Prior. Leonardo, knowing that the intellect of that Prince was acute and discerning, was pleased to discourse at large with the Duke on the subject, a thing which he had never done with the Prior—and he reasoned much with him about art, and made him understand that men of lofty genius sometimes accomplish the most when they work the least, seeking out inventions with the mind, and forming those perfect ideas which the hands afterwards express and reproduce from the images already conceived in the brain. And he added that two heads were still wanting for him to paint; that of Christ, which he did not wish to seek on earth; and he could not think that it was possible to conceive in the imagination that beauty and heavenly grace which should be the mark of God incarnate. Next, there was wanting that of Judas, which was also troubling him, not thinking himself capable of imagining features that should represent the countenance of him who, after so many benefits received, had a mind so cruel as to resolve to betray his Lord, the Creator of the world. However, he would seek out a model for the latter; but if in the end he could not find a better, he should not want that of the importunate and tactless Prior. This thing moved the Duke wondrously to laughter, and he said that Leonardo had a thousand reasons on his side. And so the poor Prior, in confusion, confined himself to urging on the work in the garden, and left Leonardo in peace, who finished only the head of Judas, which seems the very embodiment of treachery and inhumanity; but that of Christ, as has been said, remained unfinished. The nobility of this picture, both because of its design, and from its having been wrought with an incomparable diligence, awoke a desire in the King of France to transport it into his kingdom; wherefore he tried by all possible means to discover whether there were architects who, with cross-stays of wood and iron, might have been able to make it so secure that it might be transported safely; without considering any expense that might have been involved thereby, so much did he desire it. But the fact of its being painted on the wall robbed his Majesty of his desire; and the picture remained with the Milanese.
[186] Edward H. Griggs, Art and the human spirit; the meaning and relations of sculpture, painting, poetry and music; a handbook of eight lectures.
[187] Chiara Rostagno, 'The refectory of the Convent of Santa Maria delle Grazie: Architecture and Restoration' in Pietro C. Marani, Leonardo da Vinci's Last Supper, pp. 67–76.

the artist was compelled to take the existing tables of the monks as a pattern. Also, the tablecloth, with its folds still visible with its worked stripes and tied corners, was taken from the wash-room of the monastery. The plates, dishes, cups and other vessels are like those which the monks used. Here was not attempt at imitating an uncertain antiquated costume . . . no, the picture must be brought near to the present; Christ must take his last supper with the Dominicans at Milan.[188]

The painting seemed to be there, at the announcement of Christ:
'Truly, truly, I say to you, one of you will betray me.' (St John's Gospel 13:21).
The disciples are arranged around the figure of Christ, in a kind of circle which is the geometric expression of the harmony. But they are troubled and deeply reacting with their bodies and facial expressions because of the statement of Christ.

The movements of men vary with the variety of accidents running thorough their minds: and each accident in itself moves these men to a greater or lesser degree according to their force and age; because the same occurrence will cause a different movement in a young man than in an old one.[189]

Goethe's reading of the refectory helps us to understand deeply the ideas of Leonardo. Let us now imagine ourselves in the place; let us consider the moral repose which prevails in such a monastic dining hall, and let us admire the artist who has infused into his picture powerful emotion, passionate movement, and at the same time has kept his work within the bounds of nature, and thus brought it in close contrast with the nearest reality.[190]

The multitude of human feelings, of emotions, is the grammar of the composition.

If we assume that this complex chain of 'motions of the soul' and emotional reactions, as reflected in attitudes, gestures, and facial expressions, is the definitive version of the programmatic manifesto that Leonardo intended to leave for posterity (perfectly rendering the visualization of a passage in the Gospels), then the spatial context—the imaginary refectory in which Jesus and the apostles are sitting . . . the space of the painting is conceived to escalate the drama and focus the scene on Christ, the main actor in the story we see unfolding.[191]

Once again, the composition of the painting offers to us a sort of drama focused on the 'movements of the soul'.[192]

The theme of 'Historia'—as described by Leon Battista Alberti's *De pictura*—is crucial and the continuity between the pictorial space and the real one is the result of a ge-

[188] Goethe, D.J. Snider and T. Davison, 'Leonardo da Vinci's Last Supper', in The Journal of Speculative Philosophy, Vol. 1, n. 4 (1867), p. 242.
[189] This sentence is a part of the Treatise on Painting—a later compilation from Leonardo's original notes and drawings provided by Francesco Melzi by the 1540s. The Treatise on Painting was published in Paris in 1651. See Juliana Barone, 'et de' suoi amici: The Early transmission of Leonardo's Treatise on Painting', in in Pietro C. Marani and Maria Teresa Fiorio, eds., Leonardo da Vinci: The Design of the World, pp. 451–461.
[190] Goethe, D.J. Snider and T. Davison, 'Leonardo da Vinci's Last Supper', in The Journal of Speculative Philosophy, Vol. 1, n. 4 (1867), p. 243.
[191] Pietro C. Marani, Leonardo da Vinci's Last Supper, p. 35.
[192] Pietro C. Marani, *'The Movements of the soul': From Leon Battista Alberti to Leonardo da Vinci,* in Pietro C. Marani and Maria Teresa Fiorio, eds., Leonardo da Vinci: The Design of the World, p. 223–233.

ometric composition, aimed to enlarge the effect of Christ's spiritual force.[193]

Jesus Christ is in the middle, also in the perspectival construction of the scene. Close to him, to his right, we find John, Judas Iscariot (the betrayer) and Simon Peter. To his left are Thomas, James the Grater and Philip. In the external part of the composition, on the right, are Andrew, James the Lesser and Bartholomew, and to the left are Mathew, Judas Thaddaeus and Simon the Zealot.

Before we go farther, we must point out a happy device whereby Leonardo principally enlivened his picture—it is the motion of the hands; this device, however, only an Italian could discover. With his motion, the whole body is full of animation; every limb participates in the expression of feeling, of passion, even of thought. By various motions and forms of the hand, he expresses, *'What do you care! Come hither! This is a rogue! Beware of him! He shall not live long! This is a main point! Observe this well, my hearers!*[194]

The 'Sfumato Leonardesco' by Leonardo to tone down and mix the colours was the technical approach adopted by him to enlarge the effects of movements and natural lighting effects on bodies.

(The) mixture of colours may be extended to an infinite variety, almost impossible to describe. . . . Black and white are not reckoned among colours; the one is representative of darkness, the other of light, that is, one is a simple privation of light, the other is the light itself. Yet I will not omit mentioning them, because there is nothing in a painting more useful and necessary, since a painting is but an effect produced by lights and shadows, viz. Chiaroscuro.[195]

The painting had already begun to deteriorate only twenty years after its completion—in 1517 it was 'very excellent, although it is beginning to be spoiled, either due to the dampness of the wall or to some other accident.'[196]

Despite its decay, 'the painting must have produced a great effect', as Goethe wrote and as a lot of historical documents attested. Today it is the same. Looking at the Da Vinci masterpiece and its decay, we understand that there are no two stronger human emotions than fear and love—love for a unique art and cultural heritage expression, and fear of losing it, because of the experimental technique adopted by Leonardo—'tempera' mixed with oil applied on two preparation layers of calcium carbonate.[197]

The *Cenacolo Vinciano*, or *The Last Supper*, started to be considered a kind of axis mundi in Europe and all over the world. The Convent of Santa Maria delle Grazie in Milan became an incomparable place of learning for art lovers and people of culture, because of its architecture, its aura

[193] Pietro C. Marani, Leonardo da Vinci's *The Last Supper*, p. 35. See also Id., 'The "Movement of the Soul": From Leon Battista Alberti to Leonardo da Vinci', in Id. and Maria Teresa Fiori, eds., Leonardo da Vinci: The Design of the World, pp. 223–233.

[194] Goethe, D.J. Snider and T. Davison, 'Leonardo da Vinci's *The Last Supper*'.

[195] John Francis Rigaud, *A Treatise on Painting* by Leonardo da Vinci, faithfully translated from the original Italian, and digested under proper Heads, p. 124–155.

[196] L. Von Pastor, Die Reise dess Cardinals Luigi D'Aragona.

[197] See the final report on the last restoration in Pietro C. Marani, Pinin Brambilla Barcilon, Leonardo. L'Ultima Cena.

and because of Leonardo da Vinci's *The Last Supper*. The Leonardo painting started to be considered a great example of art from the first half of the 16th century, but two feelings were immediately present—astonishment for its beauty and fear of losing it.[198] During the last five centuries, several restorations were done, some even before the birth of the discipline itself, to stop the degradation and to preserve the painting.

Santa Maria delle Grazie Convent, at the time of Leonardo, was located outside the city walls and its building was the first visible image of Milan for people who came to the city from the north-west. In few decades the site became known worldwide as a symbol of Milan. More than two million people apply to visit the refectory every year, but for reasons of conservation, only about a half a million are permitted to do so.

3. Leonardo's Legacy: the dream to travel around the world (some notes regarding Leonardo and his interest in travelling)

Leonardo's interest in landscape paintings opened for him an ideal place to 'develop a vision of the world and the nature . . . that contemplates the possibility of overcoming the real, disrupting its balance with the force and fury of the imagination'.[199]

Also, in *The Last Supper*, landscape is a summa of all the existing beauty because it is continuously changing—the real meraviglia! 'How to draw a landscape', how to fix 'the colours of the sea from different aspects', 'why the same prospect appears larger at some time than at others' and again observations 'of the sun-beams passing through the openings of clouds', 'of the beginning of the rain', 'of dust', 'of the horizon seen in the water'.

The descriptions were so evocative and clear that, reading Leonardo's papers and notes regarding 'Asia', J.P. Richter, at the end of the 19th century, believed Leonardo travelled to the Middle East (Egypt, Cyprus and Turkey). Latest studies, however, attest that Leonardo da Vinci's Asia travel was a flight of his mind—perhaps the first draft of a novel or the effect of the tales of Italian travellers he may have heard during his time at the court of Ludovico Sforza and in Florence. Leonardo da Vinci's capability to imagine scenarios and landscapes is 'now recognized as forming an intriguing whole that demonstrates Leonardo's attempt at fantasy literature'.[200] Using words and sketches, Leonardo was able to describe landscapes and scenarios of the Levant, by matching reality and imagination.

Leonardo's writings about quick sketches and the creative imagination have proved to be perhaps the most revolutionary in historical hindsight, because they acknowledge and attempt to verbalize the role of the conscious, semiconscious and unconscious mind in the creative impulse. In this, Leonardo's notes represent an entirely new manner of conceptualizing the design process of a storia.[201]

---

[198] D. Pino, Storia genuina del Cenacolo insigne dipinto da Leonardo da Vinci nel Refettorio de' Padri domenicani di Santa Maria delle Grazie. See also F. Wittgens, Il Cenacolo di Leonardo da Vinci, p. 12.

[199] Marco Verserio suggests us to see, on this specific point, Pietro C. Marani in Leonardo: Una carriera di pittore, pp. 333–334; rep. in English edition Id., The Leonardo da Vinci Complete Paintings.

[200] Marco Verserio, Leonardo's 'Deluges': Prophecy, Legend and History, in Pietro C. Marani and Maria Teresa Fiorio, eds., Leonardo da Vinci: The Design of the World. p. 409.

[201] Carmen C. Bambach, 'Porre le figure disgrossante: The Sketches of Leonardo and the Creative Imagination', in

Leonardo's topographical notebooks 'The Levant' were surely inspired by travellers' tales and historic events. The result was amazing—an imaginative journey in the countries of the western end of the Mediterranean Sea, the Red Sea region and to the site of a temple of Venus.[202]

In Leonardo's manuscripts, there are some notes regarding Asia and India. These attest to his interest in other cultures and how strong the interest was in people of art and science like him to extend the horizons of their cultural experience.[203]

'*Piata d'Elefante d'India che à Antonello Merciaio 'da maestro Maffeo.*'
Map of Elephanta in India which Antonello Merciaio has from maestro Maffeo; there for seven years the earth rises and for seven years it sinks; enquire at the stationers about Vitruvius.[204]

The descriptions of Leonardo's imaginary journeys are original—they direct people's eyes and feelings.
'Descrivi i paesi con vento e con acqua, e con tramontare e levare del sole.'[205]
Describe the countries with wind and water, and with setting and rising of the sun.

'Descrivi uno vento terrestre e marittimo, descrivi una pioggia.'[206]
Describe a land and sea wind, describe a rain.

Descrivi, 'Come si devono figurare le età dell'uomo.'[207]
Describe, 'How should the ages of man appear.'

Leonard's travel narratives are strongly autobiographical and 'bear the imprint of his great spirit',[208] of his sensibility. In this light, even his '*Travel to the East*', although never accomplished, has its own truth.

Pietro C. Marani and Maria Teresa Fiorio, eds., Leonardo da Vinci: The Design of the World, p. 51.
[202] J.P. Richter, ed., Scritti letterari di Leonardo da Vinci cavati dagli Autografi e pubblicati, Parte II, 259–270.
[203] Carmen C. Bambach, 'Porre le figure disgrossante: The Sketches of Leonardo and the Creative Imagination', in Pietro C. Marani and Maria Teresa Fiorio, eds., Leonardo da Vinci: The Design of the World, p. 51.
[204] Nonius Marcellus and Sextus Pompeius Festus were Roman grammarians of about the 4th century AD. Early publications of the works of Marcellus are: De proprietate sermonis, Romae (about 1470), and (place of publication unknown), Compendiosa doctrina, ad filium, de proprietate sermonum, Venice (1471).
[205] Leonardo da Vinci, Manuscript, f. 172 verso.
[206] Leonardo da Vinci, Manuscript, f. 169 recto.
[207] Leonardo da Vinci, Manuscript, f. 27 recto.
[208] Francesco Novati and Rodolfo Reiner, Giornale storico della letteratura italiana diretto e redatto. Supplementon. 10–11, p. 318.

// Bibliography

Albanese, M. and Gabriella Cella Al-Chamali, Mandala, Il linguaggio del profondo, Edizioni Xenia (1997).

Albanese, M., Gabriella-Cella Al-Chamali and Fiorenza Zanchi, I Chakra, L'universo in noi, Edizioni Xenia (1996).

Alberti, De pictura (On paintings), 1435, a cura di Walter Raffaelli, Raffaelli Editore (2019).

Angelillo M., I Mandala, Edizioni Xenia.

Arielli, E., La mente estetica. Introduzione alla psicologia dell'arte, Editore Mimesis (2012).

Aristotle, Metaphysics, Book iv, 3, 1005b:19–20

Aurora, 11.16, page 144

Bambach, C.C., 'Porre le figure disgrossante (The Sketches of Leonardo and the Creative Imagination)' in Leonardo da Vinci: The Design of the World, eds. Pietro C. Marani and Maria Teresa Fiorio (Skira Milan, 2015).

Bambach C.C., ed., 'Leonardo da Vinci Master Draftsman', exhibition catalogue (New York: The Metropolitan Museum of Art, 2003).

Barone, Juliana, 'Et de' suoi amici: The Early transmission of Leonardo's Treatise on Painting' in Leonardo da Vinci: The Design of the World, eds. Pietro C. Marani and Maria Teresa Fiorio (Skira Milan, 2015).

Bernini, E., C. Campanini and C. Casoli, Arti nella storia, Con materiali per docente. Per le scuole superiori, Edizioni Laterza Scolastiche, Collana Collezione Scolastica (2009).

Boheme, J., Viertzig Fragen von der Seele, 1620; Forty Questions Concerning the Soul English edition of 1647

Borla, Madness Removed, by Healthy People (1987).

Botella, C. and S. Botella, La raffigurabilità psichica, Editore Borla (Roma, 2004).

Bradley, N., 'The vulture as mother symbol: a note on Freud's Leonardo', American Imago, 1965 Spring 22 (1), 47–56.

Bragalia, Anton Giulio, Futuristic Photodynamism, 1914.

Breton A., 'Manifeste du surréalisme (The Futurist Manifesto)', Éditions du Sagittaire, 1924.

Caroli, F., La storia dell'arte, Editore Mondadori Electa.

Chah, Ven. Ajahn, Living Dhamma, The Sangha, 1992.

Coley, T., Leonardo e la coda, in A. Verdiglione, a cura di 'L'arte e la psicoanalisi', Feltrinelli, Milano, 1979.

Coomaraswamy, Ananda K., Introduction to Indian Art, 1923.

Cruttwell, Maud, Verrocchio (London: Duckworth and Co., 1904).

Da Vinci, Leonardo, Atlantic Codex C-61.

Da Vinci, Leonardo, Manuscript, The British Museum, f. 172 verso.

Daverio, P., Il secolo lungo della modernità. Il museo immaginato, Editore Rizzoli (2012).

De Saint-Exupéry, A., The Little Prince (New York: Reynal & Hitchcock, 1943).

Eco, U., Storia della bellezza, Ediz. illustrata, Bompiani.

Eissler, K.R., Leonardo da Vinci: Psychoanalytic notes on the enigma (New York: International University Press, 1961).

Farquhar, Maria and Ralph N. Wornum, Biographical catalog of the principal Italian Painters: With a Table of the Contemporary Schools of Italy. Designed as a Hand-book to the Picture gallery (London: J. Murray, 1855).

Fincher, F.S., I Mandala: una via all'introspezione, alla guarigione all'espressione di sé, Edizioni Astrolabio, 1996
Freud, S., Delusion and Dream in Jensen's Gradiva, 1907 (Green Integer, 2003).
Freud, S. Leonardo da Vinci and a Memory of His Childhood, 1910
Freud, S., Civilizations and its Discontents, Reprint Edition (W. W. Norton & Company, 2010).
Freud, S., 'Essays on Art, Literature and Language' (Turin, 1991).
Freud, S., Five Lectures on Psycho-Analysis, The Standard Edition (W.W. Norton & Company, 1990)
Freud, S., Freud in a letter to Jung, Letter from Sigmund Freud to C. G. Jung, (17 October 1909).
Freud, S., 'Leonardo da Vinci and a Memory of His Childhood', The Standard Edition (W.W. Norton & Company, 1990).
Freud, S., 'Mourning and Melancholia', The Standard Edition of the Complete Psychological Works of Sigmund Freud, Vol. XIV (1914–1916): On the History of the Psycho-Analytic Movement, Papers on Metapsychology and Other Works.
Freud, S., Saggi sull'arte la letteratura e il linguaggio, Editore Bollati Boringhieri (Torino, 1991).
Freud, S., The Interpretation of Dreams, First Thus Edition (Modern Library, 1995).
Freud, S., Totem and Taboo (Digireads.com, 2009)
Freud, S., Un ricordo d'infanzia di Leonardo da Vinci. Editore Boringhieri, Vol. 6 (Torino, 1909).
Fumagalli, G., Leonardo omo senza lettere, Firenze, 1939, Edizioni del Faro.
Giornale storico della letteratura italiana diretto e redatto da Francesco Novati e Rodolfo Reiner, Supplementon 10–11, (Torino, 1908).
Goethe, D.J. Snider and T. Davison, 'Leonardo da Vinci's Last Supper' in The Journal of Speculative Philosophy, Vol. 1, n. 4 (1867), Penn State University Press.
Gombrich, Ernst H., La storia dell'arte raccontata da Gombrich Ernest H., edizioni Leonardo, Collana Arte.
Griggs, Edward H., Art and the human spirit; the meaning and relations of sculpture, painting, poetry and music, a handbook of eight lectures (New York: B W. Huebsch, 1908).
Hessemer, Friedrich Maximilian, Lettere dalla Sicilia, Hudson, 1919.
Jens, Peter Thiis, Leonardo da Vinci: The Florentine years of Leonardo & Verrocchio, (London: H. Jenkins, Ltd., 1913).
Jung, C.G., Analytical Psychology and Poetic art (1922).
Jung, C.G., The Black Book.
Jung, C.G., 'Che cosa sono I mandala', (1950) in Opera, Editore Boringhieri, Vol. 9 (Torino, 1988).
Jung, C.G., 'Empiria del processo deindividuation', (1939) in Opera, Editore Boringhieri, (Torino, 1988).
Jung, C.G., Erinnerungen.
Jung, C.G., 'Gli archetipi dell'inconscio collettivo', (1934/1954) in Opera, Editore Boringhieri, Vol. 9 (Torino, 1988)

Jung, C.G., 'Il concetto dell'inconscio', (1936) in Opera, Editore Boringhieri, Vol. 9 (Torino, 1988).
Jung, C.G., Kommentar.
Jung, C.G., La dimensione psichica, Editore Boringhieri (Torino, 1972).
Jung, C.G., L'uomo e i suoi simboli, Editore Tea (Milano 2007).
Jung C.G., Mandala Symbolism (Princeton University Press, 1950).
Jung, C.G., Memories, Dreams, Reflections, (Vintage Books, 1989).
Jung C.G., Mysterium coniunctionis (1955–56).
Jung, C.G., On the relation of Analytical Psychology to Poetry (1922).
Jung C.G., 'Psicologia analitica e arte poetica', (1922) in Opera, Editore Boringhieri, Vol. 10–11 (Torino, 1985).
Jung, C.G., Psychology and Alchemy (1944).
Jung, C.G., The Red Book.
Jung, C.G., Ricordi, sogni, riflessioni, raccolti ed editi da Aniela Jaffè, Edizione riveduta e accresciuta, BUR (Milano, 1978).
Jung, C.G., Septem Sermones ad Mortuos, (1961) Giovanni Oggero, Carmagnola, 1989.
Jung, C.G., 'Sezione prima: Religioni occidentali', in Opera, Editore Boringhieri, Vol. 2 (Torino, 1988)
Jung, C.G., 'Sezione seconda: Religioni occidentali', in Opera, Editore Boringhieri, Vol. 2 (Torino, 1988).
Jung, C.G., 'Simbolismo del mandala', (1950) in Opera, Editore Boringhieri, Vol. 9 (Torino, 1988).
Jung, C.G., 'Sull'archetipo, con particolare riguardo al concetto di anima', (1936/1954) in Opera, Editore Boringhieri, Vol. 9 (Torino, 1988).
Jung, C.G., The Archetypes and the Collective Unconscious.
Jung C.G., The Philosopher Tree (1945–54).
Jung, C.G., 'Tipi psicologici', (1921) in Opera, Editore Boringhieri, Vol. 6 (Torino, 1988).
Jung C.G., What are the Mandalas (1955).
Jung, C.G. and Aniela Jaffe, Memories, Dreams, Reflections (Milan, 1965).
Kandinsky, W., Concerning the Spiritual in Art, M.T. Sadler tr., Adrian Glew ed. (New York: MFA Publications and London: Tate Publishing, 2001).
Kandinsky, W., Kandinsky, Complete Writings on Art (Da Capo Press).
La Scala, M. 'Immagine dai confini, immagine come confine', Rivista di Psicoanalisi, Monografie, Borla (Roma, 2005).
Longhi, R., Breve ma veridica storia della pittura italiana, Editore Abscondita.
Marani, Pietro C., 'The movements of the soul: From Leon Battista Alberti to Leonardo da Vinci' in Leonardo da Vinci: The Design of the World, eds. Pietro C. Marani and Maria Teresa Fiorio (Skira Milan, 2015).
Marani P. and M.T. Fiorio, 'The movement of the soul: From Leon Battista Alberti to Leonardo da Vinci' in Leonardo da Vinci: The Design of the World, ed. (Skira Milan, 2015).
Marani, Pietro C. and Maria Teresa Fiorio, eds., 'Introduction' in Leonardo da Vinci: The Design of the World (Skira Milan, 2015).
Marani, Pietro C. and Pinin Brambilla Barcilon, 'Final report on the last restoration', Leonar-

do L'Ultima Cena (Milan, 1999).
Marra, C., Fotografia e pittura nel Novecento (e oltre) (Mondadori Bruno, 2012).
Marinetti, Manifesto on Futurist photography in Futurism.
Merleau-Ponty, M., Il visibile e l'invisibile, Editore Bompiani, Sonzogno, (1969).
Muzzarelli, F., L'invenzione del fotografico. Storia e idee della fotografia dell'Ottocento, Piccola biblioteca Einaudi.
Müntz, Eugène, Leonardo da Vinci, artist, thinker and man of science (London: W. Heinemann; New York, C. Scribner's Sons, 1898).
Neumann, E. Art and the Creative Unconscious (Princeton University Press, 1971)
Nietzsche F., 'Aurora e Frammenti Postumi', Traduzione di Mazzino Montinari, Ferruccio Masini (Adelphi, 1964).
Pedrini, M., 'La storia che non si smarrisce' in Atlas Italiae (Roma, 2015).
Pino, D., Storia genuina del Cenacolo insigne dipinto da Leonardo da Vinci nel Refettorio de' Padri domenicani di Santa Maria delle Grazie (Milan, 1796).
Raghavan V., The Aesthetics of Ananda Coomaraswamy (Bengaluru: Indian Institute of World Culture, 1982).
Richter, J.P., ed., Scritti letterari di Leonardo da Vinci cavati dagli Autografi e pubblicati Parte II, (Londra: Sampson Low, Marston, Searle & Rivington, 1883).
Rigaud, J.F., A treatise on painting by Leonardo da Vinci, faithfully translated from the original Italian, and digested under proper Heads; (London: J.B. Nicholas and Son, 1835).
Rinaldi, Furio, 'The Academia Leonardi Vinci: Leonardo's Pupils, Followers and Legacy of the Masters's Works' in Leonardo da Vinci: The Design of the World, eds. Pietro C. Marani and Maria Teresa Fiorio (Skira Milan, 2015).
Riolo, F., Sulla fantasia. Rivista di Psicoanalisi 3 (1980).
Rostagno, Chiara, 'The refectory of the Convent of Santa Maria delle Grazie: Architecture and Restoration' in Leonardo da Vinci's Last Supper, ed. Pietro C. Marani (Skira Milan, 2016).
Rudenstine, Angelica Zander, The Guggenheim Museum: Paintings 1880–1945, Vol. 1 (New York: Solomon R. Guggenheim Foundation, 1976).
Samajda, Eric, Freud and Culture, 2015.
Schapiro, M., Leonardo and Freud, Journal of the history of the ideas (1956).
Schofield, Richard, 'Reality and Utopia in Leonardo's Thinking about Architecture' in Leonardo da Vinci: The Design of the World, eds. Pietro C. Marani and Maria Teresa Fiorio (Skira Milan, 2015).
Smiraglia, Scognamiglio N., Ricerche e documenti sulla giovinezza di Leonardo da Vinci (1452–1482) (Napoli, 1900).
Smith, C.M., Jung e lo sciamanesimo, l'anima tra psicoanalisi e sciamanesimo, Edizioni Amrita (2014).
Strachey, James, Anna Freud, Alix Strachey and Alan Tyson, translators, 'Mourning and Melancholia' in The Standard Edition of the Complete Psychological Works of Sigmund Freud, Volume XIV (1914–1916): On the History of the Psycho-Analytic Movement, Papers on Metapsychology and Other Works.
Sukranitisara VII.

'The intelligence of Vision: An interview with Rudolf Arnheim'.
The Bloomsbury Research Handbook of Indian Aesthetics and the Philosophy of Art, Bloomsbury Academic
The Vishnudharmottara, Part III.
Trabucco, L., 1899: esplorazioni dell'inconscio tra psicoanalisi e arte, Rivista di Psicoanalisi, 3 (2007).
Vasari, G., Le vite de' più eccellenti pittori, sculturi e architettori (1550).
Vasari, Giorgio, Lives of the Most Eminent Painters Sculptors and Architects, tr. Gaston Dec. De Vere (London: Philip Lee Warner, 1912–1914).
Verserio, Marco, Leonardo's 'Deluges': Prophecy, Legend and History in Leonardo da Vinci: The Design of the World, eds. Pietro C. Marani and Maria Teresa Fiorio (Skira Milan, 2015).
Von Pastor, L., Die Reise dess Cardinals Luigi D'Aragona (Freiburg, 1905).
Wittgens, F., Il Cenacolo di Leonardo da Vinci, (Milano: A. Martello, 1958).

http://new-territories.com/blog/2013GSAPP-UPENN/wp-content/uploads/2013/08/Pag-es-de-manisfesto2.pdf
https://www.nikonschool.it/corso-breve-storia-fotografia/1840-1887.php
https://ir.uiowa.edu/cgi/viewcontent.cgi?referer=https://www.google.com/&httpsre-dir=1&article=5236&context=etd
https://www.britannica.com/topic/Mona-Lisa-painting
http://www.iiwcindia.org/transactions/transaction56.pdf
http://www.photo-museum.org/photography-history/
https://www.napoleon.org/en/young-historians/napodoc/the-birth-of-photography/
http://www.bl.uk/learning/timeline/item106980.html
https://artlandapp.com/what-is-dadaism/
https://www.britannica.com/art/Dada
https://www.britannica.com/art/Cubism
https://manhattanarts.com/what-is-cubism/
https://www.britannica.com/art/Surrealism
https://www.britannica.com/art/Futurism
https://www.tate.org.uk/art/art-terms/f/futurism
https://www.theartstory.org/movement-futurism.htm
https://forestsangha.org/teachings/books/living-dhamma?language=English
https://www.goodreads.com/book/show/10254713-living-dhamma
http://www.english.upenn.edu/~cavitch/pdf-library/Freud_MourningAndMelancholia.pdf
http://classics.mit.edu/Aristotle/metaphysics.4.iv.html
https://onlinelibrary.wiley.com/doi/abs/10.1111/j.2044-8341.1923.tb00450.x
http://www.studiocleo.com/librarie/jung/essay.html
https://commons.wikimedia.org
https://www.paintingmania.com/
https://www.plazzart.com
https://www.moma.org/
https://arthive.com/
https://www.guggenheim.org/
https://www.smithsonianmag.com/
https://www.arthipo.com/
https://www.finestresullarte.info/
https://www.erikjo.com/

| Paola Martani |

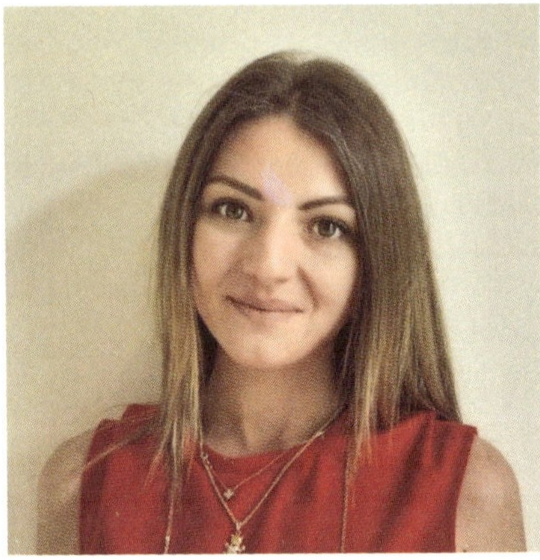

Paola Martani holds the academic title of 'Dottore' in Philosophy from University of Milan, as well as an MPhil in linguistics. She was the course coordinator and lecturer at the Italian Embassy Cultural Centre in New Delhi from 2014 to 2019.

She has been a lecturer in many universities, including Jamia Millia Islamia, New Delhi. She has six books to her credit: *A Student Handbook of Italian —Learning Italian through Design A1* (2017), *A Student Handbook of Italian —Learning Italian through Design A2* (2018), *Travelling between Fables* (2017) (which has also been translated into Italian), *Art and Culture of Italy—From the Roman Empire to Present Day* (2019), *Pocket Book for Students in Italy* (2019) and *Life Wants to Live: Real Stories of Tibetan Refugees* (2019).

In April 2018, she was awarded for her work by the Women Economic Forum, and in June 2019, she received the award Young Personality of the Year (below 40 years) from the International Academic and Research Excellence Award.

She also writes a bimonthly column, 'Culture and Influence', in *AsiaOne*.

| Chiara Rostagno |

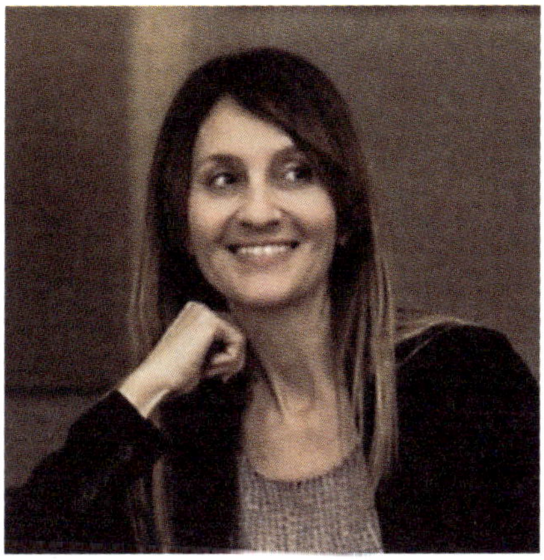

Chiara Rostagno, architect, PhD and MD in Restoration of Monuments, works at Mibac (Italian Ministry of Cultural Heritage and Activities). She is an adjunct professor at the Polytechnic of Milan, where she teaches in the field of conservation of cultural heritage. At present she is in charge of 'Landscape as Heritage'.

Since 2015, she has been the coordinator of a multidisciplinary research group for the conservation of the fragile cultural heritage, composed of resources from Polytechnic of Milan, Bocconi University, University of Milano-Bicocca, University of Salerno, University of Bologna, University of Ljubljana and Jožef Stefan Institute Ljubljana and Institute for the Conservation and Promotion of Cultural Heritage.

She was the director of the National Museum of the Last Supper from 2015 to November 2018 and director of the Cappella Espiatoria museum in Monza.

She is the author of several books and papers in the field of conservation and history of cultural heritage.